WHO AM I?

A NEW
CONSCIOUSNESS
READER

This New Consciousness Reader is part of a new series of original and classic writing by renowned experts on leading-edge concepts in personal development, psychology, spiritual growth, and healing. Other books in this series include:

SERIES EDITOR: CONNIE ZWEIG

WHO AM I?

Personality Types

for Self-Discovery

Edited by

ROBERT FRAGER, PH.D.

A JEREMY P. TARCHER/PUTNAM BOOK

Published by G. P. Putnam's Sons

New York

A Jeremy P. Tarcher/Putnam Book
Published by G. P. Putnam's Sons
Publishers Since 1838
200 Madison Avenue
New York, NY 10016

Library of Congress Cataloging-in-Publication Data
Who am I? : personality types for self-discovery / edited by
Robert Frager.
p.   cm.
Includes bibliographical references.
ISBN 0-87477-761-5
1. Typology (Psychology)   2. Archetype (Psychology)   3. Astrology
and psychology.   I. Frager, Rogert, date.
BF698.3.W46   1994
155.2'6—dc20   93-32401
                                                         CIP

Design by Irving Perkins Associates
Cover design by Susan Shankin
Printed in the United States of America
1 2 3 4 5 6 7 8 9 10
This book is printed on acid-free paper.

*To my wife, Ayhan, whose loving support
has been essential in this project as in all else in my life.*

CONTENTS

ACKNOWLEDGMENTS

Putting together this book has been a long and sometimes convoluted process. It would not have been possible without the help and encouragement of many people.

First of all, I want to thank my editor at Tarcher, Connie Zweig, for her creative support and her unfailing insistence that I keep improving the book in general and my own writing in particular. I could always count on her to help raise my work to the next level.

I am grateful to Helen Palmer, who originally suggested that I do this book and whose original chapter and helpful suggestions have been wonderful contributions to the enneagram section. I am deeply appreciative of the creativity, hard work, and patience of all those who have contributed original chapters to this book: Jim Shere, Angeles Arrien, Stuart Heller, and Helen Palmer.

I am also indebted to those friends and colleagues who have suggested book resources, articles, and authors appropriate for this book—Jeremy Taylor, Belinda Brent, Stuart Heller, and many others who have shared their enthusiasm about the topic of typologies. A thank you to Danielle Light, who helped me develop my course on personality types, and to all those who participated, students and presenters alike. I am obliged to Linda Loos and Jean Harbin, who made encouraging comments and also sat down and laboriously figured out the word counts on several critical chapters.

Finally, I am deeply grateful to my family members who have been patient with me and allowed me to devote the time needed to complete this book, more time than any of us would have preferred.

A NOTE ON LANGUAGE

Sexist language supports the kind of stereotyping that is a disservice to women and men alike. I apologize for the antiquated use of *he* in some chapters, which were written when that was standard usage.

WHO AM I?

INTRODUCTION

SOME PERSONAL REFLECTIONS

TYPOLOGY SYSTEMS have interested me for many years, although I have never become completely devoted to any single system. I believe in all of the typology systems and have found value in each one. But I have never become a "true believer" in any single system. I have studied each of the systems covered in this book and typed myself and others according to each system. Sometimes this has yielded amazingly clear and useful insights. At other times, the results have been murky and confusing. I am convinced that each of these systems has the potential to be of real benefit for certain people.

Most people who write about personality typology tend to be strong advocates of one particular system. I hope that my own eclectic interest in all of the type systems has helped to make this book a balanced and fair presentation of all the major approaches to typology.

I remember visiting the noted astrologer Dane Rudhyar some years ago. Rudhyar looked closely at me and commented that I obviously had a great many "Cancerian" traits. I thought to myself, "This man is the dean of American astrology, but he has certainly blown it this time!"

I replied that I had almost no Cancer in my astrology chart. My sun and rising signs are both Gemini and I always had thought of myself as very much a "Gemini personality."

Rudhyar then asked when I was born. When I answered, "June 20," he commented, "You were born on the cusp of Cancer. The whole universe was moving into Cancer at that time, so in many ways you are more strongly affected by Cancer than by Gemini."

This caused a minor astrological identity crisis for me. I usually read the Gemini section when I looked at an astrology book or newspaper column and had totally ignored Cancer. Now I had a whole new set of personality patterns to consider.

For me this story illustrates both the strengths and weaknesses of any typology system. There are often real and powerful insights to be gained by studying one's "type." However, overidentification with a particular type can close us off to the possible relevance of other categories and their characteristics.

I believe that *all* of the various types found in each system describe different parts of each of us. Even though certain types seem to fit better than others, each type in every system has something to teach us about ourselves. Nothing that is human is truly alien to us and we can find at least something of ourselves in everyone we encounter.

When the enneagram system first came out, Charles Tart, a friend and a gifted psychologist, introduced me to the system. He had been typed as a "seven" and was sure that I was one too. Although Charles and I have different backgrounds and somewhat disparate lifestyles, the enneagram "seven" description did seem to fit both of us and illustrated several important ways in which we were very much alike. The seven type is optimistic, dedicated to pleasure and enjoying life, somewhat narcissistic, often occupied with planning, fantasizing, intellectualizing, and keeping pleasantly busy with many different activities. After reviewing the "seven" description, we became aware of how many similar interests we each enjoyed, for example, how much we both love speculation and fantasy. We have been science-fiction fans since childhood, and we both love games and have well-developed senses of humor. The enneagram description highlighted some basic shared patterns we had not known.

Since I founded the Institute of Transpersonal Psychology in 1975, almost all of my psychology graduate students have been exposed to one or more enneagram classes. Over and over again, I have seen this powerful typology system well used and abused.

Many students have used the enneagram to improve their self-knowledge, and some have found it to be a powerful tool in working as psychotherapists. Others have made the enneagram into a new way of stereotyping themselves and others. They say things like, "I have a messy house *because* I am a 'nine.' " Or, "You are so critical *because* you are a 'one.' " Instead of helping them understand themselves and others more deeply, the enneagram types became labels that ended the search and closed off further understanding. These students saw them as the *causes* of certain behavior patterns, rather than as descriptions of a preferred behavior.

A good typology description may tell us that certain kinds of behavior are more probable in a particular type of person. However, our behavior is not caused by our typology. Members of a given type *may* share a similar constitutional or psychological makeup which leads to certain kinds of behavior. The type description alone, no matter how rich and detailed, is not a cause of behavior. To put it simply, a label is only a label; it is not a cause or an explanation.

Body types and their psychological correlates generally have been ignored in psychology, in spite of the obvious relevance of the body to everything we do. Sheldon's system of body typing interested me years ago, when I was a graduate student in psychology. As I observed myself and others, I could see Sheldon's three body types all around me. Ectomorphs were skinny intellectuals; mesomorphs were muscular jocks; and endomorphs were flabby couch potatoes. However, Sheldon's system did not seem to work perfectly. Everyone I met in graduate school was bright and highly intellectually oriented, yet not everyone was an ectomorph. I saw plenty of athletic intellectuals and overweight scholars.

In studying Sheldon, I have been confused about my own type. When I was younger, I felt like an pudgy endomorph. However, as I became more involved with sports and other physical activities, my body and also my lifestyle began to resemble more and more that of the mesomorphic, athletic type. In his typology, Sheldon focuses on body structure and ignores function, yet the two are certainly interrelated.

As I have reflected on my own shifts from times of relatively little physical activity to periods of intense physical training, I have concluded that Sheldon and most other typology theorists tend to ignore the effects of experience and the environment. When I was deeply immersed in college and graduate study, I had relatively little time for sports. It was easy to slip into a fairly sedentary existence, as the pressure of schoolwork meant that I spent most of my time behind a desk. I looked and felt more like an endomorph. On the other hand, during the years I studied Aikido in Japan, my martial arts training was the most important activity in my life. The level of Aikido training in Japan was extremely arduous. Most of my friends were also involved in Aikido and my environment strongly supported intense physical activity. As a result I almost immediately lost twenty pounds and began to look and feel more like a mesomorph.

I returned to graduate school at Harvard after two years in Japan devoted to study and research in psychology as well as the daily practice of Aikido. I was pleasantly surprised to find myself seeing the world through the eyes of a mesomorph. I had never noticed it before, but I was suddenly aware, as I walked through the Harvard campus, that almost all of the students lived so much in their minds that they were unaware of their bodies and only barely aware of the world around them. Most students and professors seemed to be completely occupied with their intellects and appeared to treat their bodies as somewhat inconvenient appendages that were useful only for carting around their heads. I also noticed that I related to people differently. I found myself appreciating and hanging out with mesomorphic "jocks" for the first time.

In the years since, I have kept up my Aikido practice and also retained my dedication to intellectual activities. However, Aikido training in the United States is not nearly as physically active and demanding as training in Japan. There are a very few people who have returned from martial arts training in Japan and kept up the same intense level of physical practice. I believe that they are highly developed mesomorphs, whose constitution and character support this kind of arduous physical activity.

As a young college professor I was able to remain fairly active. However, once I founded the Institute of Transpersonal Psychology, administration took so much time and energy that my physical training suffered. I feel that, in many ways, I have slipped back into old and comfortable endomorphic patterns. If my constitution does have a strong basic endomorphic component, then perhaps I am fated to struggle with those tendencies all my life. Most of my family members are overweight endomorphs. They have been on and off diets all their lives, and I could certainly lose at least twenty pounds these days. It may be that we are able to transcend our constitutional types at times and with a supportive environment, but that we tend to slip back into our old patterns once that support is gone.

Each system has its own strengths and shortcomings. Like a good lens, a typology system will help us focus more clearly on some important issues. But whatever lies outside the system's area of focus is often blurred or even invisible. Like any tool, a good typology system may be excellent for certain tasks and ineffective for others.

After studying various typology systems, I now believe that we need to take into account the founders of each system and their own personality types, which should give us an idea of their strengths and limitations. A theorist who is primarily intellectually oriented is far more likely to develop a mental typology. Sheldon had a strong body orientation, which led to his development of a physical typology.

When I was first introduced to the Jungian typology system, I was struck by the intuition/sensation dimension. According to the type tests I took, I was fairly well balanced on introversion and extraversion and on thinking and feeling. However, I rated at the top of the scale on intuition with almost no sensation function.

This made a great deal of sense to me. It explained why, at school, I loved the abstract theories of geometry but got lost in algebra, which required that I keep track of all kinds of trivial details, like working with numbers. It explained why I never managed to balance my checkbook unless I made a special effort. It wasn't that I *couldn't* pay attention to sensate details, I simply *didn't*, most of the time.

Jung calls the least-developed function the "inferior function." In its negative aspect, the inferior function is our most unconscious, most primitive part. In our inner growth work, it is important to remember that each of us has that primitive part, that we all have feet of clay. The most intelligent person may have extremely undeveloped feelings. The most sensitive artist may find it extremely difficult to think logically. When we identify our inferior function, we come to know where we need to develop, where we need to stretch ourselves.

We tend to become self-important and inflated when we engage in activities involving our inferior way of functioning. A small glimpse into the inner world that is familiar and comfortable to an introvert may throw an extravert completely off balance. For example, extraverts who have just begun to meditate may extravagantly overestimate the depth and profoundness of their newfound mystical experiences.

In dreams, the inferior function is often represented by a shadow image of a wild, barbaric, or exotic figure. In a thinking type, for example, it will appear in a primitive or relatively inferior feeling person. In a thinking type, feeling may not go beyond a dog's level, and an intuitive's sensation may also operate on a similarly primitive, animal level. For instance, an introverted intuitive might stretch out luxuriously in the sun, filled with the intense enjoyment of his or her inferior sensation function, just like a cat stretched out in the sunshine.

Jung wrote that working with our inferior function is one of the great tasks of individuation or personal growth. If we ignore it, we become frustrated and bored with everything. If we simply jump into it, we operate at a primitive or ineffectual level. Jung recommended working on the inferior function through art, such as writing or painting. As a highly developed intuitive, Jung chose to sculpt, which was an effective way of calling on his inferior sensation function.

TYPOLOGY AND THE SEARCH FOR SELF-KNOWLEDGE

The perennial question "Who am I?" has been asked throughout the ages. In many cultures, it has been answered by the spiritual traditions, in particular with maps of the psyche known as typologies. These ancient typological systems reveal universal patterns among human beings. They also reveal our differences, or uniqueness.

Many of the greatest minds throughout history have been fascinated with why we are different and the nature of our differences. In the third century BC., a student of Aristotle named Theophrastus asked, "Why is it that while all Greece lies under the same sky and all Greeks are educated alike, we are all different with respect to personality?"

Theophrastus defined thirty personality types, each organized around a central, dominant trait, such as stinginess. He wrote that the central trait could be found in all aspects of a person's life. Today, we would seriously question the accuracy of defining an individual's personality on the basis of a single trait, such as a tendency to be tight with money. But perhaps a central, dominant trait is actually an important symptom of a deeper and more complex personality pattern.

We still use this single-trait approach to some extent in typology systems today. In the enneagram system, for example, each of the nine enneagram types has been characterized by a particular dominant trait. The enneagram "five," for example, also has been called "ego-stinge," referring to a tendency to be stingy with time, energy, and information, as well as with money. Although it tends toward oversimplification and stereotyping, we can make a typology system easier to understand and apply by hanging a clear and dramatic label on each personality type.

Hippocrates' Four Humors

In the fifth century BC., even before Theophrastus, Hippocrates, the father of Western medicine, formulated a "scientific" theory of personality based on the Greek theory of the four elements. Many Greek philosophers believed that everything in nature is composed of four basic elements: air, earth, fire, and water. In the human body, each element is associated with a different humor, or body fluid: blood, phlegm, black bile, and yellow bile. According to Hippocrates, health and illness as well as personality type depend on the relative balance of the humors in each person.

Hippocrates described four temperaments generated by a predominance of one of the four humors. Air is associated with the humor of blood and the sanguine, or optimistic, temperament. Earth is associated with the humor of "black choler," or bile, and the melancholic, or easily depressed, personality. Fire is associated with "yellow choler," or adrenaline, and the choleric, or volatile, easily angered, type. Water is associated with "white choler," or lymph and mucuous fluids, and the phlegmatic, or calm, easygoing, temperament.

Physicians, philosophers, educators, and psychologists have worked with Hippocrates' fourfold model for over two thousand years. One modern, sophisticated application of this model was developed by Rudolf Steiner, the Austrian philosopher and educator who founded the Waldorf School system. Steiner taught teachers to recognize these four temperaments in their students. He provided detailed and sophisticated guidance concerning the different educational and emotional needs of each type of child. Chapter 25 outlines Steiner's approach to the four temperaments by

Roy Wilkinson, a Waldorf teacher who has used this system in the classroom for over thirty years.

The Ayurvedic Temperaments

The belief that all things in nature are composed of basic elements is common in many civilizations. Before the development of modern chemistry and physics, early scientists and philosophers tried to order the universe according to basic, universal principles. In addition to the four elements of the Greeks, Indian philosophers postulated the fifth element of ether, an element even more insubstantial and refined than the element of air.

Indian Ayurvedic physicians developed three constitutional or body-mind types based on combinations of these elements. *Vata* is composed of air and ether, *pitta* is fire and water, and *kapha* is earth and water. The vata type is active, enthusiastic, and quick. The pitta type is sharp, enterprising, and articulate. The kapha type is strong, steady, and tolerant.

Ayurveda comes from two root words, *ayus* or "life" and *veda* or "knowledge" or "science." Ayurveda, often translated as "the science of life," is over five thousand years old. For each type, there is an ideal diet, lifestyle, and also herbal remedies designed to bring the system into harmony and balance. In Chapter 6, noted physician and author Deepak Chopra describes the Ayurvedic personality typology.

The Chinese Five-Element Typology

Chinese philosophers and physicians worked with a different five-element theory: earth, water, fire, wood, and metal. Each person is thought of as a miniature of the cosmos composed of these five elements, and everyone can be characterized by one of the elements. Metal is controlled, cool, and calm. Fire is flamboyant and intense. Wood is assertive, expansive, and determined. Earth is patient, nurturing, and connecting. Water conceives, concentrates, and conserves. In Chapter 7, Beinfield and Korngold, two of the foremost American practitioners of Chinese medicine, translate the five Chinese elements into five personality archetypes: pioneer, wizard, peacemaker, alchemist, and philosopher.

Typologies for Self-Discovery

The systems included in this book have all sprung from a desire to map human nature, to peer into the hidden reaches of the psyche. Some typologies stem from the psychotherapeutic tradition pioneered by Freud and his successors. Mental, relationship, and body typologies have been developed out of modern psychological and sociological research. Other systems are really folk psychologies that evolved centuries before the field of modern psychology was developed, and are time-tested approaches to understanding human nature. These folk psychologies developed in many cultures, including the Greek, Indian, Chinese, and Native American.

Each system of personality typology in this book provides its own unique contributions to self-understanding. Each system describes certain relationships among body, mind, and emotions. Often these relationships are not intuitively obvious, at least until they are pointed out to us. For example, emotional reactions carry the most weight for some people, while intellectual conclusions are most important for others. Yet most of us unconsciously assume that everyone else operates just as we do, and we are often taken by surprise when others respond differently. Typology systems teach us that there are important and systematic dissimilarities among individuals.

We all want to understand ourselves and others more clearly. That is the fascination and the promise of the many rich and varied typology traditions. Each system provides us with a distinct and illuminating picture of the varied ways in which people function in the world. Ideally, they enable us to perceive other people from a more accurate perspective, rather than see everyone else from our own point of view.

William Sheldon points out that the great fictional detective Sherlock Holmes is, in many ways, the epitome of the perfectly intellectual ectomorph. Holmes is described as thin and intense. Unswayed by the emotions and passions that flow through most of humanity, Holmes seems at times to become pure intellect—coldly rational and logical and capable of intense intellectual focus and remarkable deductive analysis.

One flaw in A. Conan Doyle's portrait of Holmes is his description of Holmes' abundant use of tobacco and opium. Doyle portrayed Holmes as a habitual pipe smoker, capable of smoking half a pound of strong tobacco a night. As Sheldon points out, Conan Doyle's own endomorphic character led him astray. Doyle was a hefty endomorph who loved tobacco and smoked constantly. However, a thin, sensitive ectomorph would be devastated by the excesses he describes in Holmes. This example is an excellent reminder that we need to know our own type and its strengths and weaknesses in order to work successfully with other types.

A good typology system helps us see our own strengths and weaknesses. Without personal insight we are likely to appreciate only our own strengths in others and to judge them harshly if they mirror our weaknesses. For example, sensation types tend to value only those who demonstrate mastery over facts and details. Intuitives think highly of others who can bring complex information into a new whole, and they tend to devalue sensation types as people who "can't see the forest for the trees." Feeling types respond to those who have a strong sense of human values and high ideals. Thinking types respect others who are clear, logical, and "smart," and are likely to put down feeling types as nice but not very bright.

A useful typology system also helps clarify our perceptions of others by guiding us to look for certain patterns and distinctive traits found in certain types of people. If I am conscious of my friend's muscular, mesomorphic constitution, I can understand and anticipate his or her preference for doing over planning and reflection. I may feel personally that action without planning is a waste of time, but I will know to expect that my mesomorphic friend is likely to want immediate activity, to "get things moving" rather than just sitting around thinking.

UNIQUENESS VS. UNIVERSALITY

While working on this book I have become particularly aware of issues related to personality types and type differences. I have noticed that most of those who write about human nature tend to focus either on the ways that people are fundamentally the same or on the ways that people are fundamentally different. At their extremes, neither approach is very useful.

To assume that we are all alike is to ignore our very real differences in such aspects as age, sex, or temperament. To assume that we are all unique is to give up on trying to develop any general theories of human behavior.

Most psychological theories ignore type differences. They tend to look for universal principles of human behavior. However, if there are, in fact, fundamental type differences among people, the search for universals is bound to end with relatively trivial generalities or with serious distortions for large segments of the population. For example, most psychological systems have been created by men, and tend to describe male behavior, ignoring fundamental differences between male and female psychology. In addition, modern personality theories have been developed by highly educated, white, middle-class professionals; they overlook styles of thinking and acting common in other socioeconomic, ethnic, and cultural groups. Yet the advocates of virtually every personality system claim that they have developed a universally applicable psychology.

In some ways we are all the same, and in others we are each unique. We share the same basic physiological structure and sensory apparatus, and we share the same existential facts of birth and death. Yet each of us has a different personal history, family constellation, and life experience.

However useful any typology system may be for understanding and working with different people, it fails to give a full account of an *individual*. Every individual is a unique combination of countless and varying factors.

In between these two extremes, we do fall into various groupings or types. Some obvious ones are age, sex, and nationality. Children share many important characteristics, as do men, women, Americans, Japanese, introverts, Virgos, and mesomorphs. Perhaps what we need most to learn is which categories are most appropriate to which issues. The psychology of the future may include various personality typologies, using different typology systems for different purposes. For example, we might use a learning-style typology system for deciding how to teach a child math, a temperament typology system for figuring out how to motivate or discipline that same child, and a relationship typology system to help the child get along better with a friend.

TYPOLOGY AND RELATIONSHIPS

Besides understanding ourselves, we seek deeper knowledge of and intimacy with others. An understanding of type helps us develop greater tolerance and respect for individual differences. We come to appreciate others' gifts. Working with any of the systems in this book may help you recognize that there are fundamental variations in ways of experiencing life, that our paths through life are not all the same. We cannot assume that other people's minds work the same way that ours do, that they take in data the same way we do, that they reason as we do, or that they value what we value.

To understand another's type is to understand their strengths and also their limitations and therefore to work with others more effectively. On the job, for instance, a good fit between a person's tasks and constitutional makeup will result in productivity and satisfaction. A poor fit will result in stress, fatigue, and poor performance. Sometimes we may expect too much from someone else who simply does not share our gifts or our interest in a certain area. Our type preferences may be relatively unimportant at some times and crucial at others, often when we least expect it.

For example, sensate types are skilled at accounting and similar activities that require keeping track of details, which would be a terrible strain on an intuitive type. One intuitive medical researcher had to spend hours every day carefully examining specimens under a microscope. She became chronically fatigued and irritable, but no physical cause could be found. The stress of constantly having to use her inferior sensation exhausted her.

In a way, personality types are like automobile models. Many distinctions among cars are relatively superficial, like color and styling. (In fact, it is not uncommon that two cars will have contrasting shapes and styles on the outside, yet have the same engine underneath the hood.) Some cars get much better gas mileage, some have far greater acceleration or speed, but these differences really don't matter for everyday driving, such as commuting to work or going to buy groceries.

There *are* times when the differences do matter. A rugged four-wheel-drive vehicle will ride easily over rough terrain that would damage a finely machined sports car. A car with a powerful engine and heavy-duty suspension can pull a heavy trailer, a load that might burn out a light car built mainly for gas economy. When you buy a car you need to match what it is built for with the kinds of tasks you are planning to use it for. Similarly, type theory can help you know others' strengths and limits and understand what kinds of tasks they are "built" for and what challenges may cause them to break down.

It is easiest to understand others whose type is the same as ours. These people are likely to have similar interests and values, to see the world as we see it. We are more likely to understand them and feel understood by them, as they tend to look at things in the same way we do and come to similar conclusions. Mesomorphs will tend to understand and appreciate the value of being active and getting things done. Thinking types are likely to agree on the importance of logic and rational organization. Most sensate types will concur on the need for attention to detail. Enneagram "sixes" will probably be in accord concerning the dangers and the attractions of power and authority.

We may be fascinated by those who operate differently in the world, confirming the old saying that opposites attract. But people who are truly of a very different type are hard to understand and hard to predict. On most issues they are likely to take a different position. Constant misunderstanding and opposition can create great strain. Unfortunately, attraction without understanding does not make for a successful long-term relationship, as evidenced by the high divorce rate in this country.

The worst kind of relationship occurs when another type style is treated as inferior. For example, someone who operates from feeling and intuition may be put down as an incompetent thinker instead of valued as someone who can bring new skills and an alternative perspective to decision making. In one couple who sought therapy, the husband complained that his wife was disorganized and untidy and, worst of all, illogical. The wife asserted that her husband was rigid and hypercritical. Each felt that the other was acting out of spite or malicious motivation, because each judged the other by the standards of his or her own type. After ten hours of therapy with a Jungian analyst, they became conscious of each other's type and learned to recognize and affirm each other's strengths. Their relationship began to blossom.

Another advantage of understanding type is that it can provide insight into our relationship with the larger society in which we live. Our society values certain types of personality more than others. Thinking is valued far more than feeling, for example. We are an extraverted society, and our institutions often fail to take into account introverts' needs for quiet and solitude, and so we even have Muzak in the elevators. Most schools and churches are like prisons to mesomorphs, who need active learning and who generally find it extremely difficult to sit still for long periods of time. For centuries Christianity has tended to favor the ascetic, intellectual ectomorphs and has devalued the sensory endomorphs and the active mesomorphs.

If your way of functioning in the world is not valued by society, your faith in your own gifts may diminish. In fact, these gifts may not develop fully because of your own doubts and also because society may provide few opportunities to exercise your own particular talents.

This may have happened on a smaller scale in your family as you grew up. If your parents understood and valued your type, you probably felt that your own particular gifts and interests were worthwhile. On the other hand, your self-confidence may have suffered severely if you felt that your parents did not value your character and your preferences, but wanted you to be "more physical" or "more intellectual," for example. Trying to change a child's personality type can be like forcing a left-handed child to be right-handed. That kind of pressure can seriously inhibit the development of anyone's natural gifts.

In one family, the daughter reported that her parents had been extremely upset when she had difficulties with arithmetic and similar tasks at school. Both parents and her younger brother were sensation types and she was an intuitive, whose inferior function was sensation. The father was an engineer and the brother later became an accountant. She could never live up to their standards for tidiness and attention to detail and eventually sought therapy.

A boy who was an introverted feeling type grew up in a family of extraverts. He was ridiculed for his love of reading and constantly badgered to become more active in school affairs. As an adult he tried business and sales with little success. He had fantasies of getting a doctorate in English literature or becoming a professional in human services, but did nothing about them. Because his basic character choices had been invalidated for so long, he literally did not know what was good for himself anymore.

In both cases, an understanding of typology helped the individuals appreciate their own strengths and accept their own character preferences.

This enabled them to move beyond the painful psychological impasse created by childhoods in which their personality type was unrecognized and unappreciated.

CATEGORIZING: A BASIC HUMAN HABIT

Descriptions of human types can be found in many cultures and eras, from Greek philosophy to Chinese medicine to the Indian caste system to modern Western psychology. It used to be taken for granted that personality varied with culture and social class. Today we tend to think that it is somehow "undemocratic" to talk of fundamental individual differences. It is as if we have forgotten that the Constitution states that all people are equal *under the law*, but does not claim that we are all the same. Equality is not uniformity, yet in our search for equal rights and equal opportunity, we may fail to acknowledge individual uniqueness. As a result, typing has gained a bad reputation in some circles and may be judged politically incorrect, although we still tend to do it unconsciously.

We frequently classify people by *stereotypes*, such as age, sex, intelligence (for example, smart, average, or dumb), race, and nationality. The term "stereotype" originally meant a one-piece printing plate which is cast from a mold. Today, "stereotype" is defined as a fixed and unchangeable idea or a mental pattern having no individuality, as though cast from a mold. Stereotyping is one of the great dangers of typing. It occurs when we ignore individuality and treat all people in a given category as if they were all stamped from the same mold.

Often we judge others by stereotypes of appearance (good-looking, average, or ugly) and of psychological state (normal, neurotic, or crazy). One of the most common categorizations we make about others is to distinguish between those we like and those we don't, such as "good guy" vs. "bad guy" or trustworthy friend vs. dishonest enemy.

It is hard *not* to categorize. Our minds tend to organize all our experience into a relatively few categories. Most of us will lump together different experiences under a single, broad label, unless we are deeply interested in the topic. For instance, most Americans think of "snow" as a single category. Skiers will differentiate snow into corn snow, powder snow, and several other varieties. Eskimos, who are far more concerned with snow than skiers, have dozens of words for different kinds of snow.

Categorization may be a basic human tendency, but there are also problems inherent in categorizing. Stereotyping occurs when we create a category and then attribute certain traits to everyone in that category. So, for example, all body builders are seen as dumb, or all Latin men are judged macho. These stereotypes distort our perceptions and our understanding of others.

Moshe Feldenkrais, a brilliant observer of human behavior and founder of the Feldenkrais Method, insisted that *all* generalizations are distortions. An expert in human movement, he worked with an extraordinary range of people, from gifted professional athletes and musicians who wanted to improve their skill to patients in wheelchairs who were partly paralyzed from serious accidents or illnesses.

Feldenkrais hated labels and generalizations. He tried to see each individual as a unique case, without prejudging or labeling. Feldenkrais wrote that when he worked with someone, he even tried to stop thinking in whole sentences. He felt that the very structure of language interfered with his developing an intimate understanding of the unique qualities of functioning and movement in that person.

Feldenkrais once discussed a serious medical error. Two patients were scheduled for surgery at the same time and somehow their charts got switched. The surgeons removed a healthy gallbladder from the patient with a diseased liver and took out a perfectly healthy liver from the patient with a malfunctioning gallbladder.

Feldenkrais commented that this was a clear example of the danger of operating in terms of labels and categories, and not *looking* at what is actually in front of us. If the doctors had looked, they certainly would have seen that the organs they were about to remove were healthy. Instead, they relied more on labels and charts than on the real bodies in front of them.

A young man once asked Feldenkrais if his system might help women in labor. He gave several dramatic examples of the short and easy labors of pregnant women he had worked with. The man then asked just which of Feldenkrais' techniques were best for pregnant women. Feldenkrais replied, "You idiot! There is no such thing as a pregnant woman!" There was a long moment of silence as we all reflected on this astonishing statement. No one knew what to say.

Feldenkrais went on, "A girl of fourteen having her first baby is nothing like a woman of thirty-five having her fourth child. What I would do with each is completely different." We realized once again how easily we can get caught by labels and categories. Because we have the term "pregnant women," we begin to think of all members of this category as alike and tend to ignore their differences.

The systems of personality typology covered in this book contain important insights into human nature. They can help us better understand ourselves and those around us. They also can obscure our understanding if we forget that the map is not the territory and pay more attention to a system than to the people it is describing.

TYPES OF TYPOLOGIES

The simplest typology systems are based on common dichotomies: male and female, light and dark, good and evil. The oldest and most complex is astrology, with twelve major types, each modified by a host of factors. However, most personality systems describe four or five basic types. Perhaps that is as much complexity as most of us can hold in categorizing others. Who could actually make use of a system that worked with as many as twenty or thirty different types? Few, if any, of us can hold that many distinct and complex categories in our minds and also apply them effectively in understanding and working with others. For most of us, a system with three or four basic categories allows us to see and respond to others with some discrimination, without becoming overwhelmed by complexity.

Twofold Typologies

There are a number of relatively simple approaches to personality typology involving just two categories. The most common binary classification is between "masculine" and "feminine" types. These include traditional definitions of gender roles in different cultures, which today we generally regard as little more than crude stereotypes that devalue women.

The Chinese distinguish between Yin and Yang, which are seen as feminine and masculine principles and are often translated as "receptive" and "expressive." Yin and Yang literally mean the shady and the sunny sides of a mountain and, as such, Yin and Yang are not viewed as rigidly separate. As the sun moves across the sky, the slope that was warmed by the morning sun falls into shade in the afternoon. The sunny and shady sides merge and alternate. Yang becomes Yin, and Yin becomes Yang.

According to Chinese philosophy, Yang and Yin are also the first differentiation in the universe. At first there was only the Tao, which is the unity of all things, an undifferentiated whole. From this oneness emerged Yin and Yang, which then gave birth to the world in all its infinite forms.

Also related to the masculine/feminine dichotomy is the Indian distinction between *purusha* and *prakriti*, or "spirit" and "nature." Purusha, seen as the masculine principle, is pure consciousness or transcendental spirit. Prakriti, the feminine, is procreation, that which gives birth to all the manifest forms in nature. It is the primordial foundation from which all the universe springs. It is interesting to note that, in Indian philosophy, the masculine principle is essentially passive and observing, while the feminine principle is active and creative.

Human beings like to think in terms of pairs or contrasting opposites. Twofold classifications have been popular throughout history. Some commonly used pairs include:

optimist–pessimist	day–night
active–passive	sun–moon
orderly–messy	hot–cold
precise–vague	dry–wet
proud–humble	happy–sad
heavenly–earthy	head–heart
sacred–profane	tenderhearted–
verbal–visual	tough-minded
logical–intuitive	once-born–twice-born
pragmatic–idealistic	inner-directed–
objective–subjective	outer-directed
type A–type B	right brain–left brain
introvert–extravert	thinking–feeling

The distinction between right- and left-brain thinking has become extremely popular in recent years. Some writers have tried to sort all kinds of human behavior into these two categories. In Chapter 16, Springer and Deutsch discuss the latest research findings on right- and left-brain functioning.

I have personally found the contrast between thinking and feeling types particularly useful. Thinking and feeling are two of the major concepts in Jung's fourfold typology of thinking-feeling, sensation-intuition. However, long before Jung, philosophers and observers of human nature had distinguished between thinking and feeling types. Closely related terms include objective vs. subjective, tough-minded vs. tenderhearted, and head vs. heart.

Several years ago one of my students heard a lecture by a noted philosopher of religion. She came to me the next day quite upset because she strongly disagreed with the speaker's classification of mystical states. The philosopher put Gnosis, or mystical Knowing, as the ultimate state of mystical development, and Love as the second-highest state. She tried to discuss this with him after the talk, but he overwhelmed her with a host of cogent reasons for putting Gnosis as the highest possible human achievement. After listening to her, I exclaimed without thinking, "What else could you possibly expect from a professional philosopher? Of course he would put Knowing as the finest state. After all, he has spent his life developing his intellect. A philosopher virtually *has* to put knowledge at the top of the list of human achievements!"

I went on to discuss the distinction between thinking and feeling types, and how we could probably classify the world's mystical traditions in terms of traditions of the head and traditions of the heart. Ever since that realization, I have noticed this basic distinction over and over again. Most mystical traditions have powerful spokespeople for each side. The great mystical poets are the most eloquent about the importance of love and of opening the heart to God. For them, God is Love. The great spiritual philosophers write brilliantly about the importance of knowing. For them, God is Truth.

This distinction between thinking and feeling has also been at the root of many of our political difficulties. Protesters and demonstrators who insist that our government act in accord with democratic ideals and human values generally present strong feeling-type arguments based on values and considerations of human suffering. Government decision makers usually operate from a thinking perspective which involves impersonal, logical appraisal and considerations such as risk factors and cost/benefit analyses. Unfortunately, feeling criteria are not terribly significant to the thinking types who tend to judge the protesters as fuzzy-minded, unreasonable, and irrational. The protesters, on the other hand, see the government officials as cold and lacking in caring and concern for others. Liberal protesters would be far more effective if they learned to couch their arguments in the kinds of logical, rational terms that government officials can hear and appreciate. The ongoing conflict and miscommunication between these two groups has been in great part a matter of type differences.

Threefold Typologies

There are a number of classical threefold systems. Plato distinguishes three primary functions in human beings—reason, feeling, and will. For will, he uses the Greek term *thymos*, literally "spirited" as in a spirited horse. Plato argues that we use our will to force ourselves to do that which reason advocates but which our feeling side shuns. Will is an essential ally of reason, as reason cannot prevail against feeling without the support of the will. This threefold distinction yields three different types of people, according to which function is dominant.

George Gurdjieff, the esoteric teacher who first introduced the concept of the enneagram to the West, built on this Platonic model. He taught that there are three types of people: the physical person, the emotional person, and the intellectual person. Gurdjieff wrote that there are three basic spiritual paths, each designed for one of the three types: the way of the fakir, the way of the monk, and the way of the yogi.

The way of the fakir is for the physically oriented person with a strong will and involves extremely rigorous, even tortuous physical discipline. For example, some fakirs may assume a particular posture and maintain it for months or even years. Through this kind of physical discipline, they develop an iron will.

The way of the monk is the path of devotion and faith, and the work is essentially emotional. This is the path for those with a strong emotional, feeling nature; it is probably the most common spiritual path in all the world's religious traditions. The monk learns to develop a profound, intense love of God that permeates all of his or her thoughts and actions.

The way of the yogi is the path of the mind and is designed for the mentally oriented person. The yogi learns to meditate, to control the mind, and to develop focused concentration. The resulting experience of deep meditative states of consciousness works to transform the mind.

Gurdjieff did not take these terms literally. There are, for example, highly devotional schools of yoga whose practitioners would be following what Gurdjieff called the way of the monk. There are also Zen monks, devoted primarily to meditation, who are following the way of the yogi.

Gurdjieff also pointed out that development in only one area generally leads to a dead end. A monk with devotion but no discrimination is likely to be a "silly saint." A fakir with a developed will but no understanding lacks any direction for application of that finely honed will. A yogi with a controlled mind may become dry and impotent.

Gurdjieff suggested that there was also a fourth way, a way that transcended individual differences. He pointed out that the traditional ways of the fakir, monk, and yogi all involved renouncing the world and devoting all one's time and energy to intense, if one-sided, practice. The fourth way is one of remaining in the world and using all of one's life experiences for self-development. The work of the fourth way also involves balancing development in all three areas—body, heart, and head. A competent teacher is essential in this work because each student progresses differently, according to individual temperament. Gurdjieff indicated that the Sufi mystical tradition is the most highly developed model of a fourth way tradition. For over a thousand years, Sufis have practiced "living in the world but not of it."

This same threefold distinction can also be found in Chapter 22, William Sheldon's body typology of endomorph, mesomorph, and ectomorph. Will and physical activity are the central core for the mesomorph. The endomorph is emotionally oriented and focused on pleasant, comfortable feelings and sensations. The ectomorph prefers the life of the intellect and operates in terms of thinking and reason.

In Chapter 18, Sandra Seagal and David Horne outline their similar modern system, which is based on the mental, emotional, and physical principles in human dynamics. They have applied this system in a variety of settings, from individual classrooms to school systems to large corporations.

The three temperaments of Ayurvedic medicine can also be related to Sheldon and to the other threefold systems. The air-ether, vata type is imaginative, sensitive, and quick and corresponds closely to the ectomorph. The fire-water, pitta type is forceful, intense, and determined, much like the mesomorph. The earth-water, kapha type is solid, steady, and tranquil and strongly resembles the endomorph.

Karen Horney also uses a threefold classification. In Chapter 10, she distinguishes between the fundamental human tendencies to move toward others, away from others, or against others. Although it is clearly an oversimplification, we can see how the mesomorph is likely to prefer moving against, the endomorph tends to move toward, and the ectomorph chooses moving away from others.

Another classic threefold system is found in Indian philosophy, in which all things are composed of a combination of three *gunas* or fundamental qualities: *tamas, rajas,* and *sattva.* Tamas is inertia, or the basic tendency to remain the same; rajas is stimulation, or the innate impulse to act; and sattva is purity, or illumination. We can see these three tendencies in many different areas. Some foods, for example, are heavy and tamasic and leave us feeling stuffed, sleepy, and almost unable to move. Other foods are stimulating and rajasic and leave us feeling nervous or so highly stimulated that we can hardly sit quietly, much less remain calm and relaxed. Still other foods are sattvic and leave us feeling fresh and calm afterwards. Some people have highly tamasic (e.g., passive, couch potato) lifestyles. Others are rajasic and always seem on edge or on the go. Others lead calm, sattvic lives.

One interesting aspect of the system of gunas is that rajas and tamas form a kind of dialectic that ideally become resolved in sattva. As opposed to most typology systems, in which each type has a balance of positive and negative qualities, Indian philosophy clearly advocates the physical, psychological, and spiritual superiority of sattva.

The founders of Neuro-Linguistic Programming, a modern psychological system, also developed a threefold typology. They decided to look at human functioning in terms of our five senses because, after all, they are the channels for all our experiences in the world. NLP argues that taste and smell are relatively trivial in most of our experience and that our most important senses are sight, hearing, and touch. They further point out that touch is more correctly referred to as our kinesthetic sense and includes awareness of both external and internal stimuli.

Most people clearly prefer one particular sense modality, and this is frequently reflected in the kind of language we use. For example, a visually oriented type will tend to use phrases like, "show me" or "I see what you mean." An auditory person will be likely to say, "tell me" or "I hear you." Someone who is more kinesthetic will say, "let me try (or feel) it" or "I feel that you are right."

Differences in sense channel preference can lead to interesting relationship problems. Take the example of a kinesthetic man and a visual woman. As they sit together, he will want to move closer to her in order to touch her, while she will want to move back in order to see him better. Each is seeking the same thing, namely, better contact with the other. Unfortunately, the strategy each employs has the opposite effect on the other. This example is a particularly good illustration of how knowledge of type differences can be of tremendous benefit in a relationship.

Fourfold Typologies

The four-element, four-temperament typology of Hippocrates is one of the oldest and most widely used fourfold typology systems. The four elements also have been part of the underpinnings of astrology for centuries. In her chapter on the astrology of relationship, Liz Greene indicates how the four elements provide an important psychological dimension in understanding astrology and also in understanding relationships. She relates the four elements to Jung's types: earth is related to sensation, water to feeling, fire to intuition, and air to thinking.

Jung's basic classification of thinking, feeling, sensation, and intuition is the best-known fourfold system. Jung postulated two dimensions to his typology: judgment and perception. Thinking and feeling are both ways of making judgments and decisions. Sensation and intuition are both ways of taking in information.

A number of other fourfold systems use the same approach. They identify two major dimensions of functioning, with two categories in each, resulting in a two-by-two table.

	Judgment	
	Thinking	Feeling
Sensation		
Intuition		

Perception

Jung's system is the basis for the Meyers–Briggs Type Indicator, which is the most widely used personality measure in the world. The MBTI adds to

Jung's four functions the two new types, perception and judgment. Perception means to remain open and receptive to new data and new developments. Judgment involves shutting off perception and coming to a decision with whatever information is at hand. The Meyers–Briggs model has been used with great success in business and education as well as in psychology.

The interpersonal style model presented by John Corbett in Chapter 19 is based on the Wilson social styles system, which is widely used in the business world. The two basic dimensions are dominance and sociability. High dominance is referred to as "dominant" and low dominance as "yielding." High sociability is called "outgoing" and low sociability is termed "reserved." The directive leader, also known as the driver, is dominant and reserved. The collaborative leader, or expressive type, is dominant and outgoing. The deliberative type, also known as analytic, is reserved and yielding. The counseling or amiable type is outgoing and yielding.

Dominance

	Yielding	Dominant
Reserved	Deliberative	Directive
Outgoing	Counseling	Collaborative

Sociability

An awareness of your employer's or colleague's style can ease communication and build a more effective team.

Fivefold Typologies

Both Chinese and Tibetan element theories have five elements instead of four. The Chinese system includes earth, water, fire, metal, and wood. The Tibetan system includes earth, water, fire, air, and ether.

In Chapter 24, "An *I Ching* of the Body," Stuart Heller uses the same five elements as the Tibetan system. His work is inspired by the Chinese *I Ching* and by *The Book of Five Rings*, the classic book on strategy by the great samurai swordsman and philosopher Miyamoto Musashi. In Heller's system, the four elements of ground, water, fire, and wind form the major types.

Ether, or space, is at the center. Space includes the other elements, and provides access to each of the other four, as needed. Each individual is a certain combination of the first four elements.

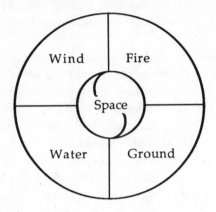

Through training and inner development you can begin to enter the realm of space, the realm of freedom, flexibility, and immediate access to all the elements.

The leadership typology of Blake and Mouton, in Chapter 21, is similar to Heller's model. It also has the classic two-dimension structure of many fourfold models. The two underlying dimensions are concern for people and concern for production. The Team manager is high on both dimensions. The Authoritarian manager is high on production and low on people. The Impoverished manager is low on both. The Country Club manager is high on people and low on production. The fifth type, the Middle-of-the-Road manager, falls right in the middle on both dimensions and is moderate on concern for people and moderate on concern for production. This type is located at the very center of the two-by-two table. In this model, as opposed to Heller's, the central type is no better than any of the other types. It simply represents a middle ground on both of the underlying dimensions that generate the types.

Using this kind of map in a company may lead to a rise in both bottom lines—profit and human satisfaction.

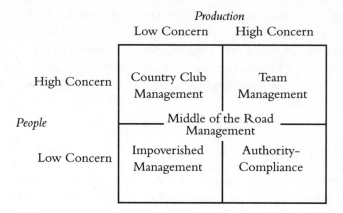

	Production	
	Low Concern	High Concern
High Concern	Country Club Management	Team Management
People	Middle of the Road Management	
Low Concern	Impoverished Management	Authority-Compliance

Sixfold Typologies

There is one sixfold typology in this book, the Goddess Wheel system of Jennifer and Roger Woolger in Chapter 13. The Goddess Wheel is composed of three pairs of Greek Goddesses: Hera and Persephone, Athena and Artemis, Aphrodite and Demeter. All six come from a single basic archetype: the Great Mother. The three pairs represent the basic dimensions of independence, power, and love, and each dimension has an introverted and an extraverted pole.

Both Athena and Artemis are independent, powerful, single women. Athena is more extraverted, enjoying the company of others and a busy urban life. Artemis prefers the quiet and solitude of the woods. Both Hera and Persephone are queens and represent power. Hera is the queen of heaven and is the extravert, concerned with the outer world. Persephone is the queen of the underworld and prefers the inner psychic world of spirits and intuition. Demeter represents the love of a mother for her children. Aphrodite is the more extraverted lover, who loves (but does not mother) the adult rather than the child.

	Independence	*Power*	*Love*
Extraverted	Athena	Hera	Aphrodite
Introverted	Artemis	Persephone	Demeter

Each woman is a particular combination of goddess energies at any given time. Life changes will tend to bring out one or more goddesses in a woman. For example, Aphrodite is likely to emerge on a honeymoon (we would hope!) and Demeter at the birth of a child. Just as Heller's system included the possibility of movement into the center of the circle, the Woolgers have organized the six goddesses into the Goddess Wheel, whose center is the underlying archetype of the Great Mother, the symbol of the transcendent unity of all the goddesses. Getting more profoundly in touch with any of the goddesses brings a woman closer to the Great Mother at the center, where all the goddesses merge.

Sevenfold Typologies

In this book there is one example of a sevenfold system: the seven chakras of Indian yoga psychology. In a sense, this is actually a complex variant of the twofold system, as the seven chakras can be divided into upper and lower chakras. The three lower chakras, located at the base of the spine, below the navel, and at the navel, are related to worldly concerns. The three upper chakras, located at the throat, between the eyebrows, and at the top of the head, are related to spiritual interests. The fourth chakra, located at the heart, is the fulcrum or bridge between the upper and lower chakras.

As Ram Dass explains it, the first chakra is connected with survival issues, the second chakra is related to sexuality, and the third is related to power. These form a part of the basic psychological makeup of everyone, although someone fixated on the second chakra, for example, will perceive everything in terms of sexuality. Freudian theory is a good example of a "second chakra" psychology.

The fourth chakra is the heart chakra. It is the turning point between the upper and lower groups of chakras. This is also the level at which we first encounter the Jungian archetypes and collective unconscious. In a sense, spiritual life truly begins when the heart is opened and psychic energy begins to travel upward to the higher chakras.

The fifth chakra is related to the perception of subtle states and higher levels of awareness. The sixth chakra is related to the perception of truth and the development of wisdom. The seventh chakra is related to unification of the individual and the universe.

The states related to the three upper chakras transcend the basic assumptions of traditional Western psychology. To understand these higher levels of human nature, we need to look at disciplines such as transpersonal and the psychology of consciousness.

Eightfold Typologies

Jung always emphasized the importance of the introversion-extraversion dimension in typology. Added to his four types, this yields a total of eight basic types, such as introverted-intuitive-feeling and extraverted-thinking-sensation. This can be seen as follows:

	Judgment				Judgment	
	Thinking	Feeling			Thinking	Feeling
Sensation				Sensation		
Perception				*Perception*		
Intuition				Intuition		
	Introverted				**Extraverted**	

The concepts of introvert and extravert provide an extremely useful twofold distinction. They strongly color the four Jungian functions. For example, extraverted sensation types will be inclined to work easily and well with details and are likely to make great accountants. On the other hand, introverted sensation types will know precisely what is going on *inside* themselves. They may not be nearly so aware of their external environment.

One of my psychology students was an introverted sensation type who would often say things like, "I don't know what is going on with a certain client, but my stomach felt funny when he brought up this topic." As she learned to trust her own inner psychic thermometer, she became an extraordinarily effective therapist. Her stomach was one of the best inner guides I've known. It was sensitive to the slightest nuances in her clients, even when she had no conscious idea of what was going on.

Ninefold Typologies

The nine-element enneagram system can be seen as having three basic positions, each of which contains three subtypes. The threefold system of mental, emotional, and body type is at the root of the enneagram, which is not surprising given its origins in Gurdjieff's teachings.

Three of the nine enneagram types are related to mental orientation (types five, six, and seven). Three types are related to a physical or will orientation (types eight, nine, and one). The final three types are related to feeling orientation (types two, three, and four). Within each group, the orientation is overdeveloped in one type, underdeveloped in another type, and the third type is out of touch with the orientation.

Twelvefold Typologies

Astrology is one of the oldest ways of accounting for differences in individual personalities. Systems of astrology developed in many if not most ancient cultures, including the Egyptian, Greek, Indian, Chinese, and Mayan.

In addition to the twelve signs of the zodiac, an individual's astrological type is modified by the position of the planets, the sun, the moon, and also the twelve houses, or twelve divisions of the person's astrological chart. The twelve houses are formed by dividing the individual's circular astrological chart into four quadrants, each containing three subsections of thirty degrees each. The four quadrants have been interpreted by Liz Greene, in Chapter 1, and others as corresponding to Jung's thinking, feeling, sensation, and intuition. The psychological meanings of each house are discussed by Jim Shere in Chapter 2, "Astrology as Psychological Cosmology."

The classic astrological zodiac was first postulated by the great Egyptian astrologer Ptolemy, who has provided the major foundations for Western astrology. The signs of the zodiac are identified with twelve constellations. As the sun passes in front of each of the twelve zodiacal constellations, the earth moves through our annual cycle. Each of the twelve zodiacal signs represents a different form of power or energy. These are grouped into the four seasons: the spring signs of Aries, Taurus, and Gemini; the summer signs of Cancer, Leo, and Virgo; the fall signs of Libra, Scorpio, and Sagittarius; and the winter signs of Capricorn, Aquarius, and Pisces.

The first signs in each seasonal group (Aries, Cancer, Libra, and Capricorn) are called cardinal signs and are related to the generation of power. The second signs (Taurus, Leo, Scorpio, and Aquarius) are called fixed signs and involve the concentration of power. The third signs of each season (Gemini, Virgo, Sagittarius, and Pisces) are known as mutable signs and involve the distribution of power. Various relationships among these signs is discussed by the noted Jungian analyst and astrologer Liz Greene in Chapter 1.

Chinese astrology also distinguishes twelve types. The Chinese lunar calendar is the longest chronological record in history, dating from 2637 BC. Twelve animals are assigned to the twelve years of the Chinese zodiac. According to legend, only twelve animals came to bid farewell to the Buddha before he left the earth. He named a year after each one, in the order that the animals arrived: Rat, Ox, Tiger, Rabbit, Dragon, Snake, Horse, Sheep, Monkey, Rooster, Dog, and Boar. In Chapter 3, Theodora Lau describes how the animal ruling the year you were born exerts a profound influence on your life. There is an old Chinese saying, "This is the animal that hides in your heart."

Native American earth astrology is also based on a lunar calendar. Sun Bear and Wabun point out, in Chapter 4, that each of the four seasons is associated with one of the four cardinal directions, the time of day, and an animal. Winter is connected with the North, night, and the white buffalo; spring is allied to the East, morning, and the eagle; summer is associated with the South, midday, and the coyote; and fall is related to the West, evening, and the grizzly bear. In addition, each month has its own animal, plant, mineral, and color.

WORKING WITH TYPOLOGY SYSTEMS

The extraordinary interest in systems like astrology, the enneagram, and the Jungian typologies reflects our intuitive understanding that there are important *qualitative* differences among individuals. Any theory that attempts to treat all people the same is bound to be of limited practical use. Typology theory assumes that much seemingly random variation in human behavior is not really random, but that it is the result of a few basic differences in how we function. This offers us a sense of order in chaos, design in a seemingly arbitrary universe.

Since no single typology system has received universal acclaim as *the* most accurate and useful approach, I think it is safe to assume that all the widely accepted typology systems are useful for some people. At a given time, one system may provide critical insights for a particular person. Another system may have equally valuable insights for someone else or for the same person at some other time. So, rather than choose one system over all the others, this book takes the approach that all typologies are potentially useful tools. As with any tool, we have to know when and how to use it best.

To take the notion of typology seriously, you might assume that your type is likely to lead you to prefer certain typology systems over others. For example, someone who is strongly oriented toward thinking is likely to prefer a complex, intellectually sophisticated system. Someone who is highly perceptual will prefer a system that includes detailed physical distinctions among types.

I have found that it works best to hold each personality typology system lightly. The various types found in any given system fit certain people better than others. In other words, some people seem to be classic "Scorpios" or Jungian "INFPs" or enneagram "nines." Sometimes, a certain system seems to fit a given individual like a glove. However, even in such cases, the fit is probably better on certain days or certain years than at other times. I personally doubt that *any* single type description fits any single person perfectly, especially if the individual has achieved a certain degree of personal growth or inner development.

I believe that the more we develop and the more conscious we become, the less we fit our original type. Most type theories have probably been developed by observation of the majority of people, who are not very deeply self-aware and who have experienced relatively little inner growth. As we grow psychologically or spiritually, we also grow out of our type. Some systems claim that our type is constitutionally given and unchangeable, that it is our destiny. Others hold that it is possible to transcend our type. Heller (Chapter 24) and the Woolgers (Chapter 13) present systems in which we can move from our original type into a deeper or more central state.

Another problem with typology systems is that they are seductive. A good typology system can be extremely useful in ordering and summarizing a lot of practical information about yourself and others. However, it can then become extremely easy to put someone in a neat little box and forget that the other person is a real and unique individual. The label becomes a substitute for seeing others as they really are.

Unfortunately, some people look to typology systems for all the answers. Perhaps because of a certain lack of self-confidence, these people come to think that all the important answers lie in a certain system and that they can be easily understood as black and white solutions. Then they do their best to fit themselves into that system. Sometimes we even feel that it is our own fault if we do not fit a system "properly," without considering that the fault may lie in the system and that *no* system can fit all people equally well.

When someone overidentifies with a certain typology, he or she begins to believe, "I *am* a Capricorn," or "I am a 'five.' " It might be better to say, "The description of Capricorn matches many of my behavior patterns and helps me understand myself better." This at least keeps the door open to other possibilities.

In a real sense, we are *all* of the types in *every* system. We all share basically the same hardware. Physiological differences among us may be real, but they are primarily a matter of degree. For example, some of us are born left-handed and others right-handed. Research has shown that this is generally a matter of brain hemisphere dominance. If the right hemisphere is dominant, the person will be left-handed and vice versa. Most people then *choose* to use their preferred hand, which further enhances their initial preference. However, it is possible for anyone to learn to use their non-dominant hand and to develop considerable skill with it. This has been demonstrated many times, for example, when the preferred hand or arm is injured and the individual has to work with the other side.

It may be correct to say, "I am left-handed" but that statement really means, "I am more comfortable and more skillful using my left hand, *and* I probably could develop much greater comfort and skill with my right hand if I choose." It does not mean "I can only use my left hand, and I cannot even understand right-handed people, much less function effectively with my right." This latter position is one of the dangers of typing ourselves and others.

Some type descriptions may be more clearly related to us than others. However, as we know from studies of the shadow, it is often in those patterns that seem most alien that we can find much of our power and creativity. To put it another way, in every introverted feeling type there is an extraverted thinking type just longing to get out. In every tough, muscular athlete, there is a hidden sensitive intellectual.

When you read over the different type descriptions found in each system, I am sure you will, as I did, look for your type. It's probably impossible to resist the temptation. However, it might help to remember that you are far richer and more complex than any single type and that you can find yourself everywhere in this book.

PART ONE

ASTROLOGICAL
TYPES

MOST OF US ARE FAMILIAR WITH ASTROLOGY only through that superficial but fascinating newspaper column in which Madame So-and-So tells us that Monday will be a rotten day. Because of this, it is easy to dismiss astrology as mere fortune-telling nonsense. Yet many people still look over the astrology columns, glancing at least at their sun sign. Newspaper astrology continues to be popular because it satisfies that favorite human pastime—reading about ourselves.

Because of interest in learning about one's own type, astrology has grown tremendously in popularity. In 1940 only two hundred daily papers carried horoscopes. Today, over twelve hundred papers have astrology columns. At present, there are at least ten thousand full-time astrologers and one hundred twenty-five thousand part-time astrologers in the United States.

In the sixth century BC., Thales of Meletus, a noted Greek philosopher, allegedly fell down a well as he was strolling along, gazing at the stars. He was rescued by a servant girl, who scolded him for paying so much attention to the sky that he didn't see what was at his feet. This may have been an important lesson for Thales, who went on to develop the theory that all things were composed of water. Perhaps there is still a lesson in this story for

31

us today, reminding us to keep our feet firmly on the ground while observing the stars.

Stargazing is an ancient human pastime, so old that we do not know its origins. As civilizations advanced, they added philosophy and mathematics to the earlier divination forms of stargazing, creating astrology. Astrology was developed by the ancient Egyptians, Babylonians, Greeks, Indians, Chinese, Mayans, and many other peoples.

There are many different ways to approach astrology. Some value it primarily as an oracle and a guide to decision making. Others see it as an aid to self-discovery and individual growth. Others view astrology as a powerful symbolic language and as a basis for a vocabulary of consciousness.

One of the basic tools of astrology is the horoscope. A birth horoscope is a map of the heavens, actually of the solar system, at the exact moment of birth. Many astrologers view the horoscope as a map of the individual's psyche, a pattern of the energies and drives which make up each person. Your horoscope illustrates who you are in relation to the universe.

Astrology addresses directly many of the central issues of typology. It acknowledges that we are all different, each of us having been born at a moment when the cosmos was in a specific, unique state. Astrology also explores ways in which we are the same, ways in which we share traits with other certain cosmological patterns and regularities, like our sun signs.

Liz Greene, a Jungian analyst and astrologer, has written over a dozen insightful books on astrology, using astrological concepts symbolically and practically, in a Jungian framework. In Chapter 1, Greene discusses the four elements of earth, air, fire, and water as they apply to the twelve signs of the zodiac. She describes four basic temperaments, each with three subtypes, which generates the twelve astrological signs. Greene also points out that someone with a particular temperament is not necessarily born under the sign of that element. Each temperament has its own characteristic modes of intellectual and emotional expression and interpersonal relationship.

Jim Shere, a psychologist and pioneer in experimental astrology, was a personal student of Dane Rudhyar, the eminent astrological theorist and author. In an article written for this book, Shere introduces the major concepts and elements of astrology as symbols that each of us can contemplate and come to understand in our own way. He argues that although most people tend to rely on professional astrologers for interpretation of their birth charts, you can gain great insight from a horoscope with a basic understanding of fundamental astrological concepts.

Chinese astrology is more oriented to the birth year than the month of birth. Each year is represented by a different animal, including the sentimental but crafty Rat, the serious and dutiful Ox, and the captivating but unpredictable Tiger. This ancient system is outlined by Theodora Lau in

Chapter 3. She has based her descriptions of the twelve Chinese astrological types on folklore, popular Chinese sayings, legends, and mythology. Each type has its own personality orientation and relates differently to each of the other signs.

In many Native American traditions, the medicine wheel is one of the most important and powerful symbols. In Chapter 4 Sun Bear, a Chippewa medicine man, seer, and Indian leader, and Wabun, his medicine helper, present an application of the medicine wheel and Native American cosmology to astrology. Each month is associated with one of the four cardinal directions, north, east, south, and west, and has a related animal, plant, mineral, and color.

One astrological research study consisted of giving personality tests to people born on the same day as a few target celebrities. The researcher found that similarities between individuals increased as differences in birth times decreased. In other words, "time twins" showed more personality similarities than people born at differing times on the same day. The experimenter pointed out that most astrologers are not interested in scientific research and treat astrology like a religion which is not to be questioned. On the other hand, most scientists are not interested in research on astrology—which is a completely unscientific attitude.

Astrology is a rich and complex approach to typology. It is the most popular and widespread type system. It was studied seriously by Carl Jung as a practical, symbolic map of consciousness, and many Jungian analysts today study their patients' horoscopes as a part of the analytical process. We need to explore still further astrology's strengths and limitations.

1. Character and the Elements in Astrology: Earth, Air, Fire, and Water

LIZ GREENE

THE BIRTH CHART is a seed or blueprint of all that potentially belongs to a man's personality—if it were in full flower, and fully conscious. It is a road map in the truest sense, for the object of studying it is not to "overcome" the "influences" of the planets, but rather to allow room in one's life to express all those qualities and drives of which the chart is a symbol. Only then can the individual approximate the original plan for his life's development as it is "conceived"—for we must in the end infer intelligent, purposeful development—by the Self.

If this seems too abstruse or lofty a definition of the birth horoscope, it is pertinent to remember that astrology, before it became the property of popular magazines and newspaper columns, was once a sacred art. Through it, the student had access to an intuitive perception of the workings of the energies behind life, which no other ancient system—except perhaps its Eastern equivalent, the *I Ching*—could offer. The great is reflected in the small, and the fact that astrology can also be used to illumine more mundane problems is not a repudiation of its deeper psychological value. It is only a reflection of the fact that even in the minutest details of our lives, we reflect that which is our essence.

When seen in this light, it will be apparent that an understanding of the birth horoscope affords a new dimension to the understanding of one's life path.

Astronomically, the birth horoscope is simply a map—accurately calculated so that it cannot be faulted by the most persnickety astronomer—of the heavens as they appear from the exact time and place of the individual's birth. The circle of the twelve zodiacal signs is a symbol of totality, and in its totality it represents all life's possibilities. In this respect, the zodiac is like any other universal symbol of wholeness, such as the egg, or the urobouros (the serpent devouring its tail), or the equal-armed cross. It is a mandala, and as Jung has shown, mandalas are the symbolic expression of the potential wholeness of life and of the human psyche. They are at the same time symbols of the Self, and symbols of God, for these two are, in terms of human perception, the same.

Against the backdrop of this circle of the zodiac (which is called the ecliptic and which is in fact the apparent circle of the sun traversing the heavens) lie the sun, the moon and the eight known planets. The positions of these planets as they are placed around the zodiacal wheel at the moment of the individual's birth form the internal pattern of the birth chart. Thus we have a symbolic picture, with the wheel of wholeness around the outside and the individual combination of psychological components on the inside. Every chart is made up of the same ingredients: twelve zodiacal signs, eight planets, and the sun and moon. Yet every chart is different because at any given moment the arrangement of all these factors is different, both within the planetary pattern and in the relationship between the planets and the horizon of the earth itself.

In other words, human beings are built of the same raw stuff, the same drives or energies, needs and possibilities; but there is an individual arrangement of these energies which gives the stamp of uniqueness to the pattern. The same forces are present in all of us, a fact with which one is confronted endlessly in any work involving counselling or therapy. But there is a creative individuality which makes of these basic energies a unique work of art, which is the individual life. This creative shaping does not, we must assume, stem from the ego, which is hardly capable of such a feat; it stems from the Self, and the Self, as such, is not mapped out on the birth chart. It is the entire zodiac. Nor can the chart show the individual's decision at any point in his life to voluntarily cooperate with his own psyche's endeavour to achieve greater consciousness, and therefore to make fuller use of those potentials which are his from the beginning. In this decision lies the deepest meaning of individual free will.

THE ELEMENT OF AIR: THE THINKING TYPE

The intellect in every one of us is God.
—MENANDER

The element of air is another way of expressing, in language more typically a product of an age when man was closer to the imagery of the unconscious, what Jung means by the function of thinking. Air, considered astrologically, is a positive, masculine element, and the airy signs—Gemini, Libra and

Aquarius—are usually described in astrological textbooks as being detached, communicative, interested in the world of ideas, and favouring rationality. They are, in short, civilised. Air is the only element in the zodiacal wheel which does not contain any animal symbolism; Gemini and Aquarius are both represented by human figures, the Twins and the Waterbearer respectively, while Libra is portrayed as an inanimate object, the Scales. Air is the element which is most typically human, the furthest removed from instinctual nature; and it is the human kingdom which has developed—or perhaps overdeveloped in the last two hundred years—the function of thinking as its great gift.

All three airy signs, although different in their modes of expression, share the need to relate life experiences to a preconceived framework of ideas. This framework may come from outside, culled from the books, teachings and conversations of others, or it may come from within, painstakingly created by one's own laborious mental processes; but the existence of the framework is all-important and there is a tendency to take all experiences and seek in them the underlying pattern of logic which will make them conform to this preconceived structure.

Thinking primarily differentiates, through logic, between "this" and "that," and it will be apparent why the air signs are associated with a temperament which collects and categorises information, weighing one thing against another, and forming a philosophical framework out of the bits and pieces.

The airy type—and this does not necessarily mean an individual born under an air sign, so much as it does one whose chart as a whole contains a predominance of airy factors—will usually resemble, in general and in particulars, the qualities of the thinking type as Jung describes him. He has all the blessings of that type—the highly developed mind, the sense of fairness and capacity for impersonal assessment of situations, the love of culture, the appreciation of structure and system, the courageous adherence to principles, the refinement. He also has all the failings of the type—in terms of the "inferior" function—and these are euphemistically expressed in the typical characteristics ascribed to the three airy signs: Gemini has a horror of being pinned down in personal relationships, Libra is notorious for sitting on the fence and refusing to commit himself, and Aquarius is known for his cool detachment and distaste for the emotional displays which so often form a part of personal relating.

In other words, the airy type has a problem with feeling. Implicit in the preponderance of air on a chart is the likelihood that the world of personal feeling exchange will be the biggest problem of the individual's life— although he may not know it until his wife leaves him—because feelings, unlike everything else which comes under his microscopic eye, cannot be classified, structured, analysed, or fitted into the framework.

There are many Aquarians, women as well as men, who pride themselves on the fact that they never cry, because they see displays of emotion as weakness. This is a rather questionable virtue considering what is inevitably building up in the unconscious through such unwarranted underestimation of the feeling function. Ask a typical Geminian what he feels about something, and he will begin, "Well, I think . . ." When you tell him you want his feelings, not his thoughts, he often simply does not know what he feels and must go off for half an hour to find out. Gemini being Gemini, he will probably not come back again; and you have lost him because you have been too "possessive" and "demanding." Then there is the characteristic Libran's habit of simply avoiding anything to do with the dark emotional undercurrents of relationships because they aren't "nice"; he prefers to dwell in the ivory tower of his romantic ideals, working out precisely how he would like his relationships to be, and wondering why things never come out that way. And we should not forget that classic Aquarian quote, made to the woman who complains that in forty years of marriage she has never received either flowers or any overt display of affection: "But I told you I loved you when we married. Isn't that enough?"

THE ELEMENT OF WATER: THE FEELING FUNCTION

Where does reality lie? In the greatest enchantment you have ever experienced.
                    —HUGO VON HOFMANNSTHAL

And so we come to the element of water and the watery signs: Cancer, Scorpio and Pisces. The true watery type—and once again, this is not necessarily an individual born with the sun in a water sign, but rather someone whose chart suggests as a whole the preponderance of this element—resembles very closely Jung's description of the feeling type. Nothing is quite so important to the water signs as personal relationships and human values, and without them the world is barren, devoid of hope or joy. Anything will be sacrificed in order to preserve relationships, and it is typical of water to create any kind of crisis necessary, even at his own expense, to evoke a feeling response from his partner. The breath of life to the water signs is the world of feeling, and this includes the entire spectrum, shading from very light to very dark. In feeling there are no fine lines of distinction based on principle—"this" is not distinct from "that." Everything, rather, is an aspect of a constantly flowing and ever changing sea in which everything is one and all differences are merged. The only differentiation water makes is whether a feeling feels right to him; but it is neither "good" nor "bad."

The symbolism of the water signs contains three cold-blooded creatures:

the crab, the scorpion, and the fish. In dreams these images are usually connected with instinctual, unconscious energies which are close to the archaic natural roots of man and very remote from the world of rational, differentiated human thought. Most of the water's evaluation of life is done at an unconscious level; and of these signs it may truly be said that the right hand doesn't know what the left is doing. Water simply responds, and his responses to any personal situation are almost unerringly accurate and appropriate. While air is busy forcing himself into behaviour consistent to a preconceived framework, water is unpredictable and will respond to each situation as though it had never happened before.

The watery type is usually well-acquainted with the darker side of human nature, which earns these signs their reputation for compassion and empathy. There is the inherent capacity to feel what another feels, and to assess things in what appears to be a totally irrational way. Water has all the blessings of the feeling type—sensitivity to atmosphere, subtlety, charm and insight, a strong sense of values in human relationships, and the capacity to bring individuals together and instinctually understand their needs. Even Scorpio, much maligned because of his impenetrable facade of cold ruthlessness and his usually unjustified reputation for sexual excess—emotional excess would be a better description—is a true feeling sign with a soft heart underneath a tough carapace. At the same time, of course, water also has the failings of the type, and these, too, are expressed in the classic sign descriptions we have inherited from ancient astrology. Cancer tends traditionally to be clingy, possessive, clannish and fearful of the future; Scorpio has a reputation for emotional fanaticism and a kind of dark, heavy, brooding atmosphere which makes every relationship resemble a scene from *Othello*; and Pisces is notorious for his gushing sentimentality, his romantic escapism, his vacillation, his unpunctuality, vagueness and lack of principles.

THE ELEMENT OF EARTH: THE SENSATION TYPE

The trouble with always keeping both feet firmly on the ground is that you can never take your pants off.

—J. D. SMITH

The element of earth correlates with the function of sensation; and since one purpose of this function is to determine that something exists, earth gives the impression of being a fairly accessible, even simple type. We relate to the world of objects through the senses, and it is difficult to discount or repress our response to objects in the way that many people discount or repress thoughts, feelings or intuitions—particularly in an age when most of the empiric sciences have given their stamp of approval only to that which has concrete form. In consequence, most people find the element of earth fairly easy to understand—except the earthy person himself.

The earthy type is usually described in the astrological textbooks as practical, efficient, full of common sense, sensual, "realistic," well-organised and fond of money, security and status. This description applies to all three earth signs: Taurus, Virgo and Capricorn. The function of sensation is the "reality function," and in this sphere the earthy type excels, managing somehow to make order out of the random array of stimuli which assault the senses by relating to each one individually, savouring it, learning its nature, and moving on to the next. In this way, he builds up a body of facts which allows him to deal with each successive situation in the most efficient manner.

The earthy type has all the virtues of Jung's sensation type. He is at home with his body, frequently identifying himself with it, and is usually healthy because he can express his physical desires directly. He is at home with things, and can usually manage money and responsibilities in an effortless way which is mystifying to those who are more intuitive by temperament. He has a gift for actualising his desires, and this capacity for "earthing" shows at its best when combined either with thinking, to produce the careful empiric thinker, the impeccable researcher and statistician, or with feeling, to produce the happy sensualist, the affectionate lover and father, the patron of nature and of all beautiful things.

The earthy type also has all the potential failings of overemphasised sensation coupled with inferior intuition, and these are once again aptly summarised in the traditional descriptions of the earthy signs. Taurus is notorious for his dogmatic narrow-mindedness, his overpossessiveness of what he considers to be his property, and his tendency to reduce the subtlest and most complex of life's experiences to a philosophy of "Either I see it or it doesn't exist." Virgo proverbially cannot "see the forest for the trees," and becomes lost in a maze of detail and irrelevant trivia without ever seeing the point of his unceasing labours or realising that some people appreciate a little chaos in their lives. And Capricorn has a rather unpleasant reputation for justifying the means by the end and moulding his behaviour to the appropriate social expectations.

THE ELEMENT OF FIRE: THE INTUITIVE TYPE

Man's perceptions are not bounded by organs of perception: he perceives more than sense (tho' ever so acute) can discover.

—WILLIAM BLAKE

We come at last to the element of fire, which in fact begins the zodiacal cycle with Aries, and which is probably the most confusing element when an attempt is made to correlate its traditional attributes with those of Jung's intuitive type. This is partially because many astrological textbooks seem to accept at face value the traditional statements that fire is "warm," "outgoing," "self-centered" and "lucky" without questioning why he is like this and what truly motivates this curious temperament. There is also a considerable amount of confusion about what Jung means by intuition. It is commonly associated with mediums, seance parlours, and other assorted oddities which belong more to the realm of feeling.

> Because intuition is in the main an unconscious process, its nature is very difficult to grasp. The intuitive function is represented in consciousness by an attitude of expectancy, by vision and penetration . . . intuition is not mere perception or vision, but an active, creative process that puts into the object just as much as it takes out.[1]

June Singer describes intuition as

> . . . a process which extracts the perception unconsciously . . . just as . . . sensation strives to reach the most accurate perception of actuality, so intuition tries to encompass the greatest possibilities.[2]

If this is confusing to the reader, it is often more so to many intuitive types, who because they are given no insight into their own psychic constitutions by science and orthodox education—who generally claim that such a function does not exist—are often unsure and mistrustful of the very aspect of themselves which is most highly developed. Intuition is generally permitted to women, with a certain patronising attitude—for it is never taken quite seriously by those who are not aware of possessing it—but there are as many intuitive men as there are women, and they suffer for this lack of understanding.

The fiery signs—Aries, Leo and Sagittarius—share a vitality and spontaneity which is often envied and sometimes resented by more peaceable types. They are children at heart, and are inclined to live in a world of fantasy where people are really knights on white horses, or princesses imprisoned in castles, or dragons which must be challenged and slain. The fiery type has a strong need to mythologise his experiences and relate them to an inner world which belongs more to the world of fairy tales than to "reality." It is no wonder that so many fiery types are drawn to the world of the theatre. The fiery type's behaviour is often exaggerated, but it is unfair to accuse him of doing this purely to get a show; he is generally perfectly acquainted with his propensity for exaggeration, dramatisation and love of colour, but he does it for himself rather than for others, and it is more important to him to experience life dramatically than to accept the apparently drab and sometimes threatening world that more pragmatic types insist he recognise as the real one. "We can accept the unpleasant more readily than we can the inconsequential," as Goethe says.

★ ★ ★

We are always unconsciously drawn to that which we lack, and these four temperaments are inexorably drawn to their opposites because relationships of this kind provide an opportunity to develop greater inner integration. There is almost always a great deal of projection in this sort of relationship, and the problems begin when each individual tries to remodel his partner. He is really trying to remodel himself, which is entirely possible if only he could realise the significance of his perpetual criticism. If we could stand on our little mountain peaks and survey the landscape while realising that others stand on different peaks and see a different landscape, we might appreciate that the richness of life only becomes available when there is a sharing of different realities, and when one recognises the worth of another's values. And we cannot do this until we have ceased to scorn, reject, and fear our own inner "inferiority." Fire can learn to live with, and learn from, his earthy partner only when he is willing to experience his senses at their fullest, and acknowledge their importance; earth can accept and learn from his fiery partner only when he has confronted his own deep longing for freedom from bondage and has recognised that vision is as important as the form in which it is housed. Water can learn to relate to and appreciate air when he understands that not everything in life can be evaluated by his own personal feeling responses; and air can begin to understand and learn from water when he acknowledges his inner feeling needs and recognises that human relationships are as valid a field of human experience as the world of ideas.

2. Astrology as Psychological Cosmology

JIM SHERE

TYPE, ARCHETYPE, AND STEREOTYPE

ANY SERIOUS DISCUSSION of astrology must take into immediate consideration the baggage of popular opinion, for it is often regarded as not much more than a primitive pseudoscience or an amusing superstition. This is not what was originally intended by those who looked deep into human nature by looking deep into the heavens that embrace it. Throughout history, and in every civilization so far, consistent attempts have been made to find the meaning of life by exploring and mapping its relationship to the mystery of the cosmos.

The popular attitude toward astrology is typical of the common attempt to reduce the rich ambiguity of the human condition to routines of comfort, convenience, and entertainment. The horoscope is generally misunderstood as a limited categorization of people into one of twelve different types, according to the "sun sign." This mistaken idea reflects the problem with typing in general, which is better understood as a holistic description of one's dynamic relationship to the entire pantheon of archetypes, rather than as a reductive, mechanistic, and static classification in terms of one particular stereotype or another. Stereotyping in fact can only reinforce the problems that mapping against an accumulated sense of cosmic order is intended to help resolve.

The meaningful usefulness of astrology as a discipline that explores and a language that describes our relationship to a cosmic order has to do with its development during the same time that the human condition itself evolved. The cycles that we may sense within ourselves today have been measured by the observation of cycles of celestial activity, ever since the cutting of the phases of the Moon into prehistoric antler bone. Sadly, the significance of these images has become dimmed by the pollution and lights of our cities, and the vitality of these natural cycles has become hemmed in by appointment calendars and prescriptions for regulating medications. We have lost the sense of order in the cosmos, and feel an increase in the need to reduce the things of life to something more manageable, but less meaningful.

In the following pages I will reintroduce the elements of the language of astrology in a way that can reclaim the power inherent in its collective, cosmic nature. To this end, various experimental techniques are included for identifying the archetypal meanings in specifically individual ways. The use of a journal or notebook is recommended for recording your personal associations, in the building up of an accumulated understanding of astrology, making this chapter an interactive experience rather than some dry reference.

For practical purposes I should note here that an accurate calculation of your natal horoscope can be obtained from any of a variety of computerized services. However, it is important to recognize that the translation of your birth chart from the language of astrology into English by computer cannot be of much personal value because it will not report more than a standardized and unintegrated view of your personal and specific scheme of health.

THE ZODIAC AS A SPECTRUM OF ARCHETYPAL QUALITIES

While the twelve signs of the zodiac may have varied to some extent from culture to culture, a basic consistency remains that demonstrates its fundamentally archetypal nature, indicating qualities that remain common to humanity in all its manifestations. The integrity of this structural consistency is made up of the rhythmic repetition of the four elements (fire, earth, air, and water) in three modes of expression (cardinal, fixed, and mutable) and two contrasting polarities (active and receptive), which give rise to the one complete cycle of the zodiac.

Traditionally, the accumulated meanings of the signs have suggested certain keywords, usually written as adjectives that modify and describe personality in certain ways. In listing my own associations here it must be emphasized that they are intended as a place to start from, to prompt your own personal associations, rather than be used in a stereotypical manner of explicit definition.

Exercise: Copy these words into your notebook, starting a separate page with each sign, and then add to them from your own experiences and considerations.

Aries (Assertive Cardinal Fire: *primal radiant spontaneous energy*): aggressive, impetuous, innocent, initiating, courageous, impulsive; **Taurus** (Receptive Fixed Earth: *primal embracing deliberate matter*): consistent, conservative, productive, sensual, strong; **Gemini** (Assertive Mutable Air: *sequel radiant deliberate life*): curious, restless, uncommitted, versatile, scattered, experimental, unprejudiced; **Cancer** (Receptive Cardinal Water: *sequel embracing spontaneous energy*): sensitive, protective, nestling, nourishing, contained, caring; **Leo** (Assertive Fixed Fire: *primal radiant spontaneous matter*): confident, proud, noble, creative, dramatic, directive, powerful; **Virgo** (Receptive Mutable Earth: *primal embracing deliberate life*): precise, analytic, ecological, detailed, harvesting, winnowing, skillful; **Libra** (Assertive Cardinal Air: *sequel radiant deliberate energy*): considerate, diplomatic, esthetic, harmonizing, social, indecisive; **Scorpio** (Receptive Fixed Water: *sequel embracing spontaneous matter*): radical, intense, investigative, sexual, raging, healing, obsessive; **Sagittarius** (Assertive Mutable Fire: *primal radiant spontaneous life*): exploratory, boisterous, hopeful, adventurous, indulgent, optimistic, extravagant; **Capricorn** (Receptive Cardinal Earth: *primal embracing deliberate energy*): having authority and integrity, austere, responsible, constructive, committed, severe; **Aquarius** (Assertive Fixed Air: *sequel radiant deliberate matter*):

idealistic, humane, inventive, altruistic, impersonal; **Pisces** (Receptive Mutable Water: *sequel embracing spontaneous life*): mystical, poetic, sensitive, vulnerable, imaginative, intuitive, inspired, confused.

Exercise: There is a tradition that associates the four elements with four ways of breathing. These breaths, together with the visualization and contemplation of certain images derived from the elements, might be used here as an experiential process to help you to identify more personal associations for each sign. Sit comfortably and breathe for a few moments as indicated below, and then begin contemplating the image provided. Notice how your body feels in each case; be aware of the emotional states that seem to be evoked and the associations that come with them. After you've considered each sign in this way, take a few minutes to write down your experiences on the pages you have begun for each sign of the zodiac.

Aries—Breathe the Fire breath, taking your breath in the mouth and releasing it out the nostrils, and visualize an image of *the igniting Spark*— perhaps in the form of a bolt of lightning or as a brief electrical shock. **Taurus**—Breathe the Earth breath, taking your breath in and releasing it out the mouth, and visualize an image of *the earthen Soil*—perhaps in the form of a newly plowed field, or hands "dirty" from gardening. **Gemini**— Breathe the Air breath, taking your breath in and releasing it out the nostrils, and visualize an image of *the moving Air*—perhaps in the form of the wind, or the breath itself. **Cancer**—Breathe the Water breath, taking your breath in the nostrils and releasing it out the mouth, and visualize an image of *the flowing Water*—perhaps in the form of a river or a refreshing glass of water. **Leo**—Breathe the Fire breath, taking your breath in the mouth and releasing it out the nostrils, and visualize an image of *the glowing Ember*—perhaps in the form of hot charcoal or the sun as it rises in the morning. **Virgo**— Breathe the Earth breath, taking your breath in and releasing it out the mouth, and visualize an image of *the fine Sand*—perhaps in the form of a desert, a beach, or the grains of sand in an hourglass. **Libra**—Breathe the Air breath, taking your breath in and releasing it out the nostrils, and visualize an image of *the radiating Light*—perhaps in the form of a brilliant flash, or a gentle rainbow. **Scorpio**—Breathe the Water breath, taking your breath in the nostrils and releasing it out the mouth, and visualize an image of *the frozen Ice*—perhaps in the form of a gradually moving glacier, or a cube of ice in a cold drink. **Sagittarius**—Breathe the Fire breath, taking your breath in the mouth and releasing it out the nostrils, and visualize an image of *the fiery Flame*—perhaps in the form of a burning candle, or a racing prairie fire. **Capricorn**—Breathe the Earth breath, taking your breath in and releasing it out the mouth, and visualize an image of *the hard Rock*—perhaps in the form of a mountain of granite or a humble cobblestone. **Aquarius—** Breathe the Air breath, taking your breath in and releasing it out the nostrils, and visualize an image of *the open Space*—perhaps in the form of a blank page, or the deeper reaches of the infinite universe. **Pisces**—Breathe the Water breath, taking your breath in the nostrils and releasing it out the mouth, and visualize an image of *the vaporous Mist*—perhaps in the form of the fogs that drift in from the sea or the way your breath might cloud a pane of glass.

THE PLANETS AS SUBPERSONALITIES WITHIN THE PSYCHE

If the signs of the zodiac are understood to be modifying adjectives in the grammatical structure of an archetypal language, the planets are the nouns which they describe. The planets are the primary actors on the stage of the natal horoscope, taking on the qualities of the signs they are located within; and as nouns they name specific parts of human nature, which are generally grouped in the following manner:

Identity

The sense of individuality; or the conscious recognition of oneself as an independent individual:

The Sun: conscious individuality as the rational, literal aspect of identity, sometimes associated with the ego, or the essential purpose of individuality; I think of it as representing the left (analytic, or exclusive) side of the brain, rather than a particularly "masculine" quality.

The Moon: the irrational, associative aspect of identity, sometimes connected with the subconscious instinct for relatedness and meaning; I think of it as representing the right (emotional, inclusive) side of the brain, rather than a "feminine" quality.

Personality

The personal nature, or the manifestation of one's identity through one's thoughts, values, and behavior:

Mercury: the mind, especially in its objective capacities of sensate perception (via the five discrete senses), cogitation, and reason (the thinking process of analysis in a detached manner), and articulation as an explicit verbal expression, written or spoken.

Venus: the heart, especially in its subjective capacities of intuitive perception, valuing, empathy, and emotion as an inner experience; the feeling process of comprehension, evaluation, and appreciation in an implicit, involved manner, and its expression through empathic relatedness.

Mars: the body, or gut, especially as its expression through affect, gesture, and emotion; advocacy, assertiveness, and activity, particularly toward those things desired.

Character

The social interface or persona, the attitude and situation one assumes within one's community:

Jupiter: the extraverted, expansive, committed aspect of the psyche: aspiration, ambition, and contentment; the urge to grow and to expand into the outer world in a fulfillment of one's inner potential; the altruistic sense of social consciousness and justice.

Saturn: the introverted, constrictive, disciplined aspect of the psyche: conscience and integrity; often represented as the superego, or the personal sense of social obligation and responsibility by an introjection of various experiences of the outer world.

Selfhood

The transcendent process of self-actualization, or the inner spiritual work undertaken in search of the ultimate meaning of life on a personal basis:

Uranus: inauguration or *initiation* (the first stage of individuation), this represents the genius for hearing a "different drummer"; generally mistaken for rebellion against social norms at first, this must eventually be recognized as the initial step in the ultimate realization of one's potential, including the expression of one's unique contribution to society.

Neptune: devotion or *consecration* (the second stage of individuation), this represents the mystic who experiences a vision that initiates personal transformation; because the focus is not upon the reality of common consent but rather upon the larger, spiritual, compassionate context of personality, it can at first express an overwhelming confusion and such hypersensitivity that a tendency to denial or indulgence in various addictions is often the result.

Pluto: embodiment or *commitment* (the third and definitive stage of individuation), this represents the self-realized soul, that part of the psyche furthest removed from the central ego and therefore its ultimate container. For this

reason, Pluto represents the effective embodiment of the individual's fundamental purpose in life; and as such it represents the justice and wealth of the
ultimate bottom line.

Exercise: You can use guided imagery to explore the planets at work in a
particular birth chart. Have a friend read the following aloud, while you
focus upon the experience of the images that rise within you: "You are
holding a party and have invited ten people. There is a knock at the door,
and you open it to greet your first guest, one of the planets in your
horoscope. Remember that it has the qualities given it by the sign of the
zodiac in which it is located. How does this guest seem?—what is the
gender, the age and clothing, the general appearance? What gift does it
present to you? How does this guest make you feel, and how do you
respond? Welcome your guest, guide it to a special place in your home, and
then prepare for the arrival of the others. Notice after a while how the
different guests, given their personalities, are interacting. Is there anything
you feel called upon to say, or do?"

Establish a page in your notebook for each planet, perhaps including
drawings or affirmations. Dialogues with the planets or conversations you
have overheard among them can also be written out as you continue to
accumulate personal associations with your horoscope over time.

THE HOUSES OF THE HOROSCOPE AS PRAXIS

The lines that divide the birth chart into twelve wedges are called "cusps";
they indicate the twelve houses of the horoscope, which collectively represent the space into which we are born. At birth we are embodied in a focus
(at a certain time and place into a particular human condition) created by the
crosshairs that are formed by the intersection of the lines of the horizon
(drawn horizontally, east to west) and the meridian (drawn vertically, above
to below). The Midheaven at the top of the chart is where the sun is at noon,
or where any other planet is when it is overhead; the Ascendant is where
planets are as they rise on the eastern horizon; the Descendant is where they
are as they set in the west; and the Nadir is at the bottom, directly beneath
your feet, where the sun is at midnight.

If you were to stand facing the south (as you must do to view the planets at
night in their orbits), the Ascendant will be at your left and the Descendant
will be at your right. The upper half of the horoscope represents the visible
sky, the accessible aspect of the psyche, and the lower half of the chart
represents what remains hidden, beneath the surface of this planet Earth
upon which you are standing. The left side of the chart is the morning side

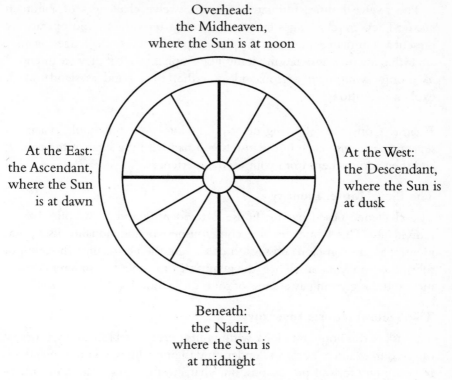

Overhead:
the Midheaven,
where the Sun is at noon

At the East:
the Ascendant,
where the Sun
is at dawn

At the West:
the Descendant,
where the Sun is
at dusk

Beneath:
the Nadir,
where the Sun is
at midnight

A Diagram of the House of the Horoscope

(from the Nadir up past the Ascendant to the Midheaven), and it represents the evolving, autonomous side of the psyche; the right side of the chart, the evening side, represents the involving, relating side of the psyche. An emphasis of planetary activity in any area is not to be ignored, but rather considered for further insight.

The cusp of each house acts as a lens that focuses the qualities of the zodiacal archetype toward which it is extended into a certain area of the human condition, as represented by the house. The signs on the cusps of the houses can be seen as setting the general tone of the environment, much as the wallpaper of a room contributes to its atmosphere. Each planet, modified by the constellation it is in, shows its primary interest or concern by its location in a particular house of the birth chart, since each house stands for a particular human activity. The planets accomplish the tasks that are represented by the houses in which they are located, using the tools that are made available by the zodiacal signs they are in. Particular attention, incidentally, should be paid to the houses of a birth chart in which more than one planet is located; this would indicate issues that are of great importance to the individual.

The twelve houses, ultimately, present twelve challenges of a human *praxis*. They are challenges to be consciously, responsibly, and operatively present as a human being upon the planet. In listing these challenges, again, I am listing my own associations; it must be emphasized that they are intended to prompt your own personal ideas, rather than stand as standardized, explicit definitions.

Exercise: Copy the following descriptions into your notebook, starting a separate page with each house just as you had with the signs of the zodiac; and then add to them from your own experiences.

The First House: Identity

The challenge posed by this house is to identify and know ourselves as individuals. This would involve consciousness of individuality itself, and identity as the conscious possession of an ego, the personality, the sense of social position and conscience, the genius that marches to a different drummer, and the growing awareness of soul, or Selfhood.

The Second House: Inventory

The task of this house is to look within ourselves to establish an inventory of our resources and to assess and understand their qualities, owning and taking responsibility for our possessions, our characteristics, our values, our interests, and our abilities.

The Third House: Environment

In this house we are confronted with the need to look about ourselves, to explore our relationship to the immediate environment, or context. This house traditionally refers to our childhood and our brothers and sisters, for it is with these seminal relationships that we establish the nature of our future relationships in the world.

The Fourth House: Centering

The challenge posed by this house is to identify a sense of groundedness, or belonging; this would include focus upon the body itself as a physical medium for operative identity, the sense of place (for example, home as a physical dwelling place), the childhood family, the family traditions, heritage and culture, and, ultimately, the archetypal (or karmic) ground.

The Fifth House: Creativity

The task of this house is to play—to risk becoming spontaneously creative and self-expressive, producing physical or psychic artifacts that contribute to the world in which we live while reflecting back to us our true nature, helping us thereby to know ourselves more clearly through our production.

This house especially refers to becoming childlike, and recognizing the meaning of the statement that "the child is father of the man."

The Sixth House: Discipline

In this house we are challenged to work upon and perfect the products of play from the previous house, and to focus upon our personal ecology in a responsible integration of ourselves with our environment; work, service, health, and devotion are issues here.

The Seventh House: Relationship

In this house (originally known as the House of Marriage) we experience our need for those human relationships that reflect our innate nature back to us—from a relationship to a "significant other" to relationships with our family members, our companions and friends, acquaintances within the community and beyond it to members of the world at large; these relationships can as well include the more negative ones with people traditionally known as enemies.

The Eighth House: Initiation

Originally known as the House of Death, this house challenges us to let go of our egoic identity, experiencing ecstasy as a global, mystical transcendence; this house rules not only death but also sneezes, bonding, orgasms, psychotic episodes, and anything else that can take us out of ourselves and into a heightened experience of existence.

The Ninth House: Philosophy

The task of this house is to understand what had taken place in the Eighth House, putting it back into the context of the world that we share with others, and to build a personal philosophy or world view that accounts for it. This generally asks that we learn to articulate the ineffable nature of our own transfiguration, or to have a fairly communicable description of our personal vision.

The Tenth House: Achievement

In this house we are confronted by the need to "amount to something." It is the house of vocation, ranging from the various jobs we take up early in life to the acceptance of the immediacy of work, providing a sense of career and perhaps profession—leading us to hear a spiritual calling to the ultimate purpose of life.

The Eleventh House: Community

The challenge posed by this house is to participate as a member of society, immersing ourselves in the human condition to take an active part in the planning and the development of its future.

The Twelfth House: Consecration

The task of this house is to let go of the material world, rather like the Eighth House, but this time into an operative personal Selfhood rather than into an impersonal ecstatic vision; this ultimate task requires inner work, dismantling, and culling the shards of personality to get at the essential nature of the Self, and to realize that (that is, to make that real).

Exercise: To make the meanings of the houses more personally significant for you as certain tasks, consider the following riddles of life in much the way one contemplates a Zen *koan*. Sit comfortably and consider one after the other, slowly. Pay close attention to the very personal responses that rise within you out of your own experience, whether they are answers or reactions, and allow them to help disclose the work that appears to be yours to do. Afterwards, write down all the answers that occurred to you for each question; and if other questions have occurred to you as more appropriate for one house or another, use them instead. Allow your own questioning to carry you deeper.

The First House asks: "Who am I?"
The Second House asks: "What do I have?"
The Third House asks: "Where am I?"
The Fourth House asks: "What nourishes me?"
The Fifth House asks: "What can I imagine?"
The Sixth House asks: "How do I work?"
The Seventh House asks: "Who am I with?"
The Eighth House asks: "How do I let go?"
The Ninth House asks: "What do I understand?"
The Tenth House asks: "What can I amount to?"
The Eleventh House asks: "What is my community?"
The Twelfth House asks: "What am I becoming?"

APPROPRIATE USES OF ASTROLOGY

If you have followed the exercises, you will have built by this time a fairly complex description of the various components of the astrological language, in terms of your own subjective process. A close examination of your birth chart in reference to the descriptions you have accumulated should help to organize and deepen your understanding of astrology as well as of yourself.

This is probably the best way to appreciate the relevance of archetypal statements regarding your own specific experience of the human condition.

The horoscope is "read" as a holographic X-ray of the psyche, for the archetypes constellated in each particular case will reappear throughout the chart in a variety of ways. The proper attitude in looking into a birth chart comes from being trained by the study of astrology in *detached attention*. It is scanned much as the horizon is scanned by a sailor in search of landfall: focus upon a search for the particular will usually overlook the actual.

An astrologer "translates" an astrological "sentence" in the way a literary critic might explicate a poem, by means of an integration of the variety of meanings of each sign, planet, and house, building up an accumulated associative description of the personality. A way of remembering the syntactical structure of the astrological language in reading the horoscope lies in remembering that *we are the total interrelationship of the planets, as described by their signs, that do what their houses require.* For instance, an Aries Sun in the First House could mean, among many other things, an assertive ego that is involved in exploring its identity. Continue in this way to explore and understand your birth chart by building up in your notebook accumulated descriptions of the ten subpersonalities that are represented by the ten planets, colored as they are by the signs in which they are located, and involved as they are in the tasks suggested by the houses they are located in.

On the other hand, professional astrologers will typically delineate, or explicate, your horoscope according to their *own* interpretation of the archetypes, a procedure dishearteningly similar to having a psychotherapist inform you of what your dream might "mean" according to another's expertise and authority.

As a discipline, astrology provides the means of consciously identifying, measuring, and participating with a higher order of reality that will put the ambiguities of the human condition into a meaningful context. This is not a translation of the horoscope from the language of astrology into the language of the reality of common consent; it is the translation of human experience from the routine into the transcendent. In short, rather than being simply a means of translating the text into the language of the reader, astrology can transport the reader directly into a healing, transformative experience of the numinous, ineffable realm that it describes.

3. The Twelve Chinese Astrological Types

THEODORA LAU

I HAVE WRITTEN THIS with the hope that it will help preserve the fast-fading folklore of Chinese horoscopes, which has endured through countless generations but is no longer popular or even encouraged in the China of today. It has been compiled from Chinese books, popular sayings, legends and mythology, interpretations of modern-day Chinese fortune-tellers as well as my own theories and observations. I also hope it will serve to bring you new insights about yourself and the people around you. It may enable you to find it easier to understand the occasional crankiness of your Dog boss, the changeable and capricious mind of a Horse client, the domineering but expansive ways of a Dragon friend or the serene but sceptical nature of a Snake-born.

You may be surprised to find that your local handyman, who is capable of fixing everything, was indeed born in the year of the dexterous Monkey, and that your slow, sure and conservative banker just happens to belong to the year of the reliable Ox. Again, you may be more patient with that annoying associate who is always the first to complain and cry wolf, when you discover she was born in the year of the Sheep. And you may laugh to learn that the fellow in your office who wears those atrocious ties will have been born in the year of the flamboyant Rooster.

It may shed light on why you dislike certain people, while with others you have an almost instant rapport. You will find the signs you will be most or least likely to be compatible with. But again, please bear in mind that there are bound to be exceptions depending on the sign that influences the time of your birth and the sign governing the month of your birth, too.

Perhaps after reading this you may believe enough to listen to the wise words of the Snake, look for sympathy from the gentle Sheep, go along with the clever schemes of the Monkey, have fun with the ever youthful and carefree Horse, rely on the Rabbit's unerring diplomacy or depend on the strength of the indomitable Dragon. And you may get your way by humoring the critical Rooster, reasoning with the Dog, going into battle with the optimistic Tiger or bargaining with the indefatigable Rat.

THE YEARS OF THE LUNAR SIGNS FROM 1900 TO 2007

RAT	1900	1912	1924	1936	1948	1960	1972	1984	1996
OX	1901	1913	1925	1937	1949	1961	1973	1985	1997
TIGER	1902	1914	1926	1938	1950	1962	1974	1986	1998
RABBIT	1903	1915	1927	1939	1951	1963	1975	1987	1999
DRAGON	1904	1916	1928	1940	1952	1964	1976	1988	2000
SNAKE	1905	1917	1929	1941	1953	1965	1977	1989	2001
HORSE	1906	1918	1930	1942	1954	1966	1978	1990	2002
SHEEP	1907	1919	1931	1943	1955	1967	1979	1991	2003
MONKEY	1908	1920	1932	1944	1956	1968	1980	1992	2004
ROOSTER	1909	1921	1933	1945	1957	1969	1981	1993	2005
DOG	1910	1922	1934	1946	1958	1970	1982	1994	2006
BOAR	1911	1923	1935	1947	1959	1971	1983	1995	2007

COMPATIBILITY AMONG THE SIGNS

Each of the twelve lunar signs in the Chinese cycle is appointed a compass point. Signs that form a triangle as shown in the affinity illustration make the best and most enduring unions.

The first triangle consists of the positive doers—the Rat, Dragon and Monkey. They are the performance and progress-oriented signs, adept at handling matters with initiative and innovation. Self-starters, they will initiate action, clear their paths of uncertainty and hesitation and forge fearlessly ahead. Restless and short-tempered when hindered or unoccupied, they are ruled by dynamic energy and ambition. They are the melting pot for ideas. They team up beautifully in any order as they possess a common modus operandi and can appreciate each other's ways of thinking.

The second triangle is made up of the most purposeful and steadfast signs. The Ox, Snake and Rooster are the dutiful and dedicated fighters who strive to achieve great heights and conquer by their constancy and unfailing determination. These three are fixed in their views and given to thought and systematic planning. They are the most intellectual signs of the cycle. They depend on their own assessment of facts and figures and give little credence to hearsay evidence. They are most likely to comply with the dictates of their heads rather than their hearts. Slow and sure in their movements, they like to act independently. They will invariably seek each other out and can intermarry and intermingle most successfully.

The third triangle is formed by the Tiger, the Horse and the Dog. These signs seek to serve humanity, promote universal understanding and heighten communications. They are made for personal contact and will develop strong bonds with their fellow human beings. They relate well to society as

they are basically honest and open and motivated by idealism. Unorthodox at times but always honorable in intent, this trio act more on impulse and heed their inner conscience. They provide their own counsel and inspire others to action by their high-spirited and aggressive personalities. Extroverted, energetic and defiant against adversity and injustice, they will get along fabulously together.

The fourth and last triangle is made up of the emotionally guided signs of the Rabbit, the Sheep and the Boar. These three signs are mainly concerned with their senses and what they can appreciate with them. They are expressive, intuitive and eloquent in aesthetic and artistic ways. They excel in the finer arts, are more diplomatic and compassionate and have generally calmer natures than other lunar signs. Dependent on others for stimulation and leadership, they are flexible because they are sympathetically tuned in to the vibrations of their environment. These three signs are drawn toward beauty and the higher aspects of love. They will extol the virtues of peaceful coexistence with their fellowmen. No doubt, these three animals will provide each other with excellent company and share the same basic philosophies.

4. Earth Astrology: A Native American Approach

SUN BEAR AND WABUN

THIS IS WRITTEN to reach out and help all people relate better to the Earth Mother and to all the rest of the creation around us. It is designed to help us understand that relationship. Many times we may feel that there is something missing in life. We may feel a longing sense to be closer to nature and the elemental forces. We hope that this will help you to find your place on the Medicine Wheel, to identify with powers that may have been lost to you. We hope that in finding a kinship with the universe you may understand why this relationship was so cherished by Native people. When you are able to completely blend with all things, then you are truly part of the whole.

The knowledge of the Medicine Wheel is needed at this time. We feel that if humanity is to grow, then we must all come to a closer understanding of our environment. It is man's alienation from natural things that causes many of his ills. Today, many people are trying to restore their balance with nature. People are turning to natural foods and natural healing, and there is a great back-to-the-land movement. Even in our industrialized society we feel the need to restore the balance with nature. It is at this time that we offer you the teachings of the Medicine Wheel.

We invite you to cast aside your preconceptions and enter, with us, a magical world where all things are connected to you, and you are connected to all things. This magical world consists of the very real and beautiful earth that is always around you and all your relations on her.

We invite you to open your eyes, your ears, your minds and your hearts and to see the magic that is always there. Today we tend to see the earth as a stable backdrop for all of the affairs of humankind. We see the minerals, the plants and the animals as servants of man. We have forgotten that they can be our teachers as well; that they can open us to ideas and emotions that have been blocked from the human heart for too long a time.

The moon, or month, during which you were born determines your starting place on the Medicine Wheel and your beginning totem in the mineral, plant and animal kingdoms. The first moon of the year, the Earth Renewal Moon, marks the time when the Father Sun returns from his journey to the south and begins, once again, to precipitate growth in the Earth Mother and all of her children. This moon begins at the time of the winter solstice, which usually occurs on December 22. This is the first moon of Waboose, Spirit Keeper of the North. It is followed by the Rest and Cleansing Moon and the Big Winds Moon. The moons of Waboose, those of rest and renewal, bring the time to contemplate the growth of the previous year and prepare for the growth of the year to come.

Following the moons of Waboose are those of Wabun, Spirit Keeper of the East. These three moons are those of awakening growth, when the Father Sun begins to illuminate all of earth's children and prepare them to bring forth their proper fruit. The first moon of Wabun is the Budding Trees Moon, which begins at the time of the spring equinox, which usually occurs on March 21. The other moons of Wabun are the Frogs Return Moon and the Cornplanting Moon. The moons of Wabun are those of illumination and wisdom, as earth's children prepare to grow in their proper way.

Next come the moons of Shawnodese, Spirit Keeper of the South. These are the moons of rapid growth, when all the earth comes to flower and bears fruit for that year. The Strong Sun Moon is the first one of Shawnodese and begins on June 21, the time of the summer solstice. It is followed by the Ripe Berries Moon and the Harvest Moon. This is the season of growth and trust. Trust is necessary in this season, since growth is so rapid there isn't time to ponder progress.

The autumn is the season of Mudjekeewis, Spirit Keeper of the West. The first moon of Mudjekeewis is the Ducks Fly Moon, which begins on September 23, the day of the autumn equinox. It is followed by the Freeze Up Moon and the Long Snows Moon. These are the moons that bring us the time of introspection, the time of gathering strength to look within and contemplate the growth and progress made in the preceding seasons. These are the times to prepare for the season of resting and renewing to come.

Each moon has a particular totem, or emblem, in the mineral, plant and animal kingdoms, which shares characteristics with the people who are born during this time. From your starting totems you will learn about yourselves, at the same time you learn more about your other relations on the earth. People do have a responsibility to their totems, to give them respect, liking and gratitude for the lessons and the energies they contribute to the continuation of life on our common Earth Mother.

As you travel around the wheel, you should strive to learn as much as you can about the totems of any place that you stand, so you are always growing more knowledgeable about those who share the earth with you. When you stand in the place of a different moon, you have the capacity to take on the characteristics of the totems for that moon and to learn from them, as well as

	DATES	MOON	ANIMAL	PLANT
NORTH	Dec. 22–Jan. 19	Earth Renewal	Snow Goose	Birch Tree
	Jan. 20–Feb. 18	Rest & Cleansing	Otter	Quaking Aspen
	Feb. 19–March 20	Big Winds	Cougar	Plantain
EAST	March 21–April 19	Budding Trees	Red Hawk	Dandelion
	April 20–May 20	Frogs Return	Beaver	Blue Camas
	May 21–June 20	Cornplanting	Deer	Yarrow
SOUTH	June 21–July 22	Strong Sun	Flicker	Wild Rose
	July 23–Aug. 22	Ripe Berries	Sturgeon	Raspberry
	Aug. 23–Sept. 22	Harvest	Brown Bear	Violet
WEST	Sept. 23–Oct. 23	Ducks Fly	Raven	Mullein
	Oct. 24–Nov. 21	Freeze Up	Snake	Thistle
	Nov. 22–Dec. 21	Long Snows	Elk	Black Spruce

Medicine Wheel Reference Chart

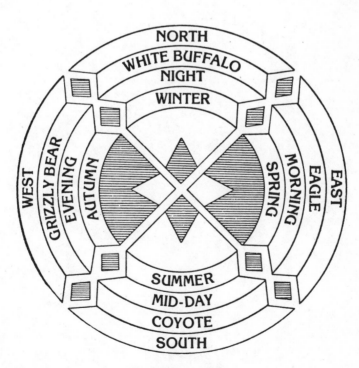

The Medicine Wheel

from your fellow two-leggeds. The more you are willing to learn, the further you can travel on your journey around the Medicine Wheel.

Remember as you read of the moons that not all people will have all of the same characteristics, even though they share the same moon and totems. All travel the wheel at their own speed. It is possible, during the time you stand at one position, to sometimes have moods or phases that seem more fitting to those of another moon. These can remind you of positions through which you have passed or give you hints of the places you'll be traveling to next. The important message of the Medicine Wheel is that you allow yourself to keep traveling, rather than tying yourself to one position and blocking your energies from growing and changing.

PART TWO

PERSONALITY TYPES IN EASTERN TRADITIONS

AMERICANS HAVE BECOME INCREASINGLY INTERESTED in Eastern philosophy. Many teachers of Eastern traditions have come to the United States, and the literature on Eastern psychology, medicine, and spiritual discipline is growing steadily. Certain Asian traditions contain sophisticated theories and practical methods of effecting psychological and physiological changes. These traditions bring us new perspectives on human functioning and potentials, as well as new techniques for psychological and physical health.

Each of the major Eastern traditions has developed a sophisticated and practical model of human nature, including a system of personality typology. These Eastern psychologies, like their Western counterparts, were derived from careful observations of human experience. They are built on centuries of empirical observations of physical and psychological variations among individuals.

The Eastern models are holistic and include diet, exercise, and general lifestyle recommendations to fit each type. They cover not only psychological dynamics but also the physical, cognitive, symbolic, and spiritual dimensions of each type.

In Chapter 5, Ram Dass, a former Harvard University psychology professor and nationally known author and teacher of spiritual issues, suggests that the ancient yoga chakra model can provide a personality diagnostic in much the same way as the Rorschach test or MMPI. Ram Dass argues that Freud, Adler, Jung, and other Western psychologists have developed psychological theories that fundamentally describe different personality types, which are represented by different chakras. For example, the second chakra is associated with sensual gratification and sexual desires. Ram Dass views Freudian psychology as a "second chakra psychology," in which everything is seen in relation to sexuality. Adlerian psychology is a "third chakra psychology," in which everything is seen in relation to power. Ram Dass classes Jungian psychology as a "fourth chakra psychology," and goes on to describe the remaining three chakras in terms of the higher levels of awareness depicted in transpersonal psychology.

Deepak Chopra, an Indian-born, Western-trained physician, is the author of several best-selling books including *Quantum Healing*, considered a classic integration of the principles of modern physics and holistic health. In Chapter 6, Chopra discusses the personality typology of the Ayurvedic tradition of India, one of the world's oldest medical traditions. There are three basic humors in Ayurveda, each composed of two elements. *Vata* contains air and ether, *pitta* is a combination of fire and water, and *kapha* is a combination of earth and water.

A central aspect of this tradition is the balancing of the different humors in each individual through diet, herbs, lifestyle, and psychological understanding. The humors are not static; they are affected by the time of day, the seasons, and a number of other variables. Developed as a medical system, Ayurveda is primarily concerned with physical health. However, psychological makeup and emotional and cognitive styles are also described as integral aspects of each typology.

Harriet Beinfield and Efrem Korngold are two of the first Westerners to become licensed in acupuncture in California. They have integrated the Chinese theory of the five elements with Western symbology, relating each element to a different archetype and personality orientation. The archetype for air is the *Pioneer*, who pushes to be on the move. The archetype for fire is the *Wizard*, who evokes passion and excitement. The archetype connected with earth is the *Peacemaker*, who sustains contact with others. Metal is associated with the *Alchemist*, who seeks to make perfect order. The water type is the *Philosopher*, who gives birth to new ideas.

The Eastern medicine typologies are active rather than static systems, and they are based on the principle that all things are undergoing constant change. One consequence of this principle is that, whatever your type, your humors or energies tend to become depleted or unbalanced. According to Ayurvedic and Chinese medicine, imbalance results in fatigue or illness. Indian and Chinese physicians work to keep their patients in balance through diet, acupuncture, herbs, and lifestyle prescriptions. For example, pitta types are more likely to become unbalanced during summer because summer heat increases their already overactive fire element. An Ayurvedic physician would prescribe a moderate lifestyle, warning the patient about the pitta tendency to overdo, and would also advise the patient to cut down on spicy foods, which are generally preferred by pitta types but which intensify the pitta humor.

In the yogic model of inner development, successful practice of the tradition's spiritual discipline is supposed to bring about personal growth, which may include a change of type. In yoga, various forms of meditation, breathing, and physical exercises are designed to awaken kundalini energy, a subtle force that resides at the base of the spine. As part of the kundalini process, yoga students are also taught to meditate on a certain shape, color, sound, and animal associated with each chakra. Kundalini then travels through each chakra, awakening and energizing them until the seventh chakra is awakened, bringing about a state of illumination or enlightenment. The yogic system provides not only a personality typology, but also a map of inner development through a series of states of consciousness and a technology to facilitate that development.

5. The Seven Chakras and Personality Types

RAM DASS

EACH PARTICULAR THERAPEUTIC SCHOOL is related to one particular type of distribution of energy in the system, or *pran*. For example, if you think in terms of *chakras* or energy centers in the body or connected with the body, there is the first, second, third, fourth, fifth, sixth, and seventh, which are called the *muladhara, sradhishthana, manipura, anahata, vishuddha, ajna,* and *sahasrara.* The first one is at the bottom of the spine, the second is sort of below the navel, the third is at the navel, the fourth is in the heart region, the fifth is at the throat, the sixth is between the eyebrows, the seventh is on the top of the head. These don't necessarily have any physiological correlates. They're just psychic localizations of psychic energy, let's put it that way, in this Hindu system. Now, instead of doing an MMPI or a Rorschach you could also do a chakra chart, just like you could do an astrological chart. And these all tell you certain things. A chakra chart tells, in a way, where the energy is fixed or localized in a person, where it's stuck.

For most people in the Western universe, in fact most people in the world, almost all of the energy is located either in the first, second, or third chakras. The first chakra can be characterized crudely as being connected with survival and survival of the individual as a separate being. It's like we're in the jungle and there's one piece of meat and who's going to get it, you or me? It's a survival-of-the-fittest-type model. It's a Darwinian assumption about the motivations of beings. When you're at that chakra, your motivation is to protect yourself as a separate being, your separateness. You can think of that as darkest Africa. And the channel up which this is all going is called the *Sushumna*—think of it as a big river. You go in the river from Africa and the next stop is like the Riviera. See, you've got your security under control and now you start to go into sensual gratification and sexual desires and reproduction. You can't be busy reproducing if you're protecting your life, but the minute your life's protected a little bit, then you can concern yourself with the next matter, which is reproducing the species. So the second chakra is primarily concerned with sexual actions, reactions, and so on—at the reproduction level. Procreative. Sex.

The third chakra . . . that's like Wall Street and Washington and London. It's primarily connected with power, with mastery, with ego control. Most of the world that we think of is connected with those particular centers. All the energy's located there. People justify their lives in terms of reproduction or sexual gratification, sensual gratification, or power or mastery. And it's interesting that pretty much any act we know of in the Western world can be done in the service of any one of those energies. So that a man can build a huge dynamic industry and we can say, "Aha, phallic," meaning second chakra. Or a person can seduce many women in order to have mastery and power over them and we say, "Aha, concerned with power and mastery," meaning third chakra. Doing sex in the service of third chakra.

Now it turns out that Freud is an absolutely unequaled spokesman and master of second-chakra preoccupation, that is, of those beings who were primarily involved in second chakra. So he could say quite honestly, because it is true at the second chakra, that religion is sublimated sex. Now it is true that in his generalized libido theories and the idea that all the body is erogenous . . . there are a lot of ways in which he slips over the edge; but his system is primarily concerned with the second chakra. Adler is primarily concerned with third chakra. Jung is primarily concerned with fourth chakra. I would point out that there are still the fifth, sixth and seventh chakras. And these are in terms of other kinds of psychic spaces and ways of organizing the universe and understanding what's happening. So that to the extent that you have "uncooked seeds" of the second chakra and you have a Freudian analyst, he's going to help you cook those seeds. He's not going to do much about where you're stuck in the third chakra, particularly. And he hasn't much to say about the fourth chakra, which is what Jung pointed out about Freud.

And when Jung starts to deal with his archetypes, collective unconscious and so on, he is starting to deal with what's called the fourth chakra, which is the same thing as Buddha's compassion. He is still in astral planes and he himself is afraid to go on. That's quite clear. He goes just so far and then he stops, because he's afraid that if he goes the next step, he will no longer be able to do what he does as Carl Jung.

As I said earlier, there are seven chakras or focal points and the transition from the third to the fourth is the first one into the transcendent state. It's the first one into the state of compassion, that is, where one experiences the shifts over figure-ground relationship so that one sees that you and I are human beings behind not only blue-suitness or dark-suitness and white-shirtness but also behind personalities and ages and bodies, and there is a place where . . . although we still see each other as separate . . . we are experiencing a feeling of a unitive nature with one another. That is another level of consciousness, where that unitive nature is *real,* rather than intellectually known. It's a real plane. And that compassion is the compassion that what is happening to you is happening to me, because in that place you and I are a unitive being. We're just two different manifestations of that one consciousness. That's already fourth chakra.

The fifth chakra is where you turn back inward, and rather than seeing the outward manifestations, you start to go deeper within or deeper up, as you might call it, and become preoccupied with higher planes of light or energy or form of it all, which are more and more subtle states of differences and similarities. It's as if we come into the place where we are energy or where we are cellular formations. It's sort of . . . different planes of perceptual organization of the universe. You could put it that way, what these planes are about. The sixth chakra is very comparable to what's called the causal plane, which is the . . . it's a place where one has broken sufficient attachments to any one perspective, so that you can stand back sufficiently far to gain what could be called cosmic perspective, to begin to see the most basic laws of the universe in operation everywhere in the universe. It's very much what the Egyptians were concerned with. It's what philosophy . . . it's what Plato's pure ideas are primarily about. That is sixth chakra. It's what we call wisdom. It's the wisdom of the ages, of these laws, these very simple laws. It could also be called the Godhead in a religious formulation of the . . . the first thought forms, the thought out of which all the rest is manifestation. At that place you are in the realm of pure ideas. That is, if you are in the sixth chakra, you have in a sense left the gross body. You are no longer identified with this body, nor are you identified with your personality, even, which is a more subtle plane. You are only identified with the ideas, all the rest is but manifestation, coming outward in planes of grossness.

The seventh chakra, the top chakra, is the chakra where you merge back into the oceanic, into the one, totally. If you would look, for example, at the cyclic process of ocean mist rising off ocean, forming clouds, clouds have raindrops, raindrops fall into ocean, ocean is made up of raindrops, but it's ocean, and it's ocean in the sense of oneness. Each raindrop does not retain its individuality as a raindrop any longer. And you can see this is merely process. The seventh chakra is the ocean. It's where it all goes back into the one. It's even behind all the laws and ideas.

Now, when one is climbing this ladder, at each new level there are certain characteristics . . . there is a new way in which you can receive energy or transmute energy in the universe. You can work with different kinds of energy when you are localized at each chakra, than you could before. You eat different foods, you can work with light, with love, and so on—different ways. Also, you see the universe in different ways and therefore your actions or responses start—your habits of thinking about it all, and thus your responses—start to change with each new level as well. At each level you are inclined to get stuck in that level. You have to, at each level, go beyond that one, too. What is usually the case for most of us who are doing this work is that we are very unevenly distributed in our energy over the different chakras or planes.

6. Body-Mind Types in Ayurvedic Medicine: Vata, Pitta, Kapha

DEEPAK CHOPRA

ONE IMPORTANT THING to know about the Ayurvedic system is that it is genetic. Body types are inherited. Long before the theory of DNA, the Ayurvedic sages realized that genetic traits come in groups: Oriental skin and hair come with brown eyes, not blue ones; solid musculature comes with heavy bones to support it, not light, thin ones. Mind, body, and behavior are consistently packaged together in subtle ways that are revealed only by knowledge of the doshas.

Your body type is the mold you were cast in, but it does not contain your fate. To be tall or short, indecisive or determined, anxious or calm is to be a type, yet there is abundant room for all the things that a body type does not control—thoughts, emotions, memories, talents, desires, and so forth. *Knowledge of your body type enables you to evolve to a more ideal state of health.* Unlike Western medicine, which aims at only physical or mental health, Ayurveda wants to lift every aspect of life to a higher level—personal relationships, work satisfaction, spiritual growth, and social harmony are all linked to mind and body very intimately; therefore, they can be influenced through one medicine, if its knowledge goes deep enough.

CHARACTERISTICS OF VATA (AIR-ETHER) TYPE

- Light, thin build
- Performs activity quickly
- Irregular hunger and digestion

- Light, interrupted sleep, insomnia
- Enthusiasm, vivaciousness, imagination
- Excitability, changing moods
- Quick to grasp new information, also quick to forget
- Tendency to worry
- Tendency toward constipation
- Tires easily, tendency to overexert
- Mental and physical energy comes in bursts

The basic theme of the Vata type is "changeable." Vata people are unpredictable and much less stereotyped than either Pittas or Kaphas, but their variability—in size, shape, mood, and action—is also their trademark. For a Vata person, mental and physical energy come in bursts, without steadiness. It is very Vata to

- Be hungry at any time of the day or night
- Love excitement and constant change
- Go to sleep at different times every night, skip meals, and keep irregular habits in general
- Digest food well one day and poorly the next
- Display bursts of emotion that are short-lived and quickly forgotten
- Walk quickly

Physically, Vatas are the thinnest of the three types, with characteristically narrow shoulders and/or hips. Some Vatas may find it difficult or impossible to gain weight and remain chronically underweight; others are pleasingly slender and supple. Though they have quite variable appetites, Vatas are the only type who can eat anything without gaining weight. (Some Vatas, however, fluctuate widely in weight over their lifetimes; they may be rangy and weedy as adolescents but overweight in middle age.)

Physical irregularity comes from an excess of Vata—hands and feet may be too large for a given body, or too small; teeth may be very small or else large and protruding; having an overbite is a Vata characteristic. Although most Vata people are well shaped, bowlegs, pigeon-toes, spinal curvature (scoliosis), deviated septum, and eyes placed too close together or too far apart are also common. Bones may be either very light or very long and heavy. Joints, tendons, and veins stand out prominently on many Vata bodies because the layer of fat beneath the skin is thin. Cracking joints are considered highly typical.

Vata dosha is responsible for all movement in the body. Your muscles move because of Vata, which also controls breathing, the movement of food through the digestive tract, and nerve impulses emanating from the brain.

Vata's most important function is to control the central nervous system. Tremors, seizures, and spasms are examples of Vata becoming disturbed. When this dosha is out of balance, nervous disorders appear, ranging from anxiety and depression (a hollow kind of depression, with feelings of being depleted, not the heavy depression of Kapha) to clinical mental disorders. Psychosomatic symptoms of all kinds are traceable to Vata aggravation. Therefore, bringing Vata back into balance often cures symptoms that defy any other treatment.

Vata is responsible for starting things, not finishing them, a characteristic that shows up strongly when a Vata type is out of balance—such people shop compulsively without buying anything, talk without coming to a conclusion, and become chronically unsatisfied. Vata types are sometimes said to spend themselves too freely, wasting money, energy, and words, but this is not true if they are in balance, since Vata dosha is responsible for balance throughout the body.

Most Vata people are prone to worry and at times suffer from insomnia, the result of restless thinking. Normal Vata sleep is the shortest of any type— six hours or less is characteristic, growing shorter as one ages. The typical negative emotion brought out by stress is anxiety (fear).

A balanced Vata person is infectiously happy, enthusiastic, and energetic. The mind is clear and alert; the inner tone is exhilarated. Vatas are extremely sensitive to change in their environment. They have quick, acute responses to sound and touch and dislike loud noise. Personalities that are vivacious, vibrant, excitable, unpredictable, imaginative, and talkative all express Vata. When out of balance, the Vata tendency to impulsiveness causes such people to overexert themselves—their excitement turns to exhaustion, then to chronic fatigue or depression.

The basic caution for Vata types is to get sufficient rest, not to overdo, and to pay close attention to regular lifestyle habits. These measures may not seem natural to many Vatas, but they often lead to quick improvements in physical or mental problems. We get our basic instinct for balance from Vata, which is absolutely vital to preserve.

CHARACTERISTICS OF PITTA (FIRE-WATER) TYPE

- Medium build
- Medium strength and endurance
- Sharp hunger and thirst, strong digestion
- Tendency toward anger, irritability under stress
- Fair or ruddy skin, often freckled
- Aversion to sun, hot weather
- Enterprising character, likes challenges

- Sharp intellect
- Precise, articulate speech
- Cannot skip meals
- Blond, light brown, or red hair (or reddish undertones)

The theme of the Pitta type is "intense." Anyone with bright red hair and a florid face contains a good deal of Pitta, as does anyone who is ambitious, sharp-witted, outspoken, bold, argumentative, or jealous. The combative side of Pitta is a natural tendency, but it does not have to be expressed. When in balance, Pittas are warm and ardent in their emotions, loving, and content. A face glowing with happiness is very Pitta. It is also very Pitta to

- Feel ravenously hungry if dinner is half an hour late
- Live by your watch (generally an expensive one) and resent having your time wasted
- Wake up at night feeling hot and thirsty
- Take command of a situation or feel that you should
- Learn from experience that others find you too demanding, sarcastic, or critical at times
- Have a determined stride when you walk

Physically, Pittas are medium in size and well proportioned. They maintain their weight without drastic fluctuations; it is not difficult for them to gain or lose a few pounds at will. Facial features are well proportioned; eyes are medium in size, often with a penetrating glance. Hands and feet are medium, too; joints are normal.

Pitta hair and skin are easily recognizable. The hair is usually straight and fine, red, blond, or sandy in color, and tends to gray prematurely. Baldness, thinning hair, or a receding hairline is also a sign of strong or excess Pitta.

Pittas generally have sharp, penetrating intellects and good powers of concentration. Their innate tendency is to be orderly and to manage their energies, money, and actions efficiently. Spending money on luxuries is one prominent exception to this—Pittas love to have fine things around them. They tend to respond to the world visually.

Heat is expressed everywhere in Pittas: by their typically short temper (hot-headedness), warm hands and feet, and burning sensations in the eyes, skin, stomach, or intestines—these are likely to appear if Pitta goes out of balance. Because they are hot themselves, Pittas are averse to long exposure to the sun. They develop heat fatigue very readily and do not take to hard physical labor. Their eyes dislike bright light.

Pittas incline toward anger as their characteristic negative emotion, and stress easily brings this out. They can be irritable and impatient, demanding and perfectionistic, particularly if out of balance. Although they are ambitious and show good leadership qualities, Pittas can be cutting and abrasive in manner, which alienates others.

Pittas speak precisely and articulately; they often make good public speakers. They hold strong opinions and like to argue. Sarcastic, critical speech identifies a Pitta imbalance, but, like people of the other doshas, Pitta types have two sides: in balance, they are sweet, joyous, confident, and brave. They like challenges and meet them vigorously, but with only medium physical energy. Pittas' stamina is moderate, and even their extremely strong digestion, the basis of their energy, can be abused. They are the kind of people who in middle age tend to say, "I used to be able to eat anything, but not anymore."

CHARACTERISTICS OF KAPHA (EARTH-WATER) TYPE

- Solid, powerful build; great physical strength and endurance
- Steady energy; slow and graceful in action
- Tranquil, relaxed personality; slow to anger
- Cool, smooth, thick, pale, often oily skin
- Slow to grasp new information, but good retentive memory
- Heavy, prolonged sleep
- Tendency to obesity
- Slow digestion, mild hunger
- Affectionate, tolerant, forgiving
- Tendency to be possessive, complacent

The basic theme of the Kapha type is "relaxed." Kapha dosha, the structural principle in the body, brings stability and steadiness; it provides reserves of physical strength and stamina that have been built into the sturdy, heavy frames of typical Kapha people. Kaphas are considered fortunate in Ayurveda because as a rule they enjoy sound health; moreover, their personalities express a serene, happy, tranquil view of the world. It is very Kapha to

- Mull things over for a long time before making a decision
- Wake up slowly, lie in bed a long time, and need coffee once you are up
- Be happy with the status quo and preserve it by conciliating others
- Respect other people's feelings, with which you feel genuine empathy
- Seek emotional comfort from eating
- Have graceful movements, liquid eyes, and a gliding walk, even if overweight

Physically, Kapha dosha gives strength and natural resistance to disease. Besides being well built, Kapha types tend to be thickset, with wide hips and/or shoulders. There is a strong tendency to gain weight easily—Kaphas have only to look at food to put on a few pounds. Since extra weight is not easily lost, Kaphas often become obese when they are out of balance. However, people with moderate builds can still be Kapha, and in two-dosha types, such as Vata-Kapha, the body can even be thin. A telltale Kapha trait is cool, smooth, thick, pale skin that is often oily. Large, soft, doelike eyes ("as if filled with milk," the ancient texts say) are also highly typical. Anything about the face or the body shape that suggests repose and stability points to an underlying dominance of Kapha. In women, to have a full, curvaceous shape or statuesque Renaissance beauty is very Kapha.

Kapha dosha is slow. Slow eaters, who usually have slow digestion, are generally Kapha types, as are slow speakers, particularly if their speaking manner is deliberate. Being calm and self-contained, Kapha types are slow to anger and want to maintain peace around themselves. Their natural response to the world is through taste and smell—Kaphas tend to place a great deal of importance on food; in a more general way, they rely on bodily feelings, being essentially earthy people.

Kaphas have steady energy. Their stamina exceeds that of other types, as does their willingness to perform physical labor. They are rarely drained by physical fatigue. It is very Kapha to store and save almost everything— money, possessions, energy, words, food, and fat. The fat is usually stored lower down, in the thighs and buttocks.

By nature Kaphas are affectionate, tolerant, and forgiving; to be motherly is to express Kapha. Kaphas are not easily shaken in a crisis, and they anchor others around them. There is a tendency to be complacent, however, and even the most balanced Kapha will procrastinate if he feels stressed. The typical Kapha negative emotion is greed or overattachment. Anyone who cannot bear to throw out old things is expressing an excess of Kapha. When out of balance, Kapha types become stubborn, dull, lethargic, and lazy.

Of the three doshas, Kaphas are the slowest learners, but, in compensation, they have good retention and in time acquire a solid command of their subject. They absorb new information slowly and take a methodical approach to it. Out of balance, they become dull and thickheaded.

The basic caution for Kapha types is to progress. Any stagnant situation turns Kapha stability into inertia—Kapha types need to make sure that they do not hold on to the past, cling to people and possessions, or balk at change. Making sure that they have a good deal of stimulation, though not natural to many Kaphas, brings out their vitality; heavy, cold food, lack of exercise, overeating, and repetitive work do not.

7. Character Types in Chinese Medicine: Pioneer, Wizard, Peacemaker, Alchemist, Philosopher

HARRIET BEINFIELD AND EFREM KORNGOLD

THE UNDERLYING ASSUMPTION of Chinese philosophy is that the forces that govern the cycles of change occurring in the external world are duplicated within our human bodies and minds. Patterns in nature are recapitulated at every level of organization—from the rotation of the planets to the behavior of our internal organs. These ancient Oriental ideas conform to what some modern thinkers call the "holographic paradigm": the organization of the whole (nature) is reflected by each and every part (plants, animals, human beings).

Within the human being, the same forces that organize the physical, sensory, and perceptual life of the organism (soma) affect the emotional, intellectual, and spiritual life of the person (psyche). Within this framework, the *Five-Phase* model has a diverse range of application.

A complex web of relationships was spun between the *Five Phases* and human culture. Affairs of state and society were conducted according to these principles. Proper times to plant and harvest, advance and retreat in battle, wed and procreate, and the methods of preserving health were prescribed by this system. The *Five Phases* are an almanac of the human cycles of momentary and lifelong change, a map that charts the course of process, a guide for comprehending our unfolding.

PHASES AS TRANSFORMATIVE STAGES

The *Five Phases* identify stages of transformation, patterns of expansion and contraction, proliferation and withering. Each *Phase* has an intrinsic primal energy, an ontological influence that shapes events. For example, human beings go through cycles in their lives similar to the seasons in nature—beginning in birth and ending in death, with stages of growth, maturity, and decay in between. Within the life cycle, the power of each *Phase* can be observed.

The *Wood Phase* is seen in birth, new life bursting forth. The newborn, at first small and fragile like a tender green shoot, mobilizes tremendous energy for swift growth. The baby moves from the *Yin* phase of gestation, corresponding to *Water,* to the *Yang* phase of growth, corresponding to *Wood.* The peak of this *Yang* phase is reached in adulthood when we are in our prime. This corresponds to *Fire.* Our "ripening," the stage during which we luxuriate in our maturity, corresponds to the *Earth Phase.* We revisit *Yin* through degeneration and aging, which corresponds to *Metal.* In our dying we return to the *Yin* state of dissolution, the *Water Phase,* and the emptiness from which we emerged.

Just as the *Five Phases* delineate transformations of the life cycle, they also describe the process of our daily existence. Our awakening is associated with *Wood,* and our movement toward a state of complete wakefulness corresponds to *Fire.* Becoming sleepy represents *Metal,* and the state of sleep itself corresponds to *Water. Earth* represents the still point, the balance between the polar movements, when neither one nor the other ascends. Our integrity is based on the proportion and rhythm of each of the *Five Phases* within us, regulating our waking and sleeping, activity and rest, arousal and inhibition.

FIVE PHASES DISTINGUISH FIVE TYPES OF PEOPLE

Our rendering of *Five-Phase Theory* postulates that we have styles of being in the world, inclinations, and gifts akin to the five seasons and powers. We are characterized by a hidden and ineffable organizing force through which all of our experience is incorporated and expressed.

Within each of us there is a particular *Phase* around which the others spin, the source from which our deepest impulses issue forth. This *Phase* is our type, the primal ontological matrix that initiates and governs the forming of our unique existence. We can distinguish five types—each of which possesses an inner landscape as distinct as the desert is from the jungle, as different as the pale dry leaves of autumn are from the flaming red dahlias of summer.

By learning how we are "put together"—how our soma and psyche are organized—our nature is revealed. When we know ourselves, we can behave accordingly. Self-recognition is a prerequisite for self-mastery. By applying the language of *Five-Phase Theory,* we can wrestle with the existential issues of identity (Who am I—how am I put together?), of purpose (What am I here to do?), and of destiny (Who will I become, and how can I make the best of it?).

Five-Phase analysis can inform us about our virtues and frailties, helping us to be wiser in our choices about what to pursue and what to avoid. Unearthing the archetypal roots of our character provides insight into our aptitudes, relationships, desires, and dreams as well as our health ailments, emotional fixations, mental doubts, and spiritual dilemmas.

Although *Five-Phase Theory* is old, the idea of *Five-Phase* "types" is our effort at grafting a Western psychospiritual branch onto the trunk of traditional Chinese medical thought. By fusing Chinese traditional meanings with Western cultural metaphors, we are expanding the ancient *Five-Phase* constructs into a phenomenological model that unifies physical, emotional, and mythical realms of human experience and behavior. We offer this version of *Five-Phase* thinking as our attempt at bridging Eastern and Western ideas about medicine and human process.

WOOD

Wood is as forceful and determined as the wind, as supple as a spreading aspen stretching into a bright, cloudless sky. Spring, a time of rebirth, sudden growth, and rapid expansion, marks the ascendance of this power. Movement surges to the surface, bursting through the confinement of winter. A crescendo of excitement builds as the life process reawakens. One day the forest appears gray and lifeless, the next day sunbeams cast warm light upon branches brimming with buds. This burgeoning of activity stirs tumultuous feeling. The change is expected yet unpredictable—like the birth of a child, the precise day or moment remains a mystery; we know spring will come but not exactly when. Anticipation foments tension as well as the promise of release.

The *Liver*, whose *Qi* is akin to the phase of *Wood*, instigates movement and arouses the mind by allowing tension and pressure to build. As spring initiates the rising of sap in the trees, so the *Liver* lifts the *Blood* and *Qi*. Alternately gathering and releasing the *Blood*, the *Liver* modulates the intensity and force of all motion and process.

The Archetype for Wood: The Pioneer

Metamorphosis is the organizing principle for the *Pioneer*. Driven by the adventure of penetrating the unknown, she contends with fate, deliberately battling adversity to tame the wilderness. Adaptive, cunning, and fiercely independent, she strikes out on her own, striving constantly to surpass her limits. Carving a broad expanse in which movement and vision are free and unfettered takes a multiplicity of forms. Inexorably drawn to travel roads not yet mapped, she treks wild mountain ridges, explores star-clustered heavens in an astronaut's suit, launches a business from scratch, or embarks upon research in yet unrecognized fields. Infatuated with what is new, curious about what is untried, she is eager to innovate, reform, and revolutionize.

Action compels the *Pioneer*. She vanquishes resistance with the thrust of a warrior's determination. Like a locomotive that gathers momentum and speed as it hurtles down the track, the *Pioneer* steers an awesome power.

FIRE

Fire is dazzling, evanescent, trembling, exciting, and all-embracing. Summer, the time when plants and creatures develop to their fullest potential, marks the ascendance of the power of *Fire*. Summer conjures up a sense of splendor and fulfillment as we stretch to the limits of our capacity. A brilliant sun climbs to its zenith over full-bloom magnolias amidst the hum of bees buzzing. In summer, *Yang* is dominant—light, warmth, activity, and interaction are at a peak. *Fire*, like summer, is expansive, radiant, outgoing, and warm. As the sun accelerates the life streams of the earth, the *Heart* squeezes the living juices of the blood through the vessels, imbuing the body with mindfulness.

The Archetype for Fire: The Wizard

Fusion is the organizing principle for the *Wizard*, who seeks to imbue the mundane with the extraordinary, merging human aspirations with divine purpose. Just as the *Fire* of love unites male and female to form new life, so the *Wizard* wields a miraculous power to annihilate separation by welding divergent elements into one. His excitement and enthusiasm generate the heat required for the reaction of fusion to occur. With this tremendous catalytic energy, he brings the transforming power of light, love, and aware-ness into the world.

Enchanting and persuasive, the *Wizard* is a natural salesman, selling not so much the product itself as the experience of possessing an instrument of magic, a veritable talisman, that endows us with the power to transcend our ordinary existence. The magic, however, is in the *Wizard*, not in the mer-chandise. So when this awesome barker of dreams vanishes, and the remark-able can opener that would open up a whole new world becomes merely a practical device, we are not dissatisfied or disappointed: the very experience of astonishment and joy that the *Wizard* inspires makes us glad.

Using personal magnetism and the gift of expression, he can assemble a group of individuals into one body. Whether as a team, chorus, classroom, audience, congregation, or political party, the *Wizard* gathers us up into a shared expanse of vision and feeling. Through this marriage with the hearts and minds of others, we realize a virtue of our humanness.

EARTH

Earth is as massive as a craggy mountain range, as gentle as a rolling grassy hill, as inviting as a verdant meadow, as absorbing as a rich alluvial valley receiving rivers of sediment and rain. Parading across boundaries, the Rockies, Appalachians, Andes, Himalayas, Alps, and Caucasus encircle and unite territories and villages, tribes and nations. In the sheltering hollows and crevices of the earth's body, creatures sculpt terraces, fields, and paddies and graze in marshes, forests, and open plains. *Earth* cradles and nurtures the life that depends upon it.

As summer wanes and fall approaches, there is a hiatus, a period in which time seems to stop and the glory of summer hangs suspended. Late summer marks the ascendance of the power of *Earth*, the time of ripening, when all that has grown and matured throughout spring and summer lies ready for harvest. Momentarily free of the cycle of birth, growth, decay, and death, this is a secure time of peace and plenty during which we appreciate the flowering of our labor. The *Spleen*, like Indian summer, corresponds with the *Phase* of *Earth*. Receiving and sharing solid and liquid, perceptions and ideas, the *Spleen* incorporates food and experience into the substance of who we are.

Earth—the soil that feeds us and the ground that locates us in time and space—imparts stability. A tree is as sturdy as the soil in which it is rooted. A sapling that grows out of gravel or sand is easily uprooted, whereas one that wraps its roots around granite stands sturdy, almost impossible to dislodge. When *Earth* is too porous, the structure that holds us securely in place erodes, whereas if too dense, we can become stuck in one spot, unable to move in any direction. *Earth's* density and mass sustains our momentum, keeping us aligned in the direction of our desired goal.

Just as a gyroscope spinning in place keeps an aircraft flying steadily along a prescribed path. *Earth* generates the capacity for changing direction without losing balance. *Earth* represents our center of gravity, the point of reference around which all other aspects of character and structure orient themselves, the axis around which they revolve.

The Archetype for Earth: The Peacemaker

Unification is the guiding principle of the *Peacemaker*. Through her power to establish and sustain relationships, she nurtures and promotes our connectedness with each other and our world. Focusing on what is mutually shared, she synthesizes what is divided and antagonistic into what is unified and interdependent. The *Peacemaker* values serenity and stability, mediating conflict with her gift for converting discord into harmony. She is the master of positioning and leverage, able to alter her perspective, grasping what is central to achieving the most cooperation with the least sacrifice. Chameleonlike, she can assume and enhance the attributes of those around her, putting people at ease in an environment of trust.

The *Peacemaker* embodies sympathy and caring, a ready advocate for those in greatest need—of friendship, sustenance, and recognition. Negotiating peace for its own sake, she tirelessly serves humanity as the great balancer and equalizer, the preserver of families and societies.

METAL

Metal is as austere as a vast arid plain before winter rains, as sharp as a high mountain peak slicing through mist into a clear empty sky. This *Phase* embodies the power of restraint, separation, and refinement.

Autumn is a time of withering and decay. Fallen leaves decompose, returning to the soil as the remains of crops are plowed under. Expired blossoms and fallen fruit fertilize the soil for next year's growth. The sap of trees settles into the interior, sinking down toward the roots. It is time for eliminating what is unnecessary, storing up only what is needed for winter. As the trees shed foliage, creatures prepare their shelters for the stark hibernation of winter as life slows down, collapsing inward. Corresponding to the temperament of this season, the *Lung*, the organ of *Metal*, sucks in and refines the *Qi*, sending it downward to nourish our roots with pure *Essence*. Ruling the skin, the outer limit of the human body, the *Lung* protects against external invasion and safeguards internal resources.

Metal, derived from the earth, is a pure substance generated by a process of reduction. Derived from the concept in alchemy of turning base metals into gold, this *Phase* represents the transformation of the gross materials of nature into pure "essence." Fall is a time for evolution through reduction. Matter returns to its source in preparation for its later re-creation—the rotting fruit leaves behind its seeds, and this corroding matter nourishes the kernels that multiply in spring.

With fall comes a sense of gathering in, stocking up, mingled with a sense of loss as the light begins to fade and the air chills. *Yin* waxes as *Yang* wanes. This is another season of change, but as spring was an expansive time of breaking through and proliferation, fall is a contractive time of pulling in and dying back. The life cycle completes itself in autumn.

The Archetype for Metal: The Alchemist

Transmutation is the guiding principle for the *Alchemist*, who seeks the perfection of form and function. Through his power of discernment, he distills what is good and pure from what is coarse and primitive. In his striving to extract order from chaos, he molds situations so that people perform their tasks with elegant precision.

Defining and refining, the *Alchemist* is the keeper of standards and measures, the source of aesthetic and moral values, the defender of virtue, principle, and beauty. He is the master of ceremony and discipline. Like an abbot ensconced in his sanctuary, serene, detached, unflappable, he instructs us in the meaning of ritual and doctrine, providing the structure that enables people to apply the metaphysical to the mundane.

WATER

Water is as subterranean as an underground stream, as dark and fertile as the womb, as enduring as the jade-colored sea. *Water* ascends to fullness in the frost of winter as plants submerge their energy into their roots, animals thicken their hides, and ponds harden into ice. Movement slackens as matter and energy concentrates. This is a time of apparent quiescence and stasis, yet beneath the surface is the hidden activity of gestation and germination that will bring forth renewal in spring. Before seeds and bulbs germinate, they demand a spell of chilly slumber. During this period of hibernation the essence of life persists in its most primitive state. The bear huddled in the corner of a darkened cave may be mistaken for dead except for his subtle warmth and slow, shallow breath. During winter he lives from accumulated reserves, resting until aroused by the hunger that swells as spring signals the intense activity of a new cycle. The *Kidney* abides within us like the bear in its cave, harboring the germ of being, the *Essence*, that feeds and renews our life force.

Like Dionysus, Greek god of nature, *Water* represents the primal inchoate forces of human nature, the realm of the collective and personal unconscious. *Water* is the primeval ooze out of which form materializes as life. It links past and future, ancestor and descendant, and is the source of our inherited intelligence.

The Archetype for Water: The Philosopher

Revelation propels the *Philosopher* in her relentless quest for truth. She brings to light that which is hidden, uncovering new knowledge, dispelling mystery, eroding ignorance. Scrutinizing life until the meaning and significance of her impressions coalesce into the germ of understanding, she is like an old-time prospector with a nose for nuggets, sifting through the gravel of notions and beliefs, tireless in her effort to apprehend the nature of reality. Just as the miner digs through tons of ore before unearthing a single gem, the *Philosopher* searches doggedly for truth, which, like a diamond, is esteemed not only for its radiant sparkle, but for its abiding hardness as a tool to advance civilization. It takes millennia to crystallize the residual mineral essence of fossils into this precious stone. Time is the pick and shovel of the *Philosopher*, who exhumes the bones of culture that endure. The *Philosopher* yearns for meaning that transcends the rudderless meandering of human affairs.

As she offers insight to the world, she relies on her hope that knowledge will be married with wisdom, power with compassion, aware that destiny is the final authority. Able to envision what can be, she is critical of what is by comparison. She discerns the inevitable disparity between apparent and ultimate reality. As the custodian of our memories and dreams, she articulates our aspirations, our ends, but does not define for us the machinery of their realization, our means.

PART THREE

PSYCHOLOGICAL TYPOLOGIES

SIGMUND FREUD, the founder of psychoanalysis at the turn of the century, has influenced everyone who has written since about human psychology. The theories of typology in this section have been directly inspired by Freud's insights.

Freud gradually developed a theory of character as he observed that his patients fell into certain personality types. He noticed, for example, that traits of orderliness, obstinacy, and stinginess seemed related to each other and also to childhood difficulties during toilet training. As psychoanalysis developed, Freud moved from concern with single symptoms to observations of themes and patterns in his patients.

Freud came to believe that the form the personality takes is determined by how the individual handles the conflicts found in the developmental, psychosexual stages of childhood. He called these the oral, anal, and phallic stages. They occur in the first three or four years of life and are followed by a latency period that ends at adolescence. After the latency period, a healthy, mature adult enters the genital stage.

These psychosexual stages of development also can be seen as distinct personality types. If someone has remained in a given developmental stage, this stage has, in effect, become his or her personality type. Or, as Freud noted, an individual can move on to other stages in some ways, yet still remain stuck on certain issues related to an earlier stage of development.

The major difference between "stage theories" and "type theories" is that the latter generally assume that we are destined to stay with one particular type for life. Stage theories make the opposite assumption, namely, that we will move from one stage to the next in the natural course of human development. Both approaches describe relatively stable, distinctive patterns of thinking, feeling, and behaving, which differentiate groups of people.

Freud believed that personality *fixation* will occur if the child receives either too little or too much gratification at any stage. This fixation will result in the development of a particular character or personality type. Oral types may be preoccupied with food, drink, or smoking. They are likely to be either strongly optimistic, gullible, and passive, or else pessimistic, suspicious, and manipulative. Anal types tend to extremes of being either stingy or overgenerous, constricted or expansive, stubborn or yielding, orderly or messy, rigidly punctual or compulsively late. Phallic types tend either to excessive vanity or self-hate, pride or humility, brashness or timidity. Genital types are mature adults who, as Freud eloquently put it, have the capacity for love and work. Freud's observations concerning the oral, anal, phallic, and genital character types have not only gained wide currency in the culture, they have also inspired a number of other psychologists to develop similar typologies.

Erik Erikson has extended Freud's theories of early development throughout the life cycle. Erikson is the most widely read and influential post-Freudian theorist. In a classic discussion of the early stages of development, Erikson makes the important point that what we learn is not simply a particular organ response to the environment, as Freud suggests, but a whole style of interacting with the world around us.

Karen Horney, another brilliant post-Freudian, was a pioneer in the exploration of the social and cultural aspects of personality and a founder of the self-help movement in psychology. Like Erikson, Horney has expanded Freud's approach to character typology into general patterns that can be seen throughout the normal population, as well as in exaggerated form in neurotics.

In Chapter 10, Horney identified types that are moving toward, moving against, and moving away from others. These tendencies are related to Plato's three functions of reason, emotion, and will and also to the three centers, head, heart, and belly, underlying the nine enneagram types. The moving-toward types are focused on love and relationship as the main solution for life's problems. The moving-against types try to dominate and control others and emphasize becoming tough-minded, hard-driving, and strong-willed in order to cope with life. The moving-away types choose privacy, independence, and intellectual detachment and seek to become detached observers, onlookers who are able to treat life as a drama acted out by others.

This brief survey of psychological typologies is far from complete. For instance, Alfred Adler, a colleague of Freud's, identified birth order as a source of type. First children, he found, tend to act more mature and responsible. They are most likely to be mother's helper. Youngest children are more likely to be family entertainers, full of charm and less quick to take on responsibility.

This section offers an introduction to the roots of typological thinking in the field of psychology.

8. *Oral, Anal, Phallic, and Genital Character Types*

SIGMUND FREUD

IT IS NOT THE CASE, then, that we recognize a sexual instinct which is from the first the vehicle of an urge towards the aim of the sexual function—the union of the two sex-cells. What we see is a great number of component instincts arising from different areas and regions of the body, which strive for satisfaction fairly independently of one another and find that satisfaction in something that we may call "organ-pleasure." The genitals are the latest of these "erotogenic zones" and the name of "sexual" pleasure cannot be withheld from their organ-pleasure. These impulses which strive for pleasure are not all taken up into the final organization of the sexual function.

The first of these "pregenital" phases is known to us as the *oral* one because, in conformity with the way in which an infant in arms is nourished, the erotogenic zone of the mouth dominates what may be called the sexual activity of that period of life. At a second level the *sadistic* and *anal* impulses come to the fore, undoubtedly in connection with the appearance of the teeth, the strengthening of the muscular apparatus and the control of the sphincter functions. We have learnt a number of interesting details about this remarkable stage of development in particular. Thirdly comes the *phallic* phase in which in both sexes the male organ (and what corresponds to it in girls) attains an importance which can no longer be overlooked. We have reserved the name of *genital* phase for the definitive sexual organization which is established after puberty and in which the female genital organ for the first time meets with the recognition which the male one acquired long before.

Our attitude to the phases of the organization of the libido has in general shifted a little. Whereas earlier we chiefly emphasized the way in which each of them passed away before the next, our attention now is directed to the facts that show us how much of each earlier phase persists alongside of and behind the later configurations and obtains a permanent representation in the libidinal economy and character of the subject.

We have been able to study transformations of instinct and similar processes particularly in anal erotism, the excitations arising from the sources of the erotogenic anal zone, and we were surprised at the multiplicity of uses to which these instinctual impulses are put. It may not be easy, perhaps, to get free from the contempt into which this particular zone has fallen in the course of evolution. Let us therefore allow ourselves to be reminded by Abraham that embryologically the anus corresponds to the primitive mouth, which has migrated down to the end of the bowel. We have learnt, then, that after a person's own faeces, his excrement, has lost its value for him, this instinctual interest derived from the anal source passes over on to objects that can be presented as *gifts*. And this is rightly so, for faeces were the first gift that an infant could make, something he could part with out of love for whoever was looking after him. After this, corresponding exactly to analogous changes of meaning that occur in linguistic development, this ancient interest in faeces is transformed into the high valuation of *gold* and *money* but also makes a contribution to the affective cathexis of *baby* and *penis*. It is a universal conviction among children, who long retain the cloaca theory, that babies are born from the bowel like a piece of faeces: defaecation is the model of the act of birth. But the penis too has its fore-runner in the column of faeces which fills and stimulates the mucous membrane of the bowel. When a child, unwillingly enough, comes to realize that there are human creatures who do not possess a penis, that organ appears to him as something detachable from the body and becomes unmistakably analogous to the excrement, which was the first piece of bodily material that had to be renounced. A great part of anal erotism is thus carried over into a cathexis of the penis. But the interest in that part of the body has, in addition to its anal-erotic root, an oral one which is perhaps more powerful still: for when sucking has come to an end, the penis also becomes heir of the mother's nipple.

If one is not aware of these profound connections, it is impossible to find one's way about in the phantasies of human beings, in their associations, influenced as they are by the unconscious, and in their symptomatic language. Faeces—money—gift—baby—penis are treated there as though they meant the same thing, and they are represented too by the same symbols.

During our studies of the pregenital phases of the libido we have also gained a few fresh insights into the formation of character. We noticed a triad of character-traits which are found together with fair regularity: orderliness, parsimoniousness and obstinacy; and we inferred from the analysis of people exhibiting these traits that they have arisen from their anal erotism becoming absorbed and employed in a different way. We therefore speak of an "anal character" in which we find this remarkable combination and we draw a contrast to some extent between the anal character and unmodified anal erotism. We also discovered a similar but perhaps still firmer link between ambition and urethral erotism. A striking allusion to this connection is to be seen in the legend that Alexander the Great was born during the same night in which a certain Herostratus set fire to the celebrated temple of Artemis at Ephesus out of a sheer desire for fame. So the ancients would seem not to have been unaware of the connection. You know, of course, how much urination has to do with fire and extinguishing fire. We naturally expect that other character traits as well will turn out similarly to be precipitates or reaction-formations related to particular pregenital libidinal structures.

9. *Three Personality Modes: To Get, To Hold On, To Make*

ERIK ERIKSON

MOUTH AND SENSES

THE FIRST ENCOUNTER occurs when the newborn, now deprived of his symbiosis with the mother's body, is put to the breast. His inborn and more or less co-ordinated ability to take in by mouth meets the breast's and the mother's and the society's more or less co-ordinated ability and intention to feed him and to welcome him. At this point he lives through and loves with his mouth; and the mother lives through and loves with her breasts. For her this is a late and complicated accomplishment, highly dependent on the love she can be sure of from others, on the self-esteem that accompanies the act of nursing—and on the response of the newborn. To him the oral zone, however, is only the focus of a first and general mode of approach, namely *incorporation*. He is now dependent on the delivery of "materia" of all kinds directly to the receptive doors of his organism. For a few weeks at least, he can only react if and when material is brought into his field. As he is willing and able to suck on appropriate objects and to swallow whatever appropriate fluids they emit, he is soon also willing and able to "take in" with his eyes what enters his visual field. (As if nearly ready also to hold on to things, he opens and closes his fist when properly stimulated.) His tactile senses too seem to take in what feels good.

As the child's radius of awareness, co-ordination, and responsiveness expands, he meets the educative patterns of his culture, and thus learns the basic modalities of human existence, each in personally and culturally significant ways. These basic modalities are admirably expressed in "basic" English, which is so precise when it comes to the definition of interpersonal patterns. To our great relief, therefore, we can at this point take recourse to some of the simplest English words instead of inventing new Latin combinations.

To get (when it does not mean "to fetch") means to receive and to accept what is given. This is the first social modality learned in life; and it sounds simpler than it is. For the groping and unstable newborn organism learns this modality only as it learns to regulate its organ systems in accordance with the way in which the maternal environment organizes its methods of child care.

One may say (somewhat mystically, to be sure) that in thus *getting what is given,* and in learning to *get somebody to do* for him what he wishes to have done, the baby also develops the necessary ego groundwork to *get to be* the giver. Where this fails, the situation falls apart into a variety of attempts at controlling by duress or fantasy rather than by reciprocity. The baby will try to get by random activity what he cannot get by central suction; he will exhaust himself or he will find his thumb and damn the world. The mother too may try to force matters by urging the nipple into the baby's mouth, by nervously changing hours and formulas, or by being unable to relax during the initially painful procedure of suckling.

Now to the second stage, during which the ability to make a more active and directed approach by incorporation, and the pleasure derived from it, grow and ripen. The teeth develop, and with them the pleasure in biting *on* hard things, in biting *through* things, and in biting pieces *off* things. With a little configurational play we can see that the biting mode serves to subsume a variety of other activities (as did the first incorporative mode). The eyes, first part of a passive system of accepting impressions as they come along, have now learned to focus, to isolate, to "grasp" objects from the vaguer background, and to follow them. The organs of hearing have similarly learned to discern significant sounds, to localize them, and to guide an appropriate change in position (lifting and turning the head, lifting and turning the upper body). The arms have learned to reach out and the hands to grasp more purposefully.

With all of this a number of interpersonal patterns are established which center in the social modality of *taking* and *holding on to* things—things which are more or less freely offered and given, and things which have more or less of a tendency to slip away. As the baby learns to change positions, to roll over, and very gradually to sit up, he must perfect the mechanisms of grasping, investigating, and appropriating all that is within his reach.

In stage II, mode 2 (incorporation by biting) dominates the oral zone. Progress here means that the child's libido moves on in order now to endow with power a second organ mode which in turn will lead to the integration of a new social modality: *taking*. A new stage does not mean the initiation of a new zone or mode, but the readiness to experience both more exclusively, to master them more co-ordinately, and to integrate their social meaning with a certain finality.

But what if this progress is impeded, accelerated, or arrested? The horizontal deviation leads to a *zone* fixation, i.e., the individual holds on to *oral* pleasures of various mode characteristics. The vertical fixation is a *mode* fixation—i.e., the individual is apt to overdevelop mode I in a variety of zones: he always wants *to get* whether by mouth and senses, or by other apertures, receptors, or behaviors. This kind of fixation will later be carried over to other zones.

ELIMINATIVE ORGANS AND MUSCULATURE

When discussing self-preservation Freud suggests that at the beginning of life the libido associates itself with the need for keeping alive by sucking drinkables and biting edibles.

It is clear that oral erotism and the development of the social modalities of "getting" and "taking" are based on the need to breathe, to drink, to eat, and to grow by absorption.

What would be the self-preservative function of anal erotism? First of all, the whole procedure of evacuating the bowels and the bladder as completely as possible is made pleasurable by a feeling of well-being which says, "Well done." This feeling, at the beginning of life, must make up for quite frequent discomfort and tensions suffered as the bowels learn to do their daily work. Two developments gradually give these anal experiences the necessary volume: the arrival of better-formed stool and the general development of the muscle system which adds the dimension of voluntary release, of dropping and throwing away, to that of grasping appropriation. These two developments together suggest a greater ability to alternate withholding and expelling at will.

What then, makes the anal problem potentially so difficult?

The anal zone lends itself more than any other to the display of stubborn adherence to contradictory impulses because, for one thing, it is the modal zone for two conflicting modes of approach, which must become alternating, namely *retention* and *elimination*. Furthermore, the sphincters are only part of the muscle system with its general duality of rigidity and relaxation, of flexion and extension. The development of the muscle system gives the child a much greater power over the environment in the ability to reach out and hold on, to throw and to push away, to appropriate things and to keep them at a distance. This whole stage, then, which the Germans called the stage of stubbornness, becomes a battle for autonomy. For as he gets ready to stand more firmly on his feet the infant delineates his world as "I" and "you," "me" and "mine." Every mother knows how astonishingly pliable a child may be at this stage, if and when he has made the decision that he *wants* to do what he is supposed to do. It is hard, however, to find the proper formula for making him want to do just that. Every mother knows how lovingly a child at this stage will snuggle up and how ruthlessly he will suddenly try to push the adult away. At the same time the child is apt both to hoard things and to discard them, to cling to possessions and to throw them out of the window. All of these seemingly contradictory tendencies, then, we include under the formula of the retentive-eliminative modes.

As to new social modalities developed at this time, the emphasis is on the simple antithesis of *letting go* and *holding on,* the nature, ratio, and sequence of which is of decisive importance both for the development of the individual personality and for that of collective attitudes.

LOCOMOTION AND THE GENITALS

I have mentioned no ages so far. We are now approaching the end of the third year, when walking is getting to be a thing of ease, of vigor. The books tell us that a child "can walk" much before this: but from the point of ego progress—i.e., of a sense of coherence and security—he cannot walk as long as he is only able to accomplish the feat, more or less well, with more or fewer props, for short spans of time. The ego has incorporated walking and running into the sphere of mastery when gravity is felt to be within, when the child can forget that he is *doing* the walking and instead can find out what he can *do with* it. Only then do his legs become an unconscious part of him instead of being an external ambulatory appendix.

To look back: the first way station was prone relaxation. The trust based on the experience that the basic mechanisms of breathing, digesting, sleeping, etc., have a consistent and familiar relation to the foods and comforts offered, gives zest to the developing ability to raise oneself to a sitting and then standing position. The second way station (accomplished only toward the end of the second year) is that of being able to sit not only securely but, as it were, untiringly, a feat which permits the muscle system gradually to be used for finer discrimination and for more autonomous ways of selecting and discarding, of piling things up—and of throwing them away with a bang.

The third way station finds the child able to move independently and vigorously. He not only is ready to visualize his sex role, but also begins either to comprehend his role in economy or, at any rate, to understand what roles are worth imitating. More immediately, he can now associate with his age mates and, under the guidance of older children or special women guardians, gradually enter into the infantile politics of nursery school, street corner, and barnyard. His learning now is intrusive; it leads away from him along aggressive associations and combinations into ever new facts and activities; and he becomes acutely aware of differences between the sexes. This, then, sets the stage for infantile genitality and for the first elaboration of the intrusive and inclusive modes.

The *intrusive mode* dominating much of the behavior of this stage characterizes a variety of configurationally "similar" activities and fantasies. These include the intrusion into other bodies by physical attack: the intrusion into other people's ears and minds by aggressive talking; the intrusion into space by vigorous locomotion; the intrusion into the unknown by consuming curiosity.

The ambulatory and infantile genital stage adds to the inventory of basic social modalities in both sexes that of "making" in the sense of "being on the make." There is no simpler, stronger word to match the social modalities previously enumerated. The word suggests head-on attack, enjoyment of competition, insistence on goal, pleasure of conquest. In the boy, the emphasis remains on "making" by phallic-intrusive modes: in the girl it sooner or later changes to making by teasing and provoking or by milder forms of "snaring"—i.e., by making herself attractive and endearing. The child thus develops the prerequisites for *initiative*, i.e., for the selection of goals and perseverance in approaching them.

PREGENITALITY AND GENITALITY

A system must have its utopia. For psychoanalysis the utopia is "genitality." This was first conceived of as the integration of the pregenital stages to a point of perfection which, later on (after puberty), would insure three difficult reconciliations: (1) the reconciliation of genital orgasm and extragenital sexual needs; (2) the reconciliation of love and sexuality; (3) the reconciliation of sexual, procreative, and work-productive patterns.

10. *Moving Toward, Moving Against, Moving Away from Others*

KAREN HORNEY

FOR THE SAKE OF SIMPLICITY I shall classify the compliant, the aggressive, and the detached personality. We shall focus in each case on the person's more acceptable attitude, leaving out in so far as possible the conflicts it conceals. In each of these types we shall find that the basic attitude toward others has created, or at least fostered, the growth of certain needs, qualities, sensitivities, inhibitions, anxieties, and, last but not least, a particular set of values.

MOVING TOWARD PEOPLE

Group I, the compliant type, manifests all the traits that go with "moving toward" people. He shows a marked need for affection and approval and an especial need for a "partner"—that is, a friend, lover, husband or wife "who is to fulfill all expectations of life and take responsibility for good and evil, his successful manipulation becoming the predominant task." However these needs may vary in their expression, they all center around a desire for human intimacy, a desire for "belonging." Because of the indiscriminate nature of his needs, the compliant type will be prone to overrate his congeniality and the interests he has in common with those around him and disregard the separating factors. His misjudging of people this way is not due to ignorance, stupidity, or the inability to observe, but is determined by his compulsive needs. He feels—as illustrated by a patient's drawing—like a baby surrounded by strange and threatening animals. There she stood, tiny and helpless, in the middle of the picture, around her a huge bee ready to sting her, a dog that could bite her, a cat that could jump at her, a bull that could gore her. Obviously, then, the real nature of other beings does not matter, except in so far as the more aggressive ones, being the more frightening, are the ones whose "affection" is the most necessary. In sum, this type needs to be liked, wanted, desired, loved; to feel accepted, welcomed, approved of, appreciated; to be needed, to be of importance to others, especially to one particular person; to be helped, protected, taken care of, guided.

The need to satisfy this urge [to feel safe] is so compelling that everything he does is oriented toward its fulfillment. In the process he develops certain qualities and attitudes that mold his character. Some of these could be called endearing: he becomes sensitive to the needs of others—within the frame of what he is able to understand emotionally. For example, though he is likely to be quite oblivious to a detached person's wish to be aloof, he will be alert to another's need for sympathy, help, approval, and so on. He tries automatically to live up to the expectations of others, or to what he believes to be their expectations, often to the extent of losing sight of his own feelings. He becomes "unselfish," self-sacrificing, undemanding—except for his un-bounded desire for affection. He becomes compliant, overconsiderate—within the limits possible for him—overappreciative, overgrateful, generous. He blinds himself to the fact that in his heart of hearts he does not care much for others and tends to regard them as hypocritical and self-seeking. But—if I may use conscious terms for what goes on unconsciously—he persuades himself that he likes everyone, that they are all "nice" and trustworthy, a fallacy which not only makes for heartbreaking disappointments but adds to his general insecurity.

These qualities are not as valuable as they appear to the person himself, particularly since he does not consult his own feelings or judgment but gives blindly to others all that he is driven to want from them—and because he is profoundly disturbed if the returns fail to materialize.

Along with these attributes and overlapping them goes another lot, aimed at avoiding black looks, quarrels, competition. He tends to subordinate himself, takes second place, leaving the limelight to others; he will be appeasing, conciliatory, and—at least consciously—bears no grudge. Any wish for vengeance or triumph is so profoundly repressed that he himself often wonders at his being so easily reconciled and at his never harboring resentment for long. Important in this context is his tendency automatically to shoulder blame. Again quite regardless of his real feelings—that is, whether he really feels guilty or not—he will accuse himself rather than others and tend to scrutinize himself or be apologetic in the face of obviously unwarranted criticism or anticipated attack.

This type has certain characteristic attitudes toward himself. One is the pervasive feeling that he is weak and helpless—a "poor little me" feeling. When left to his own resources he feels lost, like a boat loosed from its moorings, or like Cinderella bereft of her fairy godmother. This helplessness is in part real; certainly the feeling that under no circumstances could one possibly fight or compete does promote actual weakness. Besides, he frankly admits his helplessness to himself and others. It may be dramatically emphasized in dreams as well. He often resorts to it as a means of appeal or defense: "You must love me, protect me, forgive me, not desert me, *because* I am so weak and helpless."

A second characteristic grows out of his tendency to subordinate himself. He takes it for granted that everyone is superior to him, that they are more attractive, more intelligent, better educated, more worth while than he. There is factual basis for this feeling in that his lack of assertiveness and firmness does impair his capacities; but even in fields where he is unquestionably able his feeling of inferiority leads him to credit the other fellow—regardless of his merit—with greater competence than his own. In the presence of aggressive or arrogant persons his sense of his own worthiness shrinks still more. However, even when alone his tendency is to undervalue not only his qualities, talents, and abilities but his material possessions as well.

A third typical feature is a part of his general dependence upon others. This is his unconscious tendency to rate himself by what others think of him. His self-esteem rises and falls with their approval or disapproval, their affection or lack of it. Hence any rejection is actually catastrophic for him. If someone fails to return an invitation he may be reasonable about it consciously, but in accordance with the logic of the particular inner world in which he lives, the barometer of his self-esteem drops to zero. In other words any criticism, rejection, or desertion is a terrifying danger, and he may make the most abject effort to win back the regard of the person who has thus threatened him. His offering of the other cheek is not occasioned by some mysterious "masochistic" drive but is the only logical thing he can do on the basis of his inner premises.

All of this contributes to his special set of values. Naturally, the values themselves are more or less lucid and confirmed according to his general maturity. They lie in the direction of goodness, sympathy, love, generosity, unselfishness, humility; while egotism, ambition, callousness, unscrupulousness, wielding of power are abhorred—though these attributes may at the same time be secretly admired because they represent "strength."

These, then, are the elements involved in "moving toward" people. It must be apparent now how inadequate it would be to describe them by any *one* term like submissive or dependent, for a whole way of thinking, feeling, acting—a whole way of life—is implicit in them.

MOVING AGAINST PEOPLE

Just as the compliant type clings to the belief that people are "nice," and is continually baffled by evidence to the contrary, so the aggressive type takes it for granted that everyone is hostile, and refuses to admit that they are not. To him life is a struggle of all against all, and the devil take the hindmost. Such exceptions as he allows are made reluctantly and with reservation. His attitude is sometimes quite apparent, but more often it is covered over with a veneer of suave politeness, fair-mindedness and good fellowship. A desire to make others believe he is a good fellow may be combined with a certain amount of actual benevolence as long as there is no question in anybody's mind that he himself is in command. There may be elements of a neurotic need for affection and approval, put to the service of aggressive goals.

His needs stem fundamentally from his feeling that the world is an arena where, in the Darwinian sense, only the fittest survive and the strong annihilate the weak. What contributes most to survival depends largely on the civilization in which the person lives; but in any case, a callous pursuit of self-interest is the paramount law. Hence his primary need becomes one of control over others. Variations in the means of control are infinite. There may be an outright exercise of power, there may be indirect manipulation through oversolicitousness or putting people under obligation. He may prefer to be the power behind the throne. The approach may be by way of the intellect, implying a belief that by reasoning or foresight everything can be managed. His particular form of control depends partly on his natural endowments.

Concomitantly he needs to excel, to achieve success, prestige, or recognition in any form. Strivings in this direction are partly oriented toward power, inasmuch as success and prestige lend power in a competitive society. But they also make for a subjective feeling of strength through outside affirmation, outside acclaim, and the fact of supremacy. Here as in the compliant type the center of gravity lies outside the person himself; only the kind of affirmation wanted from others differs. Factually the one is as futile as the other. When people wonder why success has failed to make them feel any less insecure, they only show their psychological ignorance, but the fact that they do so indicates the extent to which success and prestige are commonly regarded as yardsticks.

A strong need to exploit others, to outsmart them, to make them of use to himself, is part of the picture. Any situation or relationship is looked at from the standpoint of "What can I get out of it?"—whether it has to do with money, prestige, contacts, or ideas. The person himself is consciously or semiconsciously convinced that everyone acts this way, and so what counts is to do it more efficiently than the rest. The qualities he develops are almost diametrically opposed to those of the compliant type. He becomes hard and tough, or gives that appearance. He regards all feelings, his own as well as others', as "sloppy sentimentality." Love, for him, plays a negligible role. Not that he is never "in love" or never has an affair or marries, but what is of prime concern is to have a mate who is eminently desirable, one through whose attractiveness, social prestige, or wealth he can enhance his own position. He sees no reason to be considerate of others. "Why should I care—let others take care of themselves." In terms of the old ethical problem of two persons on a raft only one of whom could survive, he would say that of course he'd try to save his own skin—not to would be stupid and hypocritical.

While the compliant type tends to appease, the aggressive type does everything he can to be a good fighter. He is alert and keen in an argument and will go out of his way to launch one for the sake of proving he is right. He may be at his best when his back is to the wall and there is no alternative but to fight. In contrast to the compliant type who is afraid to win a game, he is a bad loser and undeniably wants victory. To admit an error when it is not absolutely necessary seems to him an unforgivable display of weakness, if not arrant foolishness.

It is consistent with his attitude of having to fight against a malevolent world that he should develop a keen sense of realism—of its kind. He will never be so "naïve" as to overlook in others any manifestation of ambition, greed, ignorance, or anything else that might obstruct his own goals. Since in a competitive civilization attributes like these are much more common than real decency, he feels justified in regarding himself as only realistic. Actually, of course, he is just as one-sided as the compliant type. Another facet of his realism is his emphasis on planning and foresight. Like any good strategist, in every situation he is careful to appraise his own chances, the forces of his adversaries, and the possible pitfalls.

Because he is driven always to assert himself as the strongest, shrewdest, or most sought after, he tries to develop the efficiency and resourcefulness necessary to being so. The zest and intelligence he puts into his work may make him a highly esteemed employee or a success in a business of his own. However, the impression he gives of having an absorbing interest in his work will in a sense be misleading, because for him work is only a means to an end. He has no love for what he is doing and takes no real pleasure in it—a fact consistent with his attempt to exclude feelings from his life altogether. This choking off of all feeling has a two-edged effect. On the one hand it is undoubtedly expedient from the standpoint of success in that it enables him to function like a well-oiled machine, untiringly producing the goods that will bring him ever more power and prestige. Here feelings might interfere. They could conceivably lead him into a line of work with fewer opportunistic advantages; they might cause him to shy away from the techniques so often employed on the road to success; they might tempt him away from his work to the enjoyment of nature or art, or to the companionship of friends instead of persons merely useful to his purpose. On the other hand the emotional barrenness that results from a throttling of feeling will do something to the quality of his work; certainly it is bound to detract from his creativity.

★ ★ ★

The aggressive type looks like an exquisitely uninhibited person. He can assert his wishes, he can give orders, express anger, defend himself. But actually he has no fewer inhibitions than the compliant type. It is not greatly to the credit of our civilization that his particular inhibitions do not, offhand, strike us as such. They lie in the emotional area and concern his capacity for friendship, love, affection, sympathetic understanding, disinterested enjoyment.

MOVING AWAY FROM PEOPLE

What is crucial is [this type's] inner need to put emotional distance between themselves and others. More accurately, it is their conscious and unconscious determination not to get emotionally involved with others in any way, whether in love, fight, co-operation, or competition. They draw around themselves a kind of magic circle which no one may penetrate. And this is why, superficially, they may "get along" with people. The compulsive character of the need shows up in their reaction of anxiety when the world intrudes on them.

All the needs and qualities they acquire are directed toward this major need of not getting involved. Among the most striking is a need for *self-sufficiency*. Its most positive expression is resourcefulness. The aggressive type also tends to be resourceful—but the spirit is different; for him it is a prerequisite for fighting one's way in a hostile world and for wanting to defeat others in the fray. In the detached type the spirit is like Robinson Crusoe's: he has to be resourceful in order to live. It is the only way he can compensate for his isolation.

A more precarious way to maintain self-sufficiency is by consciously or unconsciously restricting one's needs. We shall better understand the various moves in this direction if we remember that the underlying principle here is never to become so attached to anybody or anything that he or it becomes indispensable. That would jeopardize aloofness. Better to have nothing matter much. For example: A detached person may be capable of real enjoyment, but if enjoyment depends in any way on others he prefers to forego it. He can take pleasure in an occasional evening with a few friends but dislikes general gregariousness and social functions. Similarly, he avoids competition, prestige, and success. He is inclined to restrict his eating, drinking, and living habits and keeps them on a scale that will not require him to spend too much time or energy in earning the money to pay for them. He may bitterly resent illness, considering it a humiliation because it forces him to depend on others. He may insist on acquiring his knowledge of any subject at first hand: rather than take what others have said or written about Russia, for instance, or about this country if he is a foreigner, he will want to see or hear for himself. This attitude would make for splendid inner independence if it were not carried to absurd lengths, like refusing to ask directions when in a strange town.

Another pronounced need is his need for privacy. He is like a person in a hotel room who rarely removes the "Do–Not–Disturb" sign from his door. Even books may be regarded as intruders, as something from outside. Any question put to him about his personal life may shock him; he tends to shroud himself in a veil of secrecy. A patient once told me that at the age of forty-five he still resented the idea of God's omniscience quite as much as when his mother told him that God could look through the shutters and see him biting his fingernails. This was a patient who was extremely reticent about even the most trivial details of his life. A detached person may be extremely irritated if others take him "for granted"—it makes him feel he is being stepped on. As a rule he prefers to work, sleep, eat alone. In distinct contrast to the compliant type he dislikes sharing any experience—the other person might disturb him. Even when he listens to music, walks or talks with others, his real enjoyment only comes later, in retrospect.

Self-sufficiency and privacy both serve his most outstanding need, the need for utter independence. He himself considers his independence a thing of positive value. And it undoubtedly has a value of sorts. For no matter what his deficiencies, the detached person is certainly no conforming automaton. His refusal blindly to concur, together with his aloofness from competitive struggle, does give him a certain integrity. The fallacy here is that he looks upon independence as an end in itself and ignores the fact that its value depends ultimately upon what he does with it. His independence, like the whole phenomenon of detachment of which it is a part, has a negative orientation; it is aimed at *not* being influenced, coerced, tied, obligated.

The need to feel superior must be stressed here because of its intrinsic association with detachment. The expressions "ivory tower" and "splendid isolation" are evidence that even in common parlance, detachment and superiority are almost invariably linked. Probably nobody can stand isolation without either *being* particularly strong and resourceful or *feeling* uniquely significant. This is corroborated by clinical experience. When the detached person's feeling of superiority is temporarily shattered, whether by a concrete failure or an increase of inner conflicts, he will be unable to stand solitude and may reach out frantically for affection and protection. Vacillations of this kind often appear in his life history. In his teens or early twenties he may have had a few rather lukewarm friendships, but lived on the whole a fairly isolated life, feeling comparatively at ease. He would weave fantasies of a future when he would accomplish exceptional things. But later these dreams were shipwrecked on the rocks of reality. Though in high school he had had undisputed claim to first place, in college he ran up against serious competition and recoiled from it. His first attempts at love relationships failed. Or he realized as he grew older that his dreams were not materializing. Aloofness then became unbearable and he was consumed by a compulsive drive for human intimacy, for sexual relations, for marriage. He was willing to submit to any indignity, if only he were loved. Only when he feels considerably stronger does he discover with immense relief that he would much rather "live alone and like it." The impression is that he has merely reverted to his former detachment. But actually it is a matter of being now for the first time on solid enough ground to admit—even to himself—that isolation is what he wants.

The need for superiority in the case of the detached person has certain specific features. Abhorring competitive struggle, he does not want to excel realistically through consistent effort. He feels rather that the treasures within him should be recognized without any effort on his part; his hidden greatness should be felt without his having to make a move. In his dreams, for instance, he may picture stores of treasure hidden away in some remote village which connoisseurs come from far to see. Like all notions of superiority this contains an element of reality. The hidden treasure symbolizes his intellectual and emotional life which he guards within the magic circle.

Another way his sense of superiority expresses itself is in his feeling of his own uniqueness. This is a direct outgrowth of his wanting to feel separate and distinct from others. He may liken himself to a tree standing alone on a hilltop, while the trees in the forest below are stunted by those about them. Where the compliant type looks at his fellow man with the silent question, "Will he like me?"—and the aggressive type wants to know, "How strong an adversary is he?" or "Can he be useful to me?"—the detached person's first concern is, "Will he interfere with me? Will he want to influence me or will he leave me alone?"

PART FOUR

JUNGIAN TYPES AND ARCHETYPES

THE JUNGIAN TYPOLOGY SYSTEM is the best known and most used type theory after astrology. Two of the basic Jungian type concepts, introversion and extraversion, have become household words. The Meyers-Briggs Type Indicator, based on Jungian typology, is the most widely used personality test in the world. The system is popular in business, where it has proven effective in enhancing team building, communication, and interpersonal relations. It is also extremely widespread among those who are seriously interested in self-understanding and personal growth.

Jung points out that no one is a pure example of type. For example, there are no pure introverts or extraverts. Jung compared these two processes to the heartbeat. There must be a rhythmic alternation between contraction (introversion) and expansion (extraversion), and without balance the heart will cease to function. However, each individual tends to favor one attitude and operates more in terms of it. The ideal is to be flexible and able to access either attitude when needed, rather than staying stuck in a fixed way of responding to the world.

Jung wrote the first edition of *Psychological Types* in 1921, partly to explain the irreconcilable differences he had with Freud. He realized that he and Freud did not simply differ on matters of factual or theoretical interpretation. They had fundamentally distinct ways of experiencing the world which were based on differences in their personality types, and their theories were reflections of these differences. In Chapter 11, Jung reflects on his development of type theory and reviews the basic attitudes of introversion and extraversion and the four orientations of thinking, feeling, sensation, and intuition.

In Chapter 12, James Hillman, the noted archetypal psychologist, presents a thoughtful critique of the misuses of typing. He argues that most people use typing to overgeneralize about others and end up cutting themselves off from their own direct perceptions of other people. He reminds us that type is meant to be an elastic, fluid, and imprecise category, as in discussing a "typical" literary style or a "typical" historical period. This is very different from the rigid and static nature of a system of *classification,* in which, for example, you are clearly defined as a member of a particular class or unequivocally excluded from that class. Hillman argues that confusion between these two approaches has led to many misuses of typing.

The remaining three chapters in this section describe archetypal typologies. The archetype, one of Jung's most difficult concepts, is composed of *arche* or "first" and *typos* or "imprint." Archetypes are basic, primordial patterns in the psyche, and operate at a deeper level of the psyche than the personal unconscious.

Jung developed the idea of archetypes from the experiences his patients reported. A number of his patients described dreams and fantasies that included remarkable ideas and images whose content could not be traced to the individual's own past experience. Jung found a close correspondence between these dream contents and the mythical and religious themes found in many widely scattered cultures. He suggested that the archetypes hold a kind of readiness to produce over and over again the same universal mythical ideas and images.

Jennifer and Roger Woolger have used the archetypes of the great Greek goddesses in developing a typology for women. Jung at times acknowledged that his typology system seemed more suited to men than women. Toni Wolff, Jung's longtime colleague and intimate companion, began to develop a type system for women, based on four female archetypes. Jennifer and Roger Woolger have extended Wolff's work into a powerful system that integrates six goddess archetypes into a Goddess Wheel. This model includes the interrelationships among the six goddess archetypes and also places at the center the Great Mother, the fundamental archetype underlying all the goddesses. Jennifer is a gestalt therapist, Roger a Jungian analyst.

Robert Moore and Douglas Gillette have developed a typology for men based on the four archetypes of King, Warrior, Magician, and Lover. Moore and Gillette present a theory of the mature male psyche and argue that most of psychology has focused on the analysis of the undeveloped male and ignored the study of masculinity in its fullness.

In Chapter 15, written for this volume, anthropologist and tarot expert Angeles Arrien presents the tarot as an archetypal personality system and shows how to find which of the major arcana cards corresponds with your birth date. Your card provides a symbolic picture of the basic archetypal forces and personality orientation operating in your life.

The tarot includes a rich, complex array of interrelated archetypal symbols. Most tarot decks contain seventy-eight cards, and each card includes dozens of symbols and images. The tarot symbols are closely related to astrology, numerology, Kabbalah, and various other symbolic systems. The tarot deck, which is the origin of our modern playing cards, is at least six centuries old, and some tarot scholars believe it originated in ancient Egypt. These old cards were conceived at a profound level of the human psyche, at a collective level that transcends the personality.

Jung was convinced of the need to maintain nonrational lines of communication with the collective unconscious, which is one of the great strengths of working with the tarot. The powerful images in each tarot card are "projection holders," or hooks to catch the imagination. The tarot deck is a symbolic map of consciousness and includes the relationships among the major archetypal symbols of inner and outer experience.

11. *Reflections on Psychological Types*

C. G. JUNG

I HAVE GIVEN A DETAILED DESCRIPTION of a purely psychological typology in my book *Psychological Types*. My investigation was based on twenty years of work as a doctor, which brought me into contact with people of all classes from all the great nations. When one begins as a young doctor, one's head is still full of clinical pictures and diagnoses. In the course of the years, impressions of quite another kind accumulate. One is struck by the enormous diversity of human individuals, by the chaotic profusion of individual cases, the special circumstances of whose lives and whose special characters produce clinical pictures that, even supposing one still felt any desire to do so, can be squeezed into the straitjacket of a diagnosis only by force. The fact that the disturbance can be given such and such a name appears completely irrelevant beside the overwhelming impression one has that all clinical pictures are so many mimetic or histrionic demonstrations of certain definite character traits. The pathological problem upon which everything turns has virtually nothing to do with the clinical picture, but is essentially an expression of character. Even the complexes, the "nuclear elements" of a neurosis, are beside the point, being mere concomitants of a certain characterological disposition. This can be seen most easily in the relation of the patient to his parental family. He is, let us say, one of four siblings, is neither the eldest nor the youngest, has had the same education and conditioning as the others. Yet he is sick and they are sound. The anamnesis shows that a whole series of influences to which the others were exposed as well as he, and from which indeed they all suffered, had a pathological effect on him alone—at least to all appearances. In reality these influences were not aetiological factors in his case either, but prove to be false explanations. The real cause of the neurosis lies in the peculiar way he responded to and assimilated the influences emanating from the environment.

By comparing many such cases it gradually became clear to me that there must be two fundamentally different general attitudes which would divide human beings into two groups—provided the whole of humanity consisted of highly differentiated individuals. Since this is obviously not the case, one can only say that this difference of attitude becomes plainly observable only when we are confronted with a comparatively well-differentiated personality; in other words, it becomes of practical importance only after a certain degree of differentiation has been reached. Pathological cases of this kind are almost always people who deviate from the familial type and, in consequence, no longer find sufficient security in their inherited instinctual foundation. Weak instincts are one of the prime causes of the development of an habitual one-sided attitude, though in the last resort it is conditioned or reinforced by heredity.

I have called these two fundamentally different attitudes *extraversion* and *introversion*. Extraversion is characterized by interest in the external object, responsiveness, and a ready acceptance of external happenings, a desire to influence and be influenced by events, a need to join in and get "with it," the capacity to endure bustle and noise of every kind, and actually find them enjoyable, constant attention to the surrounding world, the cultivation of friends and acquaintances, none too carefully selected, and finally by the great importance attached to the figure one cuts, and hence by a strong tendency to make a show of oneself. Accordingly, the extravert's philosophy of life and his ethics are as a rule of a highly collective nature with a strong streak of altruism, and his conscience is in large measure dependent on public opinion. Moral misgivings arise mainly when "other people know." His religious convictions are determined, so to speak, by majority vote.

The actual subject, the extravert as a subjective entity, is, so far as possible, shrouded in darkness. He hides it from himself under veils of unconsciousness. The disinclination to submit his own motives to critical examination is very pronounced. He has no secrets he has not long since shared with others. Should something unmentionable nevertheless befall him, he prefers to forget it. Anything that might tarnish the parade of optimism and positivism is avoided. Whatever he thinks, intends, and does is displayed with conviction and warmth.

The psychic life of this type of person is enacted, as it were, outside himself, in the environment. He lives in and through others; all self-communings give him the creeps. Dangers lurk there which are better drowned out by noise. If he should ever have a "complex," he finds refuge in the social whirl and allows himself to be assured several times a day that everything is in order. Provided he is not too much of a busybody, too pushing, and too superficial, he can be a distinctly useful member of the community.

In this short essay I have to content myself with an allusive sketch. It is intended merely to give the reader some idea of what extraversion is like, something he can bring into relationship with his own knowledge of human nature. I have purposely started with a description of extraversion because this attitude is familiar to everyone; the extravert not only lives in this attitude, but parades it before his fellows on principle. Moreover it accords with certain popular ideals and moral requirements.

Introversion, on the other hand, being directed not to the object but to the subject, and not being oriented by the object, is not so easy to put into perspective. The introvert is not forthcoming, he is as though in continual retreat before the object. He holds aloof from external happenings, does not join in, has a distinct dislike of society as soon as he finds himself among too many people. In a large gathering he feels lonely and lost. The more crowded it is, the greater becomes his resistance. He is not in the least "with it," and has no love of enthusiastic get-togethers. He is not a good mixer. What he does, he does in his own way, barricading himself against influences from outside. He is apt to appear awkward, often seeming inhibited, and it frequently happens that, by a certain brusqueness of manner, or by his glum unapproachability, or some kind of malapropism, he causes unwitting offence to people. His better qualities he keeps to himself, and generally does everything he can to dissemble them. He is easily mistrustful, self-willed, often suffers from inferiority feelings and for this reason is also envious. His apprehensiveness of the object is not due to fear, but to the fact that it seems to him negative, demanding, overpowering or even menacing. He therefore suspects all kinds of bad motives, has an everlasting fear of making a fool of himself, is usually very touchy and surrounds himself with a barbed wire entanglement so dense and impenetrable that finally he himself would rather do anything than sit behind it. He confronts the world with an elaborate defensive system compounded of scrupulosity, pedantry, frugality, cautiousness, painful conscientiousness, stiff-lipped rectitude, politeness, and open-eyed distrust. His picture of the world lacks rosy hues, as he is over-critical and finds a hair in every soup. Under normal conditions he is pessimistic and worried, because the world and human beings are not in the least good but crush him, so he never feels accepted and taken to their bosom. Yet he himself does not accept the world either, at any rate not outright, for everything has first to be judged by his own critical standards. Finally only those things are accepted which, for various subjective reasons, he can turn to his own account.

For him self-communings are a pleasure. His own world is a safe harbour, a carefully tended and walled-in garden, closed to the public and hidden from prying eyes. His own company is the best. He feels at home in his world, where the only changes are made by himself. His best work is done with his own resources, on his own initiative, and in his own way. If ever he succeeds, after long and often wearisome struggles, in assimilating something alien to himself, he is capable of turning it to excellent account. Crowds, majority views, public opinion, popular enthusiasm never convince him of anything, but merely make him creep still deeper into his shell.

His relations with other people become warm only when safety is guaranteed, and when he can lay aside his defensive distrust. All too often he cannot, and consequently the number of friends and acquaintances is very restricted. Thus the psychic life of this type is played out wholly within. Should any difficulties and conflicts arise in this inner world, all doors and windows are shut tight. The introvert shuts himself up with his complexes until he ends in complete isolation.

In spite of these peculiarities the introvert is by no means a social loss. His retreat into himself is not a final renunciation of the world, but a search for quietude, where alone it is possible for him to make his contribution to the life of the community. This type of person is the victim of numerous misunderstandings—not unjustly, for he actually invites them. Nor can he be acquitted of the charge of taking a secret delight in mystification, and that being misunderstood gives him a certain satisfaction, since it reaffirms his pessimistic outlook. That being so, it is easy to see why he is accused of being cold, proud, obstinate, selfish, conceited, cranky, and what not, and why he is constantly admonished that devotion to the goals of society, clubbableness, imperturbable urbanity, and selfless trust in the powers-that-be are true virtues and the marks of a sound and vigorous life.

The introvert is well enough aware that such virtues exist, and that somewhere, perhaps—only not in his circle of acquaintances—there are divinely inspired people who enjoy undiluted possession of these ideal qualities. But his self-criticism and his awareness of his own motives have long since disabused him of the illusion that he himself would be capable of such virtues; and his mistrustful gaze, sharpened by anxiety, constantly enables him to detect on his fellow men the ass's ear sticking up from under the lion's mane. The world and men are for him a disturbance and a danger, affording no valid standard by which he could ultimately orient himself. What alone is valid for him is his subjective world, which he sometimes believes, in moments of delusion, to be the objective one. We could easily charge these people with the worst kind of subjectivism, indeed with morbid individualism, if it were certain beyond a doubt that only one objective world existed. But this truth, if such it be, is not axiomatic; it is merely a half truth, the other half of which is the fact that the world *also* is as it is seen by human beings, and in the last resort by the individual. There is simply no world at all without the knowing subject. This, be it never so small and inconspicuous, is always the other pier supporting the bridge of the phenomenal world. The appeal to the subject therefore has the same validity as the appeal to the so-called objective world, for it is grounded on psychic reality itself. But this is a reality with its own peculiar laws which are not of a secondary nature.

For the extravert the object is interesting and attractive *a priori*, as is the subject, or psychic reality, for the introvert. We could therefore use the expression "numinal accent" for this fact, by which I mean that for the extravert the quality of positive significance and value attaches primarily to the object, so that it plays the predominant, determining, and decisive role in all psychic processes from the start, just as the subject does for the introvert.

But the numinal accent does not decide only between subject and object; it also selects the conscious function of which the individual makes the principal use. I distinguish four functions: *thinking, feeling, sensation,* and *intuition.* The essential function of sensation is to establish that something exists, thinking tells us what it means, feeling what its value is, and intuition surmises whence it comes and whither it goes. Sensation and intuition I call irrational functions, because they are both concerned simply with what happens and with actual or potential realities. Thinking and feeling, being discriminative functions, are rational. Sensation rules out any simultaneous intuitive activity, since the latter is not concerned with the present but is rather a sixth sense for hidden possibilities, and therefore should not allow itself to be unduly influenced by existing reality. In the same way, thinking is opposed to feeling, because thinking should not be influenced or deflected from its purpose by feeling values, just as feeling is usually vitiated by too much reflection. The four functions therefore form, when arranged diagrammatically, a cross with a rational axis at right angles to an irrational axis.

The four orienting functions naturally do not contain everything that is in the conscious psyche. Will and memory, for instance, are not included. The reason for this is that the differentiation of the four orienting functions is, essentially, an empirical consequence of typical differences in the functional attitude. There are people for whom the numinal accent falls on sensation, on the perception of actualities, and elevates it into the sole determining and all-overriding principle. These are the fact-minded men, in whom intellec-tual judgment, feeling, and intuition are driven into the background by the paramount importance of actual facts. When the accent falls on thinking, judgment is reserved as to what significance should be attached to the facts in question. And on this significance will depend the way in which the individ-ual deals with the facts. If feeling is numinal, then his adaptation will depend entirely on the feeling value he attributes to them. Finally, if the numinal accent falls on intuition, actual reality counts only in so far as it seems to harbour possibilities which then become the supreme motivating force, regardless of the way things actually are in the present.

The localization of the numinal accent thus gives rise to four function-types, which I encountered first of all in my relations with people and formulated systematically only very much later. In practice these four types are always combined with the attitude-type, that is, with extraversion or introversion, so that the functions appear in an extraverted or introverted variation. This produces a set of eight demonstrable function-types. It is naturally impossible to present the specific psychology of these types within the confines of an essay, and to go into its conscious and unconscious manifestations. I must therefore refer the interested reader to the aforementioned study.

It is not the purpose of a psychological typology to classify human beings into categories—this in itself would be pretty pointless. Its purpose is rather to provide a critical psychology which will make a methodical investigation and presentation of the empirical material possible. First and foremost, it is a critical tool for the research worker, who needs definite points of view and guidelines if he is to reduce the chaotic profusion of individual experiences to any kind of order. In this respect we could compare typology to a trigonometric net or, better still, to a crystallographic axial system. Secondly, a typology is a great help in understanding the wide variations that occur among individuals, and it also furnishes a clue to the fundamental differences in the psychological theories now current. Last but not least, it is an essential means for determining the "personal equation" of the practising psychologist, who, armed with an exact knowledge of his differentiated and inferior functions, can avoid many serious blunders in dealing with his patients.

12. The Dark Side of Typing

JAMES HILLMAN

THE TYPE CONCEPT: Originally, the way *typos* was used in Greek gave it the meaning of an empty or hollow form for casting, a kind of rough-edged mold. From the beginning of its use by Plato and Aristotle the word had a sketchy, incomplete relief, or outline character that emphasizes a visible shaping quality rather than a sharply struck definition. Even today in modern logic and epistemology, a type differs from other ordering categories just by virtue of its imprecision.

Owing to this uncertain boundary, types are used most frequently in lifesciences and humanities. Types can flow into one another: there is no sharp border between typical historical periods (Mediaeval and Renaissance), between typical literary styles (heroic and tragic), or between typical groupings of mental disorders, social functions or even animal species. Fluidity, relativity, elasticity is a most distinctive aspect of the type concept.

Therefore, there cannot be any pure types because they are not meant to be pure, by definition. A pure type has already become a class where a different sort of logic obtains. My name begins with H, and I was called to military service in 1944. That puts me into two classes with hard edges. There is nothing typical about persons whose names begin with H or who were called up in 1944. We can, however, be classified with H and 44. Classes require an "either/or," types a "more/less," kind of thinking. I am either an H or I am not; I cannot be more of an H than an L or a T, or a lesser H or a little H, etc. But with types I am rather more an extravert than an introvert, a point which Jung made at the very beginning of his *Psychological Types* (§§ 4–6). Extraversion does not *per se* exclude introversion.

But it is not easy to keep this distinction between classes and types. Often types are used as classes, and we begin to classify ourselves by means of types, thereby severing our fluid natures into well-defined and mutually exclusive parts. To use a type concept as a class concept has crippling results.

Also for the body-politic: when we use types as classes, they become literal stereotypes and work in a procrustean manner. A typical German or a typical American brings a typical image to mind, and this image has nothing to do with the legal definition of nationality. But should the typical be implemented by the national, that is, should the typical image become the class definition for the national, then all German and American nationals must conform to a stereotypical image, resulting in political exclusion and even genocide.

We tend to speak of types wherever we try to combine wide general principles together with single particular instances. Then types help to organize a vast number of similar events into rough groupings. Vast numbers of events are hard to work with. For example, in the 1930s Gordon Allport and Henry Odbert at the Harvard Psychological Laboratory compiled a list of 17,953 trait-names in English applicable to human personality, about as many different words as in all of Shakespeare, as in Joyce— descriptive terms such as alert, aloof, alone, alcoholic, altruistic, alluring, altered, alive, all-round, almighty, etc. and etc., to 18,000. This list reveals the immense vocabulary at our disposal in only one tongue for describing human nature.

If rich language and rich insight do bear on each other, then here already is one of the reasons for our falling off in psychological acuity, compared with just fifty years ago. We no longer allow ourselves to use naive language of the old days; much of the words regularly used for character perception are old hat or taboo: ethnic-racial words (Jew, Turk, Okie, Prussian), Biblical words for character (Jeremiah, Ruth, John); class words (blue-blood, servant class, street-urchin, pickaninny, bastard). The new "Ologies" insist that such terms are prejudices and stereotypes, which do not help seeing but block it. The "Ologies" have substituted another objectified language instead. So now we say "Fascist," "neurotic," "overcompensated," "overweight," "underdeveloped," "under-achiever," "elitist," "unrelated," "chauvinist"; and our perception by means of obscene epithets has moved from a landscape of low race, birth and region to a landscape of the low body.

Let us say that I have good thinking and poor feeling. Yet, there are specific traits of thinking which I cannot perform—keeping my checkbook accurately, understanding the principles of information theory, or symbolic logic, or how the television can be repaired; I may still stumble over the correct grammar of "that" and "which" in clauses, daylight-saving-time or Celsius-Fahrenheit conversions. These may each be miserable inferiorities in my thinking, even though I can perform many other analytical, logical, and systematic activities with precision, speed, and ease. Similarly, there are specific qualities in my supposedly poor feeling function that not only do not conflict with thinking but enhance it, such as feeling the value of a first-rate idea and subtly and aesthetically differentiating it from a second-rate one, or experiencing the ethical consequences of trains of thought or organizational planning. As well, despite this poor feeling function I may nonetheless be a loyal friend, a magnanimous host, a charitable critic of my students, admit and inwardly contain my despairs, and not be afraid to call a spade a spade in behalf of my values. In other words, particular moral and characterological, and even technical proficiencies, are altogether drained off into typological notions. A type consists in traits. Because usually a type is defined as the axial system that holds traits together or simply as their principle of correlation, it has no substance of its own. Its substance is in the traits. To let go the multiplicity and exquisite variety of the 18,000 traits is to lose the stuff and gut of persons and turn them into types.

The emptiness of types, the hollowness implied by the very word, their "invisibility," causes another problem. Whenever we talk of types we soon begin talking of examples and cases. Types call for living instances. Jung's book needs its Chapter X to make visible images with anecdotes and persons so that we can imagine all that has gone before. This peculiar process of thought—the need for examples—casts a shadow over all uses of typological thinking, especially in psychology and psychiatry. Is there not the danger of filling in the empty notion with concrete persons, creating cases even in the pathological sense to fill in our typical forms of pathology?

Jung did not intend his typology to be used for typing persons. Precisely the way in which his types are used and experimented with in the Grey-Wheelwright and Briggs-Myers tests—the clinical scientism—is what Jung expressly did not intend. He writes:

> "It is not the purpose of a psychological typology to classify human beings into categories—this in itself would be pretty pointless."[1]

> "Far too many readers have succumbed to the error of thinking that Chapter X ("General Description of the Types") represents the essential content and purpose of the book, in the sense that it provides a system of classification and a practical guide to a good judgement of human character . . . This regrettable misunderstanding completely ignores the fact that this kind of classification is nothing but a childish parlour game . . . My typology . . . [is not meant] to stick labels on people at first sight. It is not a physiognomy . . . For this reason I have placed the general typology . . . at the end of the book . . . I would therefore recommend the reader . . . to immerse himself first of all in chapters II and V. He will gain more from them than from any typological terminology superficially picked up, since this serves no other purpose than a totally useless desire to stick on labels."[2]

What then was the "fundamental tendency" of the book if it was not to type persons? Jung sets it out most clearly:

> "Its purpose is rather to provide a critical psychology . . . First and foremost, it is a critical tool for the research worker" (§986). "The typological system I have proposed is an attempt . . . to provide an explanatory basis and theoretical framework for the boundless diversity . . . in the formation of psychological concepts."[3]

Note that: not diversity of *human beings,* but diversity of *psychological concepts.* As a critical psychology, a psychology that offers a critical tool for examining ideas, it belongs to epistemology, and it was a necessary consequent of Jung's placing psyche first. As Aniela Jaffé has said, "The soul cannot be the object of judgement and knowledge, but judgement and knowledge are the object of the soul." The types were to provide the fundamental psychological antinomies which enter into every judgement in psychology.

The consequence of using a multiple tool is psychological relativism. This Jung knew; and it is even a corollary purpose of this *Types* to see through and relativize any psychological position. He says in the Epilogue to that work:

". . . in the case of psychological theories the necessity of a plurality of explanations is given from the start" . . . "an intellectual understanding of the psychic process must end in paradox and relativity."[4]

13. *The Goddess Within: A Jungian Typology for Women*

JENNIFER BARKER WOOLGER AND ROGER J. WOOLGER

WHEN THE AUTHORS began teaching workshops about the return of the Goddess in her many forms several years ago, we were not prepared for the variety and intensity of the reactions we received everywhere from the women and men we met. After an evening slide-show lecture women would report staying up half the night talking passionately about their love lives, what it meant to have children, and the frustrations of their careers. "You gave me a whole new way of talking about myself," they would say. "I have never before been so clear."

Nevertheless, we don't want to give the impression that working with this new language of the feminine is simply about having intellectual insights. What it really entails is engaging deeply and courageously with these feminine forces as they live within and through us. We have to get to know them as spiritual and psychological presences—what psychologist Carl Jung called *archetypes,* which is to say, living transformers of our lives and our consciousness.

WHAT IS A "GODDESS"?

By *goddess* we mean a psychological description of a complex female character type that we intuitively recognize both in ourselves and in the women around us, as well as in the images and icons that are everywhere in our culture. For example, the smartly dressed, intelligent young career woman we see everywhere in our cities is the living embodiment of a goddess type we call *the Athena woman,* named after the Greek goddess who was patroness of the ancient city of Athens. Magazines, movies, and novels all reproduce her as a stereotype because she is so prevalent today.

Yet a goddess type such as Athena is much more than just a media stereotype or cliché, Athena also represents a complex and highly evolved style of consciousness that characterizes everything about the way this type of woman thinks, feels, and acts. The most prominent features of the Athena woman are that she is hardworking, achievement-oriented, independent, and intellectual. She values education, a high degree of political and social awareness, and generally puts her career before her children and husband.

There is a fundamental *dynamic* behind the behavior of such a woman that makes her unique as a type. Part of it is socially acquired and part seems to be innate. When such a psychological dynamic is observed in a whole group of individuals, it is what Jung called an archetype. He was the first to observe that dynamic types of this sort are to be found in their purest forms in mythology and literature and that they show up, in disguise, in everyone's dream and fantasy life. Today they can easily be observed in movies, television soap operas, and the way the media treat the lives of prominent people.

A goddess, then, is the form that a feminine archetype may take in the context of a mythological story or epic. In a fairy tale this archetype may appear as a princess, a queen, or a witch. When we ourselves dream or fantasize, our unconscious mind may draw upon the common pool of archetypal images in our culture (Jung called this pool the *collective unconscious*). Instead of a queen or goddess like the Hera of Greek myth to represent the feminine archetype of power, we may dream of Margaret Thatcher or a soap opera matriarch like Jane Wyman.

THE MAJOR GODDESS TYPES

We have selected six major Greek goddess archetypes that strike us as the most active in the lives of modern women and in contemporary society.

The basic characteristics of all six types can be summarized as follows:

• The Athena woman is ruled by the goddess of wisdom and civilization and is concerned with achievement, career, education, intellectual culture, social justice, and politics.

• The Aphrodite woman is ruled by the love goddess, and her chief concerns are relationships, sexuality, intrigue, romance, beauty, and the inspiration of the arts.

• The Persephone woman is ruled by the goddess of the underworld; she is mediumistic and is attracted to the spirit world, to the occult, to visionary and mystical experience, and to matters associated with death.

• The Artemis woman is ruled by the goddess of the wilds; she is practical, athletic, adventurous; she likes physical culture, solitude, the outdoors, animals, and is concerned with the protection of the environment, alternative life-styles, and women's communities.

• The Demeter woman is ruled by the corn goddess; she is an earth mother who loves bearing, nurturing, and raising children; she is concerned with all aspects of childbirth and women's reproductive cycles.

• The Hera woman is ruled by the queen of heaven; she is concerned with marriage, partnerships with men, and with issues of power wherever women are rulers and leaders.

What we want to emphasize is that not just one but several of these goddess types, in various combinations, underlie every woman's behavior and psychological style. Unlike sun-sign astrology, in which one is fixed as a Pisces or a Leo, every woman is a complex mixture of all the goddess types. To know oneself more fully as a woman is to know which goddess one is primarily ruled by and to be aware of how different goddesses influence the various stages and turning points of one's life.

Men, too, are influenced by the goddess types. The goddesses most certainly mirror feminine energies in the male psyche, although men usually experience them as being more external to themselves in the shape of women they are either attracted to or else have strong reactions to. Psychologically we would say that men experience the goddesses projected onto the women around them as well as onto particular media images that arouse or repel them.

All of men's relationships with women are, we believe, determined by one or more of the goddess energies and the particular archetypal patterns that belong to each. One man may unconsciously look for Demeter in a woman; another may want Hera to take power in their partnership, and so on.

THE SIX MAJOR GODDESSES

The Goddess Wheel

Each section of the Wheel summarizes the attributes of a particular goddess and gives her major area of influence, her rulership. Here are the six goddesses described in terms of major areas and styles of life they pursue:

Athena rules everything to do with *civilization,* which is to say all aspects of cities, urban life, and what we call "civilized" pursuits, which may include anything that maintains the city or the nation-state it commands. Athena rules technology and science and all practical crafts, as well as the literary arts, education, and intellectual life in all its forms. For the modern woman living in the city, Athena would guide all aspects of her career, her profession, and how she relates to the patriarchal world of the city fathers.

Aphrodite rules *love and eros,* which is to say all aspects of sexuality, intimacy, and personal relationships. Because hers is the power to entice and attract the senses, she is the goddess of beauty and hence of all the visual arts, such as painting, sculpture, and architecture, as well as poetry and music. She is a "cultured" goddess like Athena in the sense that her influence is private, but she is individual rather than public and collective. Thus she rules salons, artistic inspiration, and all creative liaisons between the sexes.

As queen of the dead, *Persephone* rules over all aspects of contact with the *underworld,* the spirit world or the realm of the departed. She is consciously or unconsciously in contact with the greater transpersonal powers of the psyche traditionally called spirits, the ones Jung called the archetypes. In modern psychological terms we could say that she rules over the deeper unconscious mind, the dream world, and everything to do with paranormal or psychic phenomena and mysticism. She is thus concerned with mediumship or channeling, visionary capacity, occult matters, and areas of psychic healing covered by certain forms of psychotherapy. Because she is a goddess of the dead, she will be present in any event or situation where a death or tragic loss occurs. She also rules all minor losses, separations, and traumas.

As ruler of the wilds, *Artemis* is a goddess of *nature* in its virgin or untamed form. She stands in strict contrast to Athena, who represents nature tamed and civilized. Artemis is especially close to animals and the hunt and those cycles of nature that rule the animal as much as the human world; she is also a goddess of midwifery. A moon goddess, she rules over all instinctual life, emphasizing the body rather than the head (as Athena would) and living for all physical, practical, and outdoor activities, which today include athletics and dance. Since she is concerned with instinctual nature and hunting, she rules over killing and blood sacrifice. She complements and aids Persephone in regard to death: Artemis understands the death of the body; Persephone, the passage of its spirit. Artemis is related to the ancient practice of shamanism, which incorporates both.

The most direct descendant of the ancient Earth Mother goddess, *Demeter* is the goddess of *motherhood* and everything connected with the reproductive functions, particularly the inner experience of the menstrual and childbearing cycles. Because she rules seed and fruit, she is sometimes called the Lady of Plants. This symbolizes her deep connection to all aspects of food, growth, the cycles of the crops, and to harvesting and preserving. She is intimately bound up with nurturing and caring for the organic growth of the body. Most of her energy goes toward nurturing and caring for all infants, children, and growing creatures.

Hera is queen of heaven, or Olympus, and is concerned with *power and rulership.* As the wife of the god Zeus, she rules over marriage, partnership, and all public roles where a woman has power, responsibility, or leadership. Very much concerned with social morality and the upholding of the integrity of the family, she also oversees all aspects of tradition and the cohesiveness of the larger community. In this she shares something of Athena's vision of civilized life and the maintenance of patriarchal values, symbolized by her husband, Zeus. When her power is restricted only to the family arena, she becomes the undisputed family matriarch.

CONTRASTS AND COMMONALITIES: THE GODDESS DYADS

One clue to the basic perspectives of the six goddesses is that they arrange themselves very easily into opposite pairs on the Wheel, thus graphically suggesting certain common areas as well as major contrasts. We call these the three *Goddess Dyads.* As you get to know them, you will notice that these pairs have distinct complementary qualities.

One dyad that we have already noted is between *Artemis and Athena.* As goddesses of the wilds, on the one hand, and civilization, on the other, they are strongly contrasted. And yet they share two major qualities: both carry weapons in quite masculine warrior fashion, and neither has a consort or male lover. We call this opposing pair on the Goddess Wheel the *dyad of independence,* because these two goddesses are temperamentally much more inclined to live and work alone than with a mate. Even when married, they require very independent, unfettered styles of partnership. In the ancient world they were "virgin" goddesses, which simply meant *unmarried.* (Chastity as a component of virginity is largely an overlaid patriarchal value.)

Their different worlds also reflect different styles of companionship. Athena is more extraverted, liking to work as part of a team of associates in the bustle and competition of the city; Artemis is more of an introvert, preferring to work alone, far from the madding crowd, with perhaps one or two close friends or in a specially chosen community of like-minded loners.

But because they are so temperamentally close in their independent spirits, both aspects of the Athena-Artemis dyad may show up in a woman. It is not uncommon to find a younger woman moving from the city to the country or vice versa in different phases of her life. On the other hand, if only one pole of this dyad is developed, many women find it relatively easy to develop the other.

A second contrasting pair of opposites is discernible in *Hera and Persephone,* though this is perhaps less immediately obvious. Their most extreme difference is how they relate to the outer and inner worlds. It is as though Hera, as supreme extravert, chooses to concern herself only with the outer world, whereas Persephone, as introvert, spurns the outer world for her inner psychic realm of the spirits. Yet, as queens of heaven and of the underworld they are both concerned with having control over their different worlds. Therefore we call theirs the *dyad of power.*

Because their worldviews are so different and their ego formations so opposite—Hera's ego is extremely strong, Persephone's weak to the point of permeability by her spirits—it is hard for them to appreciate and understand each other. Nevertheless they have much to learn from each other if they can let go of their individual prejudices. Hera often needs to go inward, Persephone to come out of her shell.

The remaining pair of contrasting opposites is that of *Demeter and Aphrodite*. Since they are both concerned with love in different ways, we call theirs the *dyad of love*. We can see in them a subtle contrast between how they express love and how they experience their bodies. Demeter reserves her love for her children, serving as a selfless container for all her loved ones both physically and spiritually. Aphrodite nurtures spiritually and physically, but not by containing or mothering those she loves. What she gives to her lover is his (or her) full maturity and otherness. She loves the adult rather than the child. Demeter's style of love is more introverted, carrying her loved ones always in her heart, no matter where they are, whereas Aphrodite, an extravert, is only fulfilled by the physical presence of her lover.

For Demeter the body is a sacred vessel, for Aphrodite it is a sacred love object, a thing of beauty. It is often difficult for an Aphrodite woman to fully enjoy her first pregnancy or for a Demeter woman to fully appreciate her body aesthetically, because they both experience and treat their body and its functions so differently. Nevertheless, they can both learn and share from the other's styles of loving and embodiment.

All three dyads arrange themselves broadly around the temperamental orientations of introversion and extraversion:

DYAD:	INDEPENDENCE	POWER	LOVE
Extraverted:	Athena	Hera	Aphrodite
Introverted:	Artemis	Persephone	Demeter

In this respect the Wheel divides itself diagonally down the middle, the three goddesses concerned more with outer realities on the upper right, those goddesses inclined more toward inwardness on the lower left. Only Demeter does not entirely fit this scheme, being blessed with a healthy mixture of introverted love and extraverted energy to care for her children and family. We should also add that Aphrodite is very private, too, in her intimacy in that she often explores a form of soul-searching or mutual introversion with her lovers.

THE GODDESSES AND THEIR MASCULINE COMPLEMENTS: THE ANIMUS

Each goddess has a distinctly different relationship to the masculine, either in terms of the kind of male figures that appear in her individual myths or in terms of the particular form of masculine psychic energy that each goddess has harnessed within herself. Hera and Persephone both have husbands or consorts, which, ideally, suggests some kind of equal power sharing. Aphrodite and Demeter have relationships that are defined more by their styles of love. Although Artemis and Athena are "virgin" goddesses who have no marital or ongoing close relationships, they manifest masculine qualities as the huntress and the warrior woman.

In the Goddess Wheel we refer in shorthand to the most typical relationship styles each goddess has with the opposite sex, calling the male counterpart her *animus*. This is Jung's term for the masculine element of every woman's psyche that is carried within her and that determines how she will be attracted to or repelled by certain kinds of men. Each of the goddesses is drawn to men who complement her style of femininity.

These, in brief are the common animus counterparts of each of the goddesses:

Athena relates to men as heroic "companions in arms," with whom she shares ideals, ambitions, career goals, and struggles. Frequently he will be an intellectual companion or friendly rival. She will not necessarily marry such men, maintaining instead close and enduring friendships. She is also drawn to father figures and usually has strong bonds to nonpersonal authority as invested in the institutions of the patriarchy or in spiritual ideals. She may also be in conflict with the fatherworld. Her major animus counterparts are therefore the companion hero and the father.

Aphrodite admires the virility of a man. She engages the phallic power of the male as either lover or warrior. She admires success and combativeness in her men, but isn't too interested in being out there fighting with them, like Athena, since her chief area of engagement is the boudoir or the salon. She is happy with multiple relationships or extramarital affairs, but will marry (and divorce) as it suits her. She also attracts creative men and often acts as a patroness or inspirer of their artistic works.

Persephone is enamored more of the spirit than of incarnated males and will frequently have male *spirit guides* in her channeling or her mystical practices. Her deep and fatalistic involvement in the darker sides of life will mean that she unwittingly attracts destructive men—the *Dark Lord*—and will sometimes marry them, with disastrous results. To protect herself from this, she often chooses the safe, but unsatisfactory alternative of a younger or soft, nonthreatening man whose masculine side is underdeveloped and whom she can safely mother and manipulate. Her type of animus is best described as the *son lover.*

Artemis, in her independence, has so much masculine energy already integrated into her personality structure that she doesn't have strong needs for a man to complement her. Nevertheless, she, like Athena, enjoys a companionable male who will work alongside her in her practical pursuits. Marriage is not, as a rule, looked for but is tolerated if her freedom is respected. Sexuality is often buried, and she can be quite shy, so she appreciates reserve and diffidence in a man. Her mythic brother, Apollo, models something of the distant friendship she wants from a man. *Friend*, companion, or *brother* best describes her animus counterpart.

Demeter is not particularly interested in sexuality or intellectual relationships, but she needs someone to bring home the bacon. She is best matched with a strong, reliable *earth father* as her mate. But since she has so much abundant mother energy, she has an irresistible tendency to mother all the men around her, regardless of their ages, and turns them into sons to idealize as heroes. Her other animus we describe as the *son hero*.

Hera wants a man to be her *partner* and ideally someone who will share his power equally with her. She wants only strong, successful men who are leaders or, if possible, rulers, as was Zeus, her mythic husband. Partnership for her means marriage, so she will usually only relate closely to one man, her husband. In this she is basically monogamous. She will always seek to marry a man for his worldly power and the social prestige he carries. She wants to pass his good name on to her children. Since she is attracted to the masculine energy of rulership, she herself will want either to rule her family as the matriarch or to rule some institution.

THE GODDESS WHEEL AS A LIVING DYNAMIC

This broad orientation should be helpful in understanding the pushes and pulls of the goddesses in your life. These are what we call the dynamics of the Goddess Wheel, the living energy that derives from the tension of opposites we all carry within us in infinite, individual combinations. As we become more open to these energies in our lives, we will find that we can harness them and not be torn apart by them.

The Wheel is designed like a flower. The six goddesses, like petals, radiate from the Great Mother at the center, who symbolizes the transcendent unity of all the goddesses belonging to a broader, transpersonal level of being that we call archetypal or universal. Although this is a unity that a single individual can rarely achieve, we can catch glimpses of it from time to time. In addition, we need the diversity of experience that the different goddesses can bring us in our ordinary lives.

Each of the Greek forms of the goddess emanated originally from the Great Mother Goddess of more ancient times. Any psychological work that you undertake in getting to know a particular goddess may take you deeper into that goddess and *closer to the center of the Wheel*. What you may find is that at their deeper levels—which correspond to the older forms of the Goddess—they tend to overlap and merge with one another.

14. Four Male Archetypes: King, Warrior, Magician, Lover

ROBERT MOORE
AND DOUGLAS GILLETTE

THE ARCHETYPES OF KING, Warrior, Magician, and Lover have been increasingly in focus in the United States and abroad. It is our belief that the psychological findings outlined in these lectures constitute a major and potentially revolutionary breakthrough in decoding the fundamental deep structures of the human self, both masculine and feminine. This decoding of what Carl Jung called the "double quaternio" builds on Jung's understanding of the archetypal Self, but extends our grasp of inner geography beyond Jung's work by clearly delineating not only the psychological contents and potentials imaged in the "four quarters," but also the two fundamental dialectical oppositions built into the dynamics of the deep self: King (or Queen)/Magician and Lover/Warrior.

THE KING

The King energy is primal in all men. It comes first in importance, and it underlies and includes the rest of the archetypes in perfect balance. The good and generative King is also a good Warrior, a positive Magician, and a great Lover. And yet, with most of us, the King comes on line last.

The King archetype comes close to being God in his masculine form within every man. It is the primordial man, the Adam, what the philosophers call the Anthropos in each of us. Hindus call this primal masculinity in men the Atman; Jews and Christians speak of it as the *imago Dei*, the "Image of God." Freud talked about the King as the "primal father of the primal horde." And in many ways the King energy is Father energy. It is our experience, however, that although the King underlies the Father archetype, it is more extensive and more basic than the Father.

The mortal king was the servant and earthly embodiment of the King archetype, which maintained order in the spiritual world, or the deep and timeless world of the unconscious. Here we see the stories of the Babylonian god Marduk fighting the forces of chaos in the form of the dragon Tiamat and beating her demon army, slaying her, and creating the ordered world from her body. Or we see the Canaanite Baal slaying the twin monsters of chaos and death, Yamm and Mot.

On a more immediate note, we see in modern dysfunctional families that when there is an immature, a weak, or an absent father and the King energy is not sufficiently present, the family is very often given over to disorder and chaos.

In conjunction with his ordering function, the second vital good that the King energy manifests is fertility and blessing. Ancient peoples always associated fertility—in human beings, crops, herds, and the natural world in general—with the creative ordering of things by the gods. It seems that in prepatriarchal times, the earth as Mother was seen as the primary source of fertility. But as patriarchal cultures rose to ascendancy, the emphasis shifted from the feminine as the source of fertility to the masculine. This was not a simple shift, and the emphasis never shifted completely. The ancient myths, true to actual biology, recognized that it was the union of male and female that was truly generative, at least on the physical plane. On the cultural plane, however, in the creation of civilization and technology, and in the mastery of the natural world, the masculine generative energies were most prominent.

When we are out of touch with our own inner King and give the power over our lives to others, we may be courting catastrophe on a scale larger than the personal. Those we make our kings may lead us into lost battles, abuse in our families, mass murder, the horrors of a Nazi Germany, or a Jonestown. Or they may simply abandon us to our own underlying weakness.

But when we are accessing the King energy correctly, as servants of our own inner King, we will manifest in our own lives the qualities of the good and rightful King, the King in his fullness. We will feel our anxiety level drop. We will feel centered, and calm, and hear ourselves speak from an inner authority. We will have the capacity to mirror and to bless ourselves and others. We will have the capacity to care for others deeply and genuinely. We will "recognize" others; we will behold them as the full persons they really are. We will have a sense of being a centered participant in creating a more just, calm, and creative world. We will have a transpersonal devotion not only to our families, our friends, our companies, our causes, our religions, but also to the world. We will have some kind of spirituality, and we will know the truth of the central commandment around which all of human life seems to be based: "Thou shalt love the Lord thy God [read, "the King"] with all thy heart, with all thy soul, and with all thy might. And thy neighbor as thyself."

THE WARRIOR

We live in a time when people are generally uncomfortable with the Warrior form of masculine energy—and for some good reasons. Women especially are uncomfortable with it, because they have often been the most direct victims of it in its shadow form. Around the planet, warfare in our century has reached such monstrous and pervasive proportions that aggressive energy itself is looked upon with deep suspicion and fear.

What is interesting to notice, however, is that those who would cut off masculine aggressiveness at its root, in their zeal, themselves fall under the power of this archetype. We can't just take a vote and vote the Warrior out. Like all archetypes, it lives on in spite of our conscious attitudes toward it. And like all *repressed* archetypes, it goes underground, eventually to resurface in the form of emotional and physical violence, like a volcano that has lain dormant for centuries with the pressure gradually building up in the magma chamber. If the Warrior is an instinctual energy form, then it is here to stay. And it pays to face it.

The Warrior traditions all affirm that, in addition to training, what enables a Warrior to reach clarity of thought is living with the awareness of his own imminent death. The Warrior knows the shortness of life and how fragile it is. A man under the guidance of the Warrior knows how few his days are. Rather than depressing him, this awareness leads him to an outpouring of life-force and to an intense experience of his life that is unknown to others. Every act counts. Each deed is done as if it were the last.

There is no time for hesitation. This sense of the imminence of death energizes the man accessing the Warrior energy to take decisive action. This means that he engages life. He never withdraws from it. He doesn't "think too much," because thinking too much can lead to doubt, and doubt to hesitation, and hesitation to inaction. Inaction can lead to losing the battle. The man who is a Warrior avoids self-consciousness, as we usually define it. His actions become second nature. They become unconscious reflex actions. But they are actions he has trained for through the exercise of enormous self-discipline.

Part of what goes into acting decisively in any life situation, along with aggressiveness, clarity of thinking, the awareness of one's own death, is training. The Warrior energy is concerned with skill, power, and accuracy, and with control, both inner and outer, psychological and physical. The Warrior energy is concerned with training men to be "all that they can be"—in their thoughts, feelings, speech, and actions. Unlike the Hero's actions, the Warrior's actions are never overdone, never dramatic for the sake of drama; the Warrior never acts to reassure himself that he is as potent as he hopes he is. The Warrior never spends more energy than he absolutely has to. And he doesn't talk too much.

The Warrior energy also shows what we can call a transpersonal commitment. His loyalty is to something—a cause, a god, a people, a task, a nation—larger than individuals, though that transpersonal loyalty may be focused through some important person, like a king.

This transpersonal commitment reveals a number of other characteristics of the Warrior energy. First, it makes all personal relationships relative, that is, it makes them less central than the transpersonal commitment. Thus the psyche of the man who is adequately accessing the Warrior is organized around his central commitment. This commitment eliminates a great deal of human pettiness. Living in the light of lofty ideals and spiritual realities such as God, democracy, communism, freedom, or any other worthy transpersonal commitment, so alters the focus of a man's life that petty squabbling and personal Ego concerns no longer matter much.

This devotion to the transpersonal ideal or goal even to the point of personal annihilation leads a man to another of the Warrior's characteristics. He is emotionally distant as long as he is in the Warrior. This does not mean that the man accessing the Warrior in his fullness is cruel, just that he does not make his decisions and implement them out of emotional relatedness to anyone or anything except his ideal.

The Warrior is often a destroyer. But the positive Warrior energy destroys only what needs to be destroyed in order for something new and fresh, more alive and more virtuous to appear. Many things in our world need destroying—corruption, tyranny, oppression, injustice, obsolete and despotic systems of government, corporate hierarchies that get in the way of the company's performance, unfulfilling life-styles and job situations, bad marriages. And in the very act of destroying, often the Warrior energy is building new civilizations, new commercial, artistic, and spiritual ventures for humankind, new relationships.

When the Warrior energy is connected with the other mature masculine energies something truly splendid emerges. When the Warrior is connected with the King, he is consciously stewarding the "realm," and his decisive actions, clarity of thinking, discipline, and courage are, in fact, creative and generative.

The Warrior's interface with the Magician archetype is what enables him to achieve such mastery and control over himself and his "weapons." It is what allows him to channel and direct power to accomplish his goals.

His admixture with the Lover energy gives the Warrior compassion and a sense of connectedness with all things. The Lover is the masculine energy that brings him back into relatedness with human beings, in all their frailty and vulnerability. The Lover makes the man under the influence of the Warrior compassionate at the same time that he is doing his duty.

THE MAGICIAN

The energies of the Magician archetype, wherever and whenever we encounter them, are twofold. The Magician is the knower and he is the master of technology. Furthermore, the man who is guided by the power of the Magician is able to fulfill these Magician functions in part by his use of ritual initiatory process. He is the "ritual elder" who guides the processes of transformation, both within and without.

The human magician is always an initiate himself, and one of his tasks is to initiate others. But of what is he an initiate? The Magician is an initiate of secret and hidden knowledge of all kinds. And this is the important point. All knowledge that takes special training to acquire is the province of the Magician energy. Whether you are an apprentice training to become a master electrician and unraveling the mysteries of high voltage; or a medical student, grinding away night and day, studying the secrets of the human body and using the available technologies to help your patients; or a would-be stockbroker or a student of high finance; or a trainee in one of the psychoanalytic schools, you are in exactly the same position as the apprentice shaman or witch doctor in tribal societies. You are spending large amounts of time, energy, and money in order to be initiated into rarefied realms of secret power. You are undergoing an ordeal testing your capacities to become a master of this power. And, as is true in all initiations, there is no guarantee of success.

The Magician is a universal archetype that has operated in the masculine psyche throughout history. It can be accessed today by modern men in their work and in their personal lives.

The Magician energy is the archetype of awareness and of insight, primarily, but also of knowledge of anything that is not immediately apparent or commonsensical. It is the archetype that governs what is called in psychology "the observing Ego."

While it is sometimes assumed in depth psychology that the Ego is secondary in importance to the unconscious, the Ego is in fact vital to our survival. It is only when it is possessed by, identified with, and inflated by another energy form—an archetype or a "complex" (an archetypal fragment, like the Tyrant)—that it malfunctions. Its proper role is to stand back and observe, to scan the horizon, to monitor the data coming in from both the outside and the inside and then, out of its wisdom—its knowledge of power, within and without, and its technical skill in channeling—make the necessary life decisions.

When the observing Ego is aligned with the masculine Self along an "Ego-Self axis," it is initiated into the secret wisdom of this Self. It is, in one sense, a servant of the masculine Self. But in another sense, it is the leader and the channeler of this Self's power. It is, then, a vital player in the personality as a whole.

The Magician archetype, in concert with the observing Ego, keeps us insulated from the overwhelming power of the other archetypes. It is the mathematician and the engineer in each of us that regulates the life functions of the psyche as a whole. It knows the enormous force of the psyche's inner dynamics and how to channel them for maximum benefit. It knows the unbelievable force of the "sun" within, and it knows how to channel that sun's energy for maximum benefit. The Magician pattern regulates the internal energy flows of the various archetypes for the benefit of our individual lives.

Many human magicians, in whatever profession or in whatever walk of life (occult practitioners as well), are consciously using their knowledge and technical proficiency for the benefit of others as well as themselves. Doctors, lawyers, priests, CEOs, plumbers and electricians, research scientists, psychologists, and many others are, when they are accessing the Magician energy appropriately, working to turn raw power to the advantage of others. This is true of the witch doctor and the shaman with their rattles, amulets, herbs, and incantations. And it is equally true of the medical research technicians who are looking for cures for our most deadly diseases.

THE LOVER

The man profoundly in touch with the Lover energy experiences his work, and the people on the job with him, through aesthetic consciousness. He can "read" people like a book. He is often excruciatingly sensitive to their shifts in mood and can feel their hidden motives. This can be a very painful experience indeed.

The Lover is not, then, only the archetype of the joy of life. In his capacity to feel at one with others and with the world, he must also feel their pain. Other people may be able to avoid pain, but the man in touch with the Lover must endure it. He feels the painfulness of being alive—both for himself and for others. Here, we have the image of Jesus weeping—for his city, Jerusalem, for his disciples, for all of humanity—and taking the sorrows of the world upon himself as the "man of sorrows, one acquainted with grief," as the Bible says.

We *all* know that love brings both pain and joy. Our realization that this is profoundly and unalterably true is archetypally based. Paul, in his famous "Hymn to Love," which proclaims the characteristics of authentic love, says that "love bears all things" and "endures all things." And so it does. The troubadours of the late Middle Ages in Europe sang of the exquisite "pain of love" that simply is an inescapable part of its power.

The man under the influence of the Lover does not want to stop at socially created boundaries. He stands against the artificiality of such things. His life is often unconventional and "messy"—the artist's studio, the creative scholar's study, the "go for it" boss's desk.

Along with sensitivity to all inner and outer things comes passion. The Lover's connectedness is not primarily intellectual. It is through feeling. The primal hungers are felt passionately in all of us, at least beneath the surface. But the Lover knows this with a deep knowing. Being close to the unconscious means being close to the "fire"—to the fires of life and, on the biological level, to the fires of the life-engendering metabolic processes. Love, as we all know, is "hot," often "too hot to handle."

The man under the influence of the Lover wants to touch and be touched. He wants to touch everything physically and emotionally, and he wants to be touched by everything. He recognizes no boundaries. He wants to live out the connectedness he feels with the world inside, in the context of his powerful feelings, and outside, in the context of his relationships with other people. Ultimately, he wants to experience the world of sensual experience in its totality.

We believe that the Lover, by whatever name, is the primal energy pattern of what we could call vividness, aliveness, and passion. It lives through the great primal hungers of our species for sex, food, well-being, reproduction, creative adaptation to life's hardships, and ultimately a sense of meaning, without which human beings cannot go on with their lives. The Lover's drive is to satisfy those hungers.

The Lover archetype is primary to the psyche also because it is the energy of sensitivity to the outer environment. It expresses what Jungians call the "sensation function," the function of the psyche that is trained in on all the details of sensory experience, the function that notices colors and forms, sounds, tactile sensations, and smells. The Lover also monitors the changing textures of the inner psychological world as it responds to incoming sensory impressions. We can easily see the survival value of this energy potential for our distant, rodentlike ancestors, who struggled for survival in a dangerous world.

15. The Tarot and Personality Types

ANGELES ARRIEN

WITH EVERY MAJOR EXOTERIC DISCIPLINE, there is also a complementary esoteric discipline. Whether objective or subjective; exoteric or esoteric; external or internal, there is a basic need to understand and systemize life experience. Examples of established systems developed by humankind to map territories of experience are illustrated in the chart below:

(Objective; Quantitative)	(Subjective; Qualitative)
Exoteric Systems	Esoteric Systems
astronomy	astrology
mathematics	numerology
physics	alchemy
science	symbols

An illustration of a symbolic map of life experience is the Tarot. Basically the Tarot is an esoteric psychology, a science that represents through visual symbols a record of known possibilities of experience. Originally a book of wisdom, known as the Book of Thoth in ancient Egypt, Tarot as we know it today was transformed into its card form during the Middle Ages. Currently, there is a resurgence of interest to use the Tarot as a self-help and transformative tool.

Just as psychological and spiritual information is revealed to us in our dreams or contemplative states, the Tarot functions as an outer mirror of external experiences and internal psychological states. Looking at the Tarot from a humanistic and psychological perspective, these symbols can teach us about our own *psycho-mythology*.

The Tarot is a symbolic map of consciousness and an ancient book of wisdom that reveals to us, visually and symbolically, the creative ideas and states of consciousness that appear in multiple existence in all cultures. The

78 symbols found in the majority of decks are portraitures and archetypes of inner and outer experiences prevalent within human experience.

The Tarot deck consists of the minor arcana, better known as the four suits, comprising the ace through ten, plus sixteen royalty cards; and the major arcana with 22 cards, which bear the number 0 and the roman numerals I to XXI. The major arcana reveal life principles, the universal laws or collective experiences shared by all humankind. The four suits represent the four levels of consciousness: swords are pictures of our thoughts, mental beliefs, and general quality of thinking; cups represent the emotional, psychological factors which include our responses, reactions, and our feelings; wands represent quality of vision, insight, perception, energy, and vitality; disks—or pentacles, as they are often referred to—represent the external reality or ability to manifest what we want in the outer world in the areas of health, finances, work, creativity and relationships.

The Tarot has the ability to reveal to us, both individually, collectively, and therapeutically, the gifts and talents inherent within the psyche; it can also reveal, through problematic symbols, our personal psycho–pathology. Within the Tarot, thirteen symbols out of the 78 represent neurotic or challenging states.

When an individual selects a Tarot symbol, the card itself represents an outer mirror of an internal process, and in that moment you could say that the seat of the soul or the human psyche is revealed in the connection between the outer portraiture of the Tarot and its reflection of an internal process.

A TYPOLOGY OF THE SHADOW IN THE TAROT

In the entire Book of Thoth, or the Book of Wisdom, we find only thirteen challenges or tests pictured. From an Egyptian point of view there were only thirteen Bardo states, or challenges, or negative states that one could experience. Six of those were in the mind, three were emotional reactions to thoughts in the mind, two affected the energy or vision or how one saw things, and two then ultimately affected one's outer reality in health, finances, work, creativity, and relationships. In Jungian psychology these thirteen tests or challenges would be referred to as *the aspects of the Shadow*, or those parts of ourselves that are negative, or fearful, and are difficult to own or claim in any way. In Shamanistic terms, perhaps these Bardo states might be found in the "Journey to the Underworld," where it is important to claim one's power animals or empower oneself. The positive function of any test or challenge is to exercise our gifts, talents, and resources, to face that which is difficult from a place of empowerment rather than constriction.

SYMBOLS OF THE SHADOW IN THE TAROT

SWORDS Mental Challenges (Beliefs, Attitudes, Thoughts)

3 of Swords — Sorrow	5 of Swords — Fear of Defeat	7 of Swords — Futility	8 of Swords — Interference Doubt/ Confusion	9 of Swords — Self-Cruelty	10 of Swords — Fear of Ruin

CUPS Emotional Challenges (Responses, Reactions, Difficult Feelings)

5 of Cups — Disappoint-ment	7 of Cups — Debauch Indulgences	8 of Cups — Indolence Over-Extension

WANDS Energetic, Intuitive, Spiritual Challenges

5 of Wands — Anxiety Strife	10 of Wands — Oppression

DISKS Physical External Challenges, Health, Finances, Work, Creativity, Relationships.

5 of Disks — Worry	7 of Disks — Fear of Failure

There is no such thing as the dark night of the soul, only the dark night of the ego.
—FRANCES VAUGHAN

In the Minor Arcana, we can take a look at these forty symbols as the archetypal motif of "Beauty and the Beast" that's within. There are thirteen Beasts we might confront, move through, or attempt to tame in our consciousness, yet there are twenty-seven gifts, talents and jewels in the consciousness that are much greater than the thorns in consciousness.

TAROT AND PERSONALITY TYPES

The twenty-two major arcana are powerful archetypal symbols. They can be used to indicate each person's lifetime purpose or life dream. To find your life-time personality and soul symbols as represented in Tarot, add the day and month of your birthday together; to this total add the year of your birth. Add the final total horizontally and reduce to a single digit.

Example: if the birthday is September 9, 1956

month	9
day	+9
	18
year	1956
	1974 = 21 = 3 (1 + 9 + 7 + 4 = 21); (2 + 1 = 3)

If your final total equals a double digit number, 21 or less, reduce to a single digit. The double digit number is your personality number, the single digit number is your soul number.

Example:

month	9
day	+9
	18
year	1956
	1974 = 21 = 3

In this case, the number 21, The Universe, is the personality symbol; number 3, The Empress, is the soul symbol.

If your final total equals a single digit number you have one number for both your personality and soul.

Example:

month	3
day	+21
	24
year	1983
	2007 = 9

Number 9, The Hermit, is both the personality symbol and the soul symbol.

If your final total equals 19 it will reduce to 10 and then 1. This is the only combination of three numbers.

Example:

month	7
day	+11
	18
year	1954
	1972 = 19 = 10 = 1

Here, 19, The Sun, is the personality symbol; 1, The Magician, is the soul symbol and 10, The Wheel of Fortune, is the creativity symbol.

If your final total equals 22, it reduces to 4 and also becomes 0. In numerology 22 is the number for 4 $(2 + 2 = 4)$ and also the number for 0 $(2 - 2 = 0)$.

Example:

month	10
day	+4
	14
year	1952
	1964 = 22 = 4

In this case, 0, The Fool, is the personality symbol, and 4, The Emperor, is the soul symbol.

If your final total equals a double digit number higher than 22, reduce to a single digit. You will have one number for both your personality and soul symbols.

Example:

month	12
day	+24
	36
year	1940
	1976 = 23 = 5

Thus 5, The Hierophant, is the personality symbol and the soul symbol.

BRIEF SUMMARY OF MAJOR ARCANA SYMBOLS

The chart below briefly summarizes the Major Arcana, which are the Tarot symbols corresponding to the numerical calculations you have just made from your birthday.

MAJOR ARCANA

0   The Fool: principle of no fear; courage; mystical ecstasy

1   The Magician: principle of communication; inspired, original mind

2   The High Priestess: principle of intuition; independence, self-trust

3   The Empress: principle of love and wisdom; beauty

4   The Emperor: principle of leadership; visionary; pioneer

5   The Hierophant: principle of learning and teaching; family and community

6   The Lovers: principle of relationship; union of opposites

7   The Chariot: principle of change and transformation

8   Adjustment/Justice: principle of balance and objectivity

9   The Hermit: principle of completion; contemplation and reflection

10   The Wheel of Fortune: principle of prosperity and abundance

11   Lust/Strength: principle of passion and luster

12   The Hanged Man: principle of surrender; breaking old patterns

13   Death: principle of release; detachment; letting go

14   Art/Temperance: principle of integration and synthesis

15   The Devil/Pan: principle of maintaining humor at our bedevilments

16   The Tower: principle of awakening; healing, and restoration

17   The Star: principle of self-esteem; confidence and self-realization

18   The Moon: principle of choice and karma; authenticity versus dutifulness

19   The Sun: principle of teamwork, partnership, and collaboration

20   Aeon/Judgment: principle of good judgment

21   The Universe/World: principle of self-actualization and individuation; building new worlds

TAROT AS MEDITATION AND AFFIRMATION TOOL

A sample model, that could be used personally and therapeutically, as a guide that would incorporate the visual Tarot symbol with an affirmation that could be used on a daily basis is listed below. Clients could select the visual Tarot symbol that best represents their experience at that time and devise their own affirmation that would support that process.

Visual Meditation Symbol	Verbal Affirmations
0 The Fool (Clown; Mime; Jester; Trickster; Genii)	"I am a radiant being/I am a living treasure"
1 The Magician (Wizard; Merlin; Mercury; Shaman)	"I create magic when I use my inherent gifts and talents"
2 The High Priestess (Isis; Goddess; Delphi Oracles)	"I am an intuitive, perceptive person/I trust myself"
3 The Empress (Earth Mother; Venus; Moon; Anima)	"I am a nurturing & supportive person/I enjoy beauty, harmony, and order"
4 The Emperor (Kings; Leaders; Father; Animus; Arthur & Grail)	"I value my leadership ability"
5 The Hierophant (Zeus; Kronos; High Priest; Buddha)	"I honor what is sacred within me/I am inspired by learning/teaching situations"
6 The Lovers (Adam and Eve; yin/yang; sun/moon)	"I am a loving and caring individual/I relate well with others"
7 The Chariot (Apollo; the Charioteer; Knights; Gladiators)	"I stimulate and motivate others positively/I am responsible for what I cause"
8 Adjustment/Justice (Scales; Dharma; Maat; Titaness)	"I am balanced & centered/I honor my word & commitment"
9 The Hermit (Pilgrim; Monk; Sage; Way-Shower; Rogue)	"I value that which is meaningful & significant/I enjoy the feeling of completion & resolution"
10 The Wheel of Fortune (Mandala; Roulet; Chakras; Prayer Wheels)	"I enjoy manifesting internal abundance externally"
11 Strength/Lust (Hercules; Samson; Basht; Skehet; Fortuna)	"I am an individual of character and strength"
12 The Hanged Man (Odin; Neptune; Poseidon)	"I value breaking ineffective old patterns"
13 Death/Rebirth (Skeleton; Phoenix; Lotus; Snake)	"I am excited about growing & becoming even more of who I am"
14 Art/Temperance (Artemis; Centaur; Sphinx)	"I am a creative, well-integrated individual"
15 Devil; Pan (Satyr; Bacchus; Dionysus; Dragon)	"I am a vital, joyful, and grounded person/I enjoy my sensuality"
16 The Tower (Tower of Babel; Leaning Tower of Pisa; Faust)	"I am able to restore my energy easily/My body is the temple of my spirit"
17 The Star (Orion; Sirus; Star of David; Pleiades)	"I am a walking star/I value who I am"
18 The Moon (Mirror; Mask; Anubis; Scarab; Txaddi)	"I value honesty & integrity in relationships/I enjoy making important decisions"
19 The Sun (Networking; Eye of Ra; Osiris; Helios)	"I work well in teamwork situations/I am a cooperative individual"
20 The Aeon/Judgment (Agni; Vulcan; Pluto; Goddess Nuit)	"I observe people in situations objectively & fairly"
21 The Universe/World (Planet Earth; The Womb; Nirvana; Siva)	"I love exploring the unknown/I am excited about bringing my ideas into tangible form"

The use of the Tarot as an outer mirror for internal and external processes aligns with the basic functions of mythology, or the essential services that mythology provides for human growth and development, and as a resource for self-revelation and self-reclamation processes. In his book *The Inner Reaches of Outer Space: Metaphor as Myth and as Religion*, Joseph Campbell cites that "The first and foremost essential service of a mythology is this one, of opening the mind and heart to the utter wonder of all being. And the second service then is cosmological: of representing the universe and the whole spectacle of nature, both as known to the mind and as beheld by the eye."

So the symbols found on each Tarot card function as a way that the mind and heart can be opened to the utter wonder of what's going on with the individual, internally and externally, at that moment in time, or be a reminder of an individual's life-time dream or purpose.

PART FIVE

MENTAL
TYPOLOGIES

WE DO NOT ALL THINK ALIKE. As often as not, two people looking at the same evidence will come to different conclusions. In order to understand why, we need to examine various thinking and learning styles.

Jung's typology provides one way to understand these differences. For example, sensory types pay close attention to details, while intuitives attend to the possibilities and varied interpretations of sense data. Thinking types are concerned with objective truth and impersonal analysis, while feeling types focus on values and judgments of good or bad, right or wrong.

One of the most basic mental typologies is the distinction between left- and right-brain functioning. In Chapter 16, Sally Springer and Georg Deutsch provide a solid, scientifically based discussion of the topic. Springer is a psychologist who works with brain damaged and split-brain patients. Deutsch is a neuropsychologist whose work includes the testing and evaluation of neurologically damaged patients.

The distinction between left- and right-brain functioning is an old and well-established one. Centuries before brain research, writers and philosophers contrasted two basic modes of functioning—rational vs. emotional, linear vs. metaphoric, words vs. images. The right brain is the seat of imagery, metaphor, and intuition. The left brain is the seat of rational, verbal, and logical thought.

However, the term "left and right *brain*" is somewhat misleading. We are actually talking about the left and right cerebral hemispheres of the brain. In some ways these hemispheres act like two separate brains, but in many other ways they function as integral parts of the brain as a whole.

One reason that the two hemispheres have been treated as distinct is that most of the basic research in this area has been done on "split-brain" patients who, for medical reasons, had radical surgery that severed the corpus callosum, a thick network of nerves joining the two halves of the brain. The surgeons were surprised that so major an operation seemed to have such small effects. It took a series of sophisticated experiments to reveal the different functions of the separated left and right hemispheres. For example, in one study, split-brain patients were given a pencil to hold without being able to see it. When they held the pencil in their right hand (the right side of the body is controlled by the verbal left hemisphere), they could immediately describe it as a pencil. When the pencil was placed in their left hand, connected to the nonverbal right hemisphere, they were unable to describe it. These patients could continue to write language with their right hand, but could no longer draw with that hand. They could draw with their left hand, but not write with that hand.

The distinction between left- and right-brain functioning became grossly oversimplified and overgeneralized when the original research findings were popularized. Everything became either a left-brain activity or a right-brain activity, and people were categorized as either "left-brainers" or "right-brainers." It is true that people differ in preferences for verbal or nonverbal activity, but Springer and Deutsch point out that, for all of us whose brains are intact, the brain operates as a whole, and we send thousands of messages across the corpus callosum, from one hemisphere to the other, every second.

Learning styles differ among individuals, and a number of highly effective learning-style theories have been developed by educators. However, they have not yet gained wide currency among the general public. In Chapter 17 Thomas Armstrong describes seven different learning styles in children. Armstrong points out that our schools have lost the ability to respond to individual differences, and as a result, schooling for many children is bland and boring. Research has shown that interest in all school subjects declines from elementary school to high school.

Armstrong's work is based on a relatively new model of intelligence developed by Harvard psychologist Howard Gardner. Gardner has found that each child demonstrates a particular strength in one of seven different kinds of intelligence—logical-mathematical, musical, bodily-kinesthetic, linguistic, spatial, interpersonal, and intrapersonal.

Gardner has argued that our society generally rewards only two or three of the seven types of intelligence. We admire the linguistically developed person who reads and writes well, the logical thinker, and the independent and strong-willed intrapersonal individual. Schools rarely reward the other kinds of intelligence, which are related to skills like dancing, singing, painting, acting, and inventing. Armstrong teaches us how to recognize these seven types of intelligence in ourselves and in children, and how to work with and cultivate each type.

The model presented by Sandra Seagal and David Horne in Chapter 18 is based on investigations involving over 30,000 people—children and adults—in different cultures, including Sweden, Canada, and the United States. Seagal and Horne's theory has direct implications for communication, learning, parenting, and personal development. It focuses on three basic dimensions found in all people: body, mind, and emotions.

These three dimensions are related to fundamental principles found in virtually all phenomena. An organization, for example, begins with an idea or a vision, which is related to the mind. Next comes the establishment of relationships among those who wish to implement the vision, which corresponds to the emotions. Finally, there is the actual work of carrying out the initial purpose or vision, which is associated with the body, the instrument through which we act in the world. This threefold division of mind, emotions, and body goes back to Plato's classic threefold distinction of reason, emotions, and will.

The three principles interact to form four basic sets of personality dynamics. These are the mentally centered, emotional-objective, emotional-subjective, and physically centered personality dynamics. Each of us has a style of learning and acting centered around our own type.

Mentally centered individuals prefer abstractions and objective expression. They want clear and well-documented information and are usually logical, focused, thorough, and careful in work. Emotional-objective people are interested in ideas and thoughts, and require a sense of self-respect and emotional as well as mental contact. Emotional-subjective people enjoy linking their own experiences with others, and want emotional and physical contact as well as a sense of being personally seen and approved. Physically centered individuals love to translate ideas into results, and prefer concrete, detailed, and practical information.

By studying mental typologies we can enhance our ability to learn new material and to communicate with others. We can come to understand how we most easily take in and retain new information and how we tend to present thoughts and ideas to others. If we understand our own and another's type, we will be able to change our own preferred style to match the kind of presentation the other person needs to appreciate and understand what we want to communicate.

16. Left Brain and Right Brain

SALLY SPRINGER AND GEORG DEUTSCH

WE HAVE SEEN EVIDENCE THAT, after the surgical division of the two hemispheres, learning and memory can continue separately in the left brain and right brain. Each half of the brain of a split-brain patient is able to sense, perceive, and perhaps even conceptualize independently of the other. Furthermore, in virtually every approach to the study of hemispheric processes, including approaches using normal individuals, findings support the existence of hemispheric differences. Some talk of a verbal-nonverbal distinction. Others argue that the halves of the brain differ in terms of how they deal with information in general.

Since the first split-brain operations, a progression of labels has been used to describe the processes of the left brain and right brain. The most widely cited characteristics may be divided into five main groups, which form a kind of hierarchy. Each designation usually includes and goes beyond the characteristics above it:

Left Hemisphere	Right Hemisphere
Verbal	Nonverbal, visuo-spatial
Sequential, temporal, digital	Simultaneous, spatial, analogic
Logical, analytic	Gestalt, synthetic
Rational	Intuitive
Western thought	Eastern thought

The descriptions near the top of the list seem to be based on experimental evidence; the other designations appear more speculative. The verbal-nonverbal distinction, for example, was the earliest to emerge from split-brain research and behavioral research with normal subjects. The sequential-simultaneous distinction reflects a current, though not universally accepted, theoretical model holding that the left hemisphere tends to deal with rapid changes in time and to analyze stimuli in terms of details and features, while the right hemisphere deals with simultaneous relationships and with the more global properties of patterns. In this model, the left hemisphere is something like a digital computer, the right like an analog computer.

Many investigators speculating on these issues have attempted to go beyond these distinctions. A popularly accepted view of the differences between the hemispheres is that the left brain operates in a logical, analytic manner and the right brain works in a Gestalt, synthetic fashion.

Once one starts using such labels to describe the operation of the hemispheres, several questions come to mind. Are they just convenient descriptions of how the hemispheres deal with information? Or do they imply that the hemispheres differ in their styles of thinking? Is it possible to view the specialized functions of the left brain and right brain as distinct modes of thought?

Historically, philosophers and students of the mind have shown a tendency to divide intellectual faculties into two types. For example, consider the following quotation from a yogic philosopher who wrote in 1910:

> The intellect is an organ composed of several groups of functions, divisible into two important classes, the functions and faculties of the right hand, the functions and faculties of the left. The faculties of the right hand are comprehensive, creative, and synthetic; the faculties of the left hand critical and analytic. . . . The left limits itself to ascertained truth, the right grasps that which is still elusive or unascertained. Both are essential to the completeness of the human reason. These important functions of the machine have all to be raised to their highest and finest working power, if the education of the child is not to be imperfect and one-sided.[1]

Many Western thinkers have also talked of mental organization as if it were divided into two parts. Rational versus intuitive, explicit versus implicit, analytic versus synthetic, are some examples of these dichotomies. More are listed in Table 1. Although these terms are quite varied, they do seem to have something in common. Perhaps, as some have suggested, they correspond to the separate processes of the two cerebral hemispheres.

TABLE 1
DICHOTOMIES

Intellect	Intuition
Convergent	Divergent
Intellectual	Sensuous
Deductive	Imaginative
Rational	Metaphoric

Vertical	Horizontal
Discrete	Continuous
Abstract	Concrete
Realistic	Impulsive
Directed	Free
Differential	Existential
Sequential	Multiple
Historical	Timeless
Analytic	Holistic
Explicit	Tacit
Objective	Subjective
Successive	Simultaneous

Why so many two-part divisions? Do they label truly distinct and separate qualities, or do they just describe the extremes of a set of continuous behaviors? In other words, are we dealing with all-or-none differences, or are there gradations in between? Some have insisted on the former view because, they claim, it conforms best to a neuroanatomical reality—the existence of the left brain and right brain capable of operating independently. Another view is that the formulation of dichotomies or opposites is just a convenient way of viewing complex situations.

The idea that different modes of knowing are reflected in hemispheric functions has become associated in recent years with psychologist Robert Ornstein. In addition to his electroencephalographic (EEG) studies of hemispheric asymmetry, Ornstein has been interested in the nature of consciousness and its relationship to hemispheric function.

In 1970, Ornstein published a book entitled *The Psychology of Consciousness.*[2] In it he set forth the message that Western men and women have been using only half of their brain and hence half of their mental capacity. He noted that the emphasis on language and logical thinking in Western societies has ensured that the left hemisphere is well exercised. He then went on to argue that the functions of the right hemisphere are a neglected part of human abilities and intellect in the West and that such functions are more developed in the cultures, mysticism, and religions of the East. In short, Ornstein identified the left hemisphere with the thought of the technological, rational West and the right hemisphere with the thought of the intuitive, mystical East.

Many outlandish claims and misinterpretations have followed in the wake of Ornstein's book. For example, some have equated the left hemisphere with the evils of modern society. Ornstein, however, has stressed that the cerebral hemispheres are specialized for different types of *thought*. He also insists that schools spend most of their time training students in what seem to be left-hemisphere skills.

Ornstein has become an advocate of the idea that there are alternate ways of knowing and alternate forms of consciousness. He feels that our intellectual training unduly emphasizes the analytic

> ... with the result that we have learned to look at unconnected fragments instead of at an entire solution. ... As a result of this preoccupation with isolated facts, it is not surprising that we face so many simultaneous problems whose solutions depend upon our ability to grasp the relationship of parts to wholes. ... Split- and whole-brain studies have led to a new conception of human knowledge, consciousness, and intelligence. All knowledge cannot be expressed in words, yet our education is based almost exclusively on its written or spoken forms. ... But the artist, dancer, and mystic have learned to develop the nonverbal portion of intelligence.[3]

As we have seen, ideas about the nature of hemispheric differences are diverse. They have evolved from verbal–nonverbal distinctions to ever more abstract notions of the relationship between mental function and the hemispheres. In this process, ideas concerning hemispheric differences have moved further and further away from basic research findings. Some have found this progression disconcerting because the distinction between fact and speculation is often blurred. The term "dichotomania" has been coined to refer to the avalanche of popular literature fostered by the most speculative notions.

17. Seven Learning Styles in Children

THOMAS ARMSTRONG

PETER CAN beat any challenger in a game of chess. Sally spends her free time listening to opera. Ed is a super-athlete. Frank entertains his peers with long-winded stories of adventure. Ann loves to draw and paint. June is always organizing a party or committee at school. David sits at home alone planning a business venture.

Although a typical IQ test might not show it, all of these children are highly intelligent. Each demonstrates a particular strength in one of seven different kinds of intelligence—logical-mathematical, musical, bodily-kinesthetic, linguistic, spatial, interpersonal, and intrapersonal—described by Harvard psychologist Howard Gardner in his prize-winning book *Frames of Mind*. This new model of intelligence has been called by Ernest Boyer of the Carnegie Foundation for the Advancement of Teaching the most exciting work currently being done in the field of learning. Gardner's theory of multiple intelligences provides a solid foundation upon which to identify and develop a broad spectrum of abilities within every child.

Gardner says that our society talks about only two or three of the seven types of intelligence when deciding who's smart in the culture. We look up to the highly linguistic person who reads and writes well, the logical thinker who reasons in clear and concise ways, and the rugged individualist with strong intrapersonal intelligence. Yet there are other equally valid forms of intelligence. What about people who sing or dance well? Or those who can paint, draw, act, sculpt, invent or design? And what about individuals who are great leaders or have good intuition? These musical, bodily-kinesthetic, spatial, and interpersonal learners often get overlooked in discussions about superior intelligence.

Everyone has all seven kinds of intelligence in different proportions. Your child may be a great reader but a poor math student, a wonderful drawer but clumsy out on the playing field. Children can even show a wide range of strengths and weaknesses within one area of intelligence. Your child may write very well but have difficulty with spelling or handwriting, read poorly but be a superb storyteller, play an excellent game of basketball but stumble on the dance floor.

As you read through the descriptions of each type of intelligence that follow, resist the temptation to categorize your child into one of the seven intelligence groups. Your child is more complex than this. You should find your child described in several of the sections. Take what seems to apply to your child in these descriptions and add to this other observed strengths and weaknesses in all seven varieties of intelligence. Taken together, these constitute your child's personal learning style.

LINGUISTIC INTELLIGENCE

Children gifted in linguistic ability have highly developed auditory skills and enjoy playing around with the sounds of language. They often think in words. They frequently have their head stuck in a book or are busy writing a story or poem. Even if they don't enjoy reading or writing, they may be gifted storytellers. They often love word games and may have a good memory for verse, lyrics, or trivia. They might want to be writers, secretaries, editors, social scientists, humanities teachers, or politicians. They learn best by verbalizing or hearing and seeing words. Linguistically gifted children:

- like to write;
- spin tall tales or tell jokes and stories;
- have a good memory for names, places, dates, or trivia;
- enjoy reading books in their spare time;
- spell words accurately and easily;
- appreciate nonsense rhymes and tongue twisters;
- like doing crossword puzzles or playing games such as Scrabble or Anagrams.

LOGICAL–MATHEMATICAL INTELLIGENCE

Youngsters strong in this form of intelligence think conceptually. Before adolescence, these children explore patterns, categories, and relationships by actively manipulating the environment and experimenting with things in a controlled and orderly way. In their teen years, they're capable of highly abstract forms of logical thinking. Children gifted in this area are constantly questioning and wondering about natural events. These are the youngsters who love hanging around computers or chemistry sets, trying to figure out the answer to a difficult problem. They often love brain teasers, logical puzzles, and games—like chess—that require reasoning abilities. These children may want to grow up to be scientists, engineers, computer programmers, accountants, or perhaps even philosophers. Logical-mathematically talented children:

- compute arithmetic problems quickly in their head;
- enjoy using computers;
- ask questions like "Where does the universe end?" "What happens after we die?" and "When did time begin?";
- play chess, checkers, or other strategy games, and win;
- reason things out logically and clearly;
- devise experiments to test out things they don't understand;
- spend lots of time working on logic puzzles such as Rubik's cube.

SPATIAL INTELLIGENCE

These kids seem to know where everything is located in the house. They think in images and pictures. They're the ones who find things that have been lost or misplaced. If you should rearrange the interior of your home, these children will be highly sensitive to the change and react with joy or dismay. They often love to do mazes or jigsaw puzzles. They spend free time drawing, designing things, building with Lego blocks, or simply daydreaming. Many of them develop a fascination with machines and contraptions, sometimes coming up with inventions of their own. They might want to become architects, artists, mechanics, engineers, or city planners. Children strong in spatial intelligence:

- spend free time engaged in art activities;
- report clear visual images when thinking about something;
- easily read maps, charts, and diagrams;
- draw accurate representations of people or things;
- like it when you show movies, slides, or photographs;
- enjoy doing jigsaw puzzles or mazes;
- daydream a lot.

MUSICAL INTELLIGENCE

Musically gifted kids often sing, hum, or whistle tunes quietly to themselves. Put on a piece of music and you can recognize these children by the way in which they immediately begin moving and singing along. They may already be playing musical instruments or singing in choirs. However, other musical children show this potential more through simple music appreciation. They will have strong opinions about the music you play on the radio or stereo. They will be the ones to lead a group sing on a family outing. They're also sensitive to nonverbal sounds in the environment—such as crickets chirping and distant bells ringing—and will hear things that others in the family have missed. Musically gifted children:

- play a musical instrument;
- remember melodies of songs;
- tell you when a musical note is off-key;
- say they need to have music on in order to study;
- collect records or tapes;
- sing songs to themselves;
- keep time rhythmically to music.

BODILY-KINESTHETIC INTELLIGENCE

These children squirm at the breakfast table and are the first ones to be excused as they zoom out the door and head for the neighborhood playground. They process knowledge through bodily sensations. They get "gut feelings" about answers on tests at school. Some are primarily graced with athletic abilities or the skills of a dancer, actor, or mime—they are great at mimicking your best and worst qualities. Others are particularly gifted with excellent fine-motor coordination and can excel in typing, drawing, fixing things, sewing, crafts, and related activities. These children communicate very effectively through gestures and other forms of body language. Sometimes they can be labeled hyperactive at home and school if there aren't appropriate outlets for them. They need opportunities to learn by moving or acting things out. Children who excel in bodily-kinesthetic intelligence:

- do well in competitive sports;
- move, twitch, tap, or fidget while sitting in a chair;
- engage in physical activities such as swimming, biking, hiking, or skateboarding;
- need to touch people when they talk to them;
- enjoy scary amusement rides;
- demonstrate skill in a craft like woodworking, sewing, or carving;
- cleverly mimic other people's gestures, mannerisms, or behaviors.

INTERPERSONAL INTELLIGENCE

These children understand people. They are frequently leaders among their peers in the neighborhood or in their class at school. They organize, communicate, and, at their worst, manipulate. They know what's going on with everybody in the neighborhood, who likes whom, who's feuding with whom, and who's going to fight whom after school. These youngsters excel in mediating conflict between peers because of their uncanny ability to pick up on other people's feelings and intentions. They might want to become counselors, business people, or community organizers. They learn best by relating and cooperating. Interpersonally gifted children:

- have a lot of friends;
- socialize a great deal at school or around the neighborhood;
- seem to be "street-smart";
- get involved in after-school group activities;
- serve as the "family mediator" when disputes arise;
- enjoy playing group games with other children;
- have a lot of empathy for the feelings of others.

INTRAPERSONAL INTELLIGENCE

Like those who have interpersonal intelligence, intrapersonal children possess strong personalities. Yet many of them tend to shy away from group activities and prefer instead to bloom in isolation. They have a deep awareness of their inner feelings, dreams, and ideas. They may keep a diary or have ongoing projects and hobbies that are semisecretive in nature. There's a certain quality of inner wisdom, intuitive ability, or even a psychic nature that accompanies many of these children throughout their lives. This deep sense of self sets them apart and causes them to go off on their own toward some goal known only to themselves. They may want to become writers, small-business people running creative enterprises, or enter into religious work. Intrapersonally talented children:

- display a sense of independence or a strong will;
- react with strong opinions when controversial topics are being discussed;
- seem to live in their own private, inner world;
- like to be alone to pursue some personal interest, hobby, or project;
- seem to have a deep sense of self-confidence;
- march to the beat of a different drummer in their style of dress, their behavior, or their general attitude;
- motivate themselves to do well on independent study projects.

Gardner cautions against using conventional tests in attempting to identify types of intelligence in children. Formal tests that require children to answer questions orally, fill in blanks, or do other paper and pencil tasks, tend to favor students who are strong in linguistic and logical-mathematical abilities while discriminating against others who are weak in these areas but strong in one or more of the other areas.

HOW TO TEACH ANYTHING SEVEN DIFFERENT WAYS

Once you get the hang of this seven-fold teaching method, you'll be able to teach anything seven different ways. If your child isn't getting it one way, then you have at least six more tries. All it takes is a little creativity and some elbow grease!

Need some examples? Let's say you want to assist your child in learning the names of the fifty states. Here are seven different ways you can help out:

- *Linguistic:* practice quizzing her orally on the names of the states;
- *Spatial:* get a nice multi-colored map and help her associate the names with the different colors or shapes of the states;
- *Kinesthetic:* find a relief map that she can feel, or a puzzle map that she can take apart and put back together, and assist her in identifying tactile features for each of the states to use in memorizing their names;
- *Logical-mathematical:* help her classify the states into different categories—by first letter, geographical size, population, entry into the union, and so on;
- *Musical:* teach her the different state songs or a song that names all fifty states (if you can't find one, make one up!);
- *Interpersonal:* play a card game such as Concentration where players must match pairs of overturned cards; in this case the name of the state matched with its outline;
- *Intrapersonal:* suggest that she write to the state governments of all fifty states (use postcards, they're cheap!) for information she can keep in a scrapbook.

What about homework? If you're lucky, your child's teacher gives your child choices at least some of the time for doing an assignment. Let's say your child comes home with an open-ended homework project to complete for a unit on bird study. Here are seven ways of going about completing the task:

- *Linguistic:* book reports, oral presentations, writing compositions, tape recordings;
- *Spatial:* charts and maps of a bird's migration patterns, pictures of birds;
- *Kinesthetic:* hiking to a bird's natural habitat, building a replica of a bird's nest;
- *Logical-mathematical:* collecting statistics about birds, answering the basic question: "How does a bird fly?";
- *Musical:* finding records or tapes of bird calls and learning to imitate them;
- *Interpersonal:* volunteering in a community project designed to safeguard the welfare of the local bird population;
- *Intrapersonal:* creating a special place of solitude in nature for bird-watching.

Finally, there's that eternal question parents are always asking: "How do I get my child to behave?" Thousands of books have been written on the subject and nobody seems to agree on what to do. Maybe that's because different folks need different strokes. Here are seven strokes for starters:

- *Linguistic:* sit down and have a good chat with your child about why she's misbehaving or ask her to tape record or write down what's bothering her;
- *Logical-mathematical:* reason with your child—show her the logical consequences of her actions (Rudolf Dreikurs based an entire discipline system on this approach);
- *Spatial:* tell your child a good, imaginative story illustrating her misbehavior and its possible causes and/or solutions (for a child who lies, tell "The Boy Who Cried Wolf");
- *Kinesthetic:* ask your child to act out the misbehavior and then act out the appropriate behavior and compare the two;
- *Musical:* find a piece of music that contains the message you want to drive home to your child or use music as a relaxing influence for an out-of-control child;
- *Interpersonal:* use group problem-solving activities;
- *Intrapersonal:* use one-on-one counseling, centering exercises, and lots of patience!

18. Mental, Emotional, and Physical Principles in Human Dynamics

SANDRA SEAGAL AND DAVID HORNE

ALL PHENOMENA can be seen as coming into being in three stages. The creation of an organization, for example, can be seen as a process which begins with an idea or initiating purpose; then establishes a dynamic set of relationships among people with the goal of implementing that purpose; finally resulting in a specific form of manifestation. Once the organization is formed, these three components co-exist in a dynamic interplay.

In looking at a human being, it is possible to equate the initiating purpose with the mind and the will; the establishment of relationships with the emotions; and the specific manifestation with the body, which is the mechanism through which the will and the emotions are expressed.

Because these three stages or components apply universally, they can be regarded as principles. Because of the nature of their expression in human beings, we term these principles the mental, the emotional (or relational), and the physical (or practical).

THE MENTALLY CENTERED PERSONALITY DYNAMIC

General

I have a basic relationship to the world of thoughts, vision, concepts, the overview. I can live easily the gift of focus and can inspire that in others. I often bring structure, objectivity and precision to projects and situations. Because my mind is more central to my personality than my emotions, my mood is generally stable. I am not given to emotional display or impulsivity.

Most central to my personality is a value system through which I structure my life. The values which I uphold do not change easily. Therefore, if you want to know more about me, ask me what I value. One of my greatest concerns is that values are more often held in the mind than lived or practiced in the world; I feel deeply when I see that values are not maintained at the practical level of daily living. I am reliable and consistent with regard to all that I value, including the relationships and endeavors to which I commit. These are carefully selected.

Body

I experience the sensory world finely and keenly, with many subtle nuances. Because I tend to be selective with respect to what I take in, I am not easily overwhelmed by either the sensory or the emotional worlds. However, it is possible for me to be "too much in my head."

I have a natural affinity for space, for solitude (which nurtures my process of making subtle feelings and values conscious) and for independent physical activity. These factors make being in Nature attractive to me.

Communication

My communications are generally thoughtful, purposeful and objective. Since clarity and precision are important to me, I am often meticulous in my choice of words. For this reason, written communication may have a particular appeal for me.

The content of my communication is more likely to be conceptual, factual and informational than concerned with the subjective experiences and processes of myself or others. Its range will depend upon the breadth of my values and the degree to which I have cultivated personal consciousness.

I am rarely fully at ease in primarily social situations. I have most comfort in gatherings with a purpose that I value. Since I am carefully selective of the people with whom, and the situations in which I will open myself in full emotional expression, people may not always be aware of how I am feeling, or that I can be compassionately aware of the feelings of others.

Function

I do not easily lose sight of the overview or purpose in any endeavor, and I like to help establish and articulate the guiding values and principles for a relationship, group, or an organization. Because I am also interested in structure, I contribute structure to what I value through whatever skills are natural to me.

Since I have an affinity for precision, focus and careful discrimination, I am usually willing and able to engage in work that is highly detailed, provided that I value its purpose.

Mine is the objective voice that expresses constancy, essentiality, principle.

Deep Purpose

One of my deep purposes is to encompass all factions and help bring unity into a divided world. From the place of deep heart, I can articulate overarching principles and essential structures to which all can subscribe. Through my receptivity, I offer a kind of loving space in which individuals may be supported and many forms may be linked so as to contribute most effectively to a valued vision.

THE EMOTIONAL-OBJECTIVE PERSONALITY DYNAMIC

General

I am a problem-solver with an affinity for innovation at the mental level. I am interested in ideas that have meaning, purpose and serve other individuals or the community as a whole. My mind is usually focused, but may pursue several ideas at once, and several alternatives to each idea. Because there is a mental note in the emotional system it is hard to tell whether I think my feelings or feel my thoughts. I identify with what I do (my work) rather than who I am.

Body

My body functions essentially as a "support" for my personality; I usually do not pick up many signals from my body, nor am I aware of absorbing the emotional environment around me. My physical energy, therefore, is usually stable, and I can work long hours without conscious fatigue. I am often identified as a "workaholic" and may need to be made aware of the body's requirement for rest.

Communication

I often do not know myself well. It is only as this becomes a value that self-disclosure becomes important. My prime orientation is towards the movement of work and events rather than towards subjective experience. I am interested in processing creative or new ideas with others and am often extremely intense in this communication.

It is within the context of a group or in teamwork that I find personal life to become real and fully realized. Groups have special significance for me as task forces capable of cooperative service. I therefore consistently devote much communication time to furthering this group process.

I am also willing to engage in extensive personal communication with my family and the few others who play a "personal" role in my life. This communication also often has the practical purpose of facilitating individual forward movement or cooperative effort.

Function

I am a natural model maker. My function is to *move* work forward, by first understanding the work that needs to be done; then designing general models and structures related to that work; then linking the models with the people to be involved. The specific ways in which the work is undertaken emerge from the people participating. I usually prefer to leave detailing to others.

Through my forward movement and the linking of goals and purposes with people, I often play a visible leadership role.

Deep Purpose

One deep purpose is to bring into manifestation ideas or principles that serve humanity. I do this by "living" them myself (embodiment), and by devising means for fostering their expression in others. The manifestation of any vision requires the empowerment of group life. I therefore engage in continuous direct work with groups, striving with others similarly motivated to create the power of group unity, for the purpose of building something new and enduring that is of service to mankind.

THE EMOTIONAL-SUBJECTIVE PERSONALITY DYNAMIC

General

All my encounters are personalized. I connect personally with everything I hear, speak and do. I am open to experiencing the people, the environment and the contexts with which I participate. This means that I pick up a great deal of information in any situation, including the feelings and sometimes even the physical condition of the people present. I can even experience these as my own condition.

I am highly intuitive although I sometimes lack the confidence to act according to my intuition. I am learning that when my thoughts and feelings contradict my intuition, it is my intuition to which I must pay attention, for it is my most reliable signal.

I have an affinity for diversity, and am attracted to a myriad of forms, to whose creation I am often gifted in contributing. I also have the capacity to see beyond the forms, appreciating the values they reflect, the skill in their construction, and their effect upon those who use them.

Because of my attraction to the diverse facets of the world, I may become over stressed or fragmented in attempting to participate in too much. Part of my life's work is to learn to value the "middle way"—to balance the extremes within myself and in my commitments. When I do so, I am able to stay focused and clear.

Body

There is a physical dimension in my emotional system; therefore my body is responsive to my feelings. How I feel emotionally is reflected in my physical condition. Emotional trauma from the past is held in the body, and will cause loss of energy and physical distress until the issues are made conscious and resolved. Because of my openness to the experience of others, it is sometimes difficult for me to make a clear distinction between my own emotions and physical sensations, and those of others with whom I am related. With this discernment I am able to function optimally. Without it, I can lose my sense of self.

Because of my sensitivity to the emotional world, I may find at times that my energy is uneven, and I experience a wide range of moods. It is important for me to develop selectivity with regard to intake, whether that intake be people, food, sound, color, etc. As I understand myself more, I find that this selection process becomes more conscious and precise.

Regular physical exercise is critical to my well-being as it acts, in part, to release any emotional or physical stress.

Communications

I value my feelings and need to take time to reflect upon them before I can clearly communicate them to others. It is critical for me to process my feelings and thoughts through communicative interaction with selected people. In this way, I come to see and understand the meaning of my experience. When I do so, I often feel a sense of completion and release within my body. I am able to help others gain insight, understanding and release through the same process. When I have achieved clarity through communication with another person or in the silence of my own contemplation, I am able to take the actions that are appropriate.

Function

I am a natural connector. One of my functions is to understand the nature of people, and to use this understanding in communication, and in the organization and linking of people, ideas and systems. My affinity for making new connections and relationships may find creative expression in the arts or sciences, as well as with regard to people. I also ensure that the life of the feelings is valued and taken into account in the world.

Deep Purpose

One of my deep purposes is to shed the light of understanding on the human condition. Through taking my personal experiences seriously, I learn to understand them deeply and to find the larger objective meanings behind my subjective experiences. I value deeply the silence of my own contemplation, which enables me to come to understanding and so take purposeful actions that are of service to others.

A visionary factor often makes me an inspirational communicator and an effective long-range "seer."

THE PHYSICALLY CENTERED PERSONALITY DYNAMICS

General

I am interested in concrete work. I want to translate thoughts and ideas into practical results which satisfy a need or solve a problem. I especially excel in the tactical implementation of work. Detailing is important to me. I am also aware of patterns and patterning, and am capable of repetition if it is required to complete a task.

I have an innate sense of continuity and a respect for the past. I am interested in the "whole" and experience life organically. I am very receptive to, and accepting of, my environment. I work *with* the environment, including the people, things and situations. I tend to think in terms of connected systems. Group life affects me deeply as it relates to the "whole." I understand teams and work well in them. I am not the point. The point is the *whole*.

Body

My body rhythm can be slow, but my mental rhythm fast. That is sometimes a problem for me. Because of my group orientation I am sometimes unaware of my personal needs and goals. When I know these, my flow of energy is much greater. I am also often unaware of signals from my body, but as I become conscious of them I realize that they provide me with much accurate information about myself and my environment.

In any situation, I take in everything about me, including the emotional and physical condition of others, all of the information, every ambiguity and paradox. I am like a giant data bank, storing information as a whole throughout my body. My memory is usually excellent. Often my limbs give me trouble as I mature and age; perhaps the amount of storage is too much for them.

It is necessary for me to continually reconnect with Nature in order to stay balanced and healthy. Because my body absorbs and records so much data, I need to synchronize myself with the slower nature—rhythms in order to become aware of my own emotional responses and release any negative input.

Communication

My verbal responses tend to be slow because I have so much data to process and distill. Moreover, like the mentally centered, I am often relatively unconscious of what "personal processing" is all about. I like to talk about what I am doing, not about who I am. Often, rather than talk about what I am doing, I'd prefer to just do it! My natural tendency is to accept "what is" and move on to action.

A challenge for me is to become more conscious of myself as an individual—to come out of the "collective" and establish my own identity. I therefore need to separate myself from people sometimes, and listen, alone, for my own clear voice. It sometimes takes courage for me to speak with that voice when I am with others.

Function

My function is to respect the "whole" by including in my thinking and my actions all the people and all the parts. This collective process takes time, which needs to be respected. Another function is to distill the requisite essentials from all of the available data. The result is the assurance that work is grounded operationally, in accordance with the initial vision, and includes all of the necessary details.

I am orderly in my working habits. This makes me reliable to myself and others. I generally follow this sequence: a) Obtain consensus for the idea or concept which is to become operational: b) Make tactical plans, taking into account strategy and environmental considerations: c) Develop and operationalize programs.

I do what is needed.

Deep Purpose

One deep purpose is the securing of vision in the manifest world. I never forget that vision must be practically operationalized if it is to have meaning and effect. Another is to create unity from diversity through maintaining my deep bonding to all group members.

Obviously none of these outlines provides a complete description for everybody who lives that dynamic. There are in each personality dynamic many more distinguishing characteristics of appearance and functioning. Moreover, though each individual's basic design, like that of the body, remains constant throughout the life span, each person lives through their personality dynamic across time with varying degrees of development and maturity, so that though the members of each of the groups share fundamental dynamics, there is always a wide range of difference in terms of expressive quality.

Nevertheless, each person in each personality dynamic shares fundamental characteristics with all others of the same design, so that it should be possible for you to identify which of the dynamics is yours. Each should be sufficiently descriptive of every member of the personality dynamic it describes, to the degree that if 80% of an outline applies to you, it is probably describing your dynamic.

Remember that all of the descriptions are in all of us, but in each of us one specific set of dynamics is central. Try to find the one with which you most identify. Should you have difficulty in finding your "fit," read the descriptions aloud. Often the addition of vocalization produces a kind of resonance in the reader as the applicable set of dynamics is voiced.

PART SIX

BUSINESS
AND LEADERSHIP
TYPOLOGIES

WE LIVE IN A WORLD of social relationships. As we grew up, we learned how to relate to our mothers, fathers, and siblings. In school, we learned to relate to a wide variety of teachers and classmates. We have had to understand relationships to survive, but generally that understanding grows below the threshold of conscious awareness.

Just as people have different body types and mental styles, individuals also differ in the characteristic ways they handle relationships. We have all noticed that some of our friends are natural leaders, while others are always followers. Some people are quiet "loners," while others love to be the lively center of attention. Learning about relationship types can help us understand our own interpersonal style and appreciate its strengths and limitations. Relationship typologies can enable us to recognize differing styles among others, create more harmonious and productive relationships, and improve group performance.

In Chapter 19, John Corbett presents one of the most popular typologies used today in the business world. Four types are derived from the two basic dimensions of dominance and sociability. The resulting four types are *directive, counseling, collaborative*, and *deliberative*. The original version of this system was known as Wilson social styles and the four types were labeled *driver, expressive, amiable*, and *analytical*.

This system makes great intuitive sense, and we can easily recognize the dimension of dominance and sociability in ourselves and in others. We have all known people who are high in dominance, and who forcefully declare their ideas and opinions, are unafraid to confront or challenge others, and are comfortable as doers, initiators, and directors. We also know individuals who are low on dominance, and who listen more than speak, ask questions rather than state their own opinions, defer to others, and observe rather than take an active part. Those high in sociability are warm, open, involved with others, and show their feelings easily. People who are reserved, or low in sociability, tend to be objective, dispassionate, distant, independent, and emotionally controlled.

The four relationship styles are also readily recognized. The directive individual is high on dominance and low on sociability. A clear example is Perry Mason, who is both cool and forceful, and who quickly snaps out orders to his assistants and associates. The collaborative person is high on both dominance and sociability. The TV character Kojak is an excellent example, a man who is forceful and expressive and also very much involved with other people. The deliberative person is low on both dominance and sociability. Sergeant Friday, the old TV detective, is a classic, wooden-faced stereotype who is concerned only for logic and accuracy, not for people. Friday's favorite expression was, "Just the facts, ma'am, just the facts." The counseling type is high on sociability and low on dominance. This type is epitomized by Columbo, who is always extremely polite, deferent, and agreeable, up until the moment he catches his quarry.

Another approach to relationship types is to look at styles of leadership. We have all been followers, yet most of us have had to take on positions of leadership at times. So it is important to understand the various dimensions of effective leadership.

We frequently encounter powerful, archetypal images of leaders and leadership styles. For example, there is the "man on a white horse," who inspires and leads others to charge, full tilt, against problems and obstacles. Films and novels often depict the tough, angry, desk-pounding boss, who frequently hides a heart of gold. Another common image is that of the cunning and unscrupulous manipulator, who exerts power behind the scenes.

Michael Maccoby, a psychoanalyst and a personal student of Erich Fromm's, describes four kinds of business leaders in Chapter 20. Maccoby coined the term "the gamesman" to describe a certain cool and calculating breed of business leader. The other basic types he discovered through extensive research on business leadership are the craftsperson, the jungle fighter, and the company person.

The craftsperson is an old-fashioned leader who is mainly respected for his or her professional skills. A craftsperson works well in training apprentices in the complexities of a demanding profession. Self-centered and perfectionist, the craftsperson will rarely be found as a leader in a large, modern organization. The jungle fighter is a classic leader whose goal is power, and who believes that work is a jungle where only the strong survive and others are either allies or enemies. The company person has a sense of identity based on being part of a powerful, prestigious, and protective company, and this type tends to be concerned with the human side of business, seeking to develop a working atmosphere of cooperation, stimulation, and mutual support. The gamesman, or gameswoman, is a strong competitor who is out to win, and enjoys risk taking and motivating others to new heights, and loves fresh ideas, new techniques, and shortcuts.

In Chapter 21, Robert Blake and Jane Mouton examine two basic orientations in business leadership—concern for people and concern for production. Combinations of these two variables result in the following leadership types: Country Club Management, Middle-of-the-Road Management, Impoverished Management, Authority-Compliance, and Team Management.

The Country Club Management style involves primary attention to human needs, friendly working relations, and a comfortable work atmosphere. This style strongly resembles Maccoby's company person. Middle-of-the-Road managers try to balance average morale and pleasant working conditions with moderate achievement of work goals. Impoverished managers have basically given up real leadership and try to get by with a minimum of effort, allowing both low morale and low accomplishment. The Authority-Compliance style puts efficiency and production first and pays as little attention as possible to the human element, which is seen as a distraction or source of interference. Team Management seeks to accomplish high productivity through well-motivated, committed people and through the development of relationships of trust and respect.

19. Four Relationship Types: Dominant, Yielding, Outgoing, and Reserved

JOHN CORBETT

WE ARE ALL CREATURES OF HABIT. We tend to be generally consistent in how dominant or outgoing we are toward most people we deal with. This notion defines the underlying principle of interpersonal style: *people develop consistent and observable behavior patterns over time.* These patterns can be observed by others and are suggestive of our interpersonal style.

The responsive acts we choose are usually consistent with the set of behaviors we feel most comfortable with, and over time these behaviors become habitual. We are creatures of habit and we reinforce and build upon behaviors that have worked for us. Behaving in habitual and therefore predictable ways is a positive aspect of our behavior. Habits free our minds for other purposes.

Our definition of Interpersonal Style then is: *a harmonious pattern of behaviors, developed over time, which can be observed, and agreed upon for describing a person's behavior.*

THE DOMINANCE SCALE

Dominance is the inclination to be forceful, aggressive, or affirmative in relationships. At one extreme of dominance are those who relate to others with force and intensity. Their non-verbal communication is punctuated by forceful body language, aggressive command of space, and the use of their voice to emphasize points as they attempt to influence the thinking and actions of others.

At the other extreme of dominance are those who relate to others with moderate, unassuming and deferential demeanor. Non-verbal communication is evident in their restrained body language, reluctance to occupy space, and the lack of intensity in voice intonation. They tend to ask questions more readily than express their opinions.

They Readily State Their Opinion

People who tend to be dominating in social situations are described as active, aggressive, and assertive. Their style of interacting with others is characterized by the tendency to state ideas, opinions, and preferences. They may become presumptuous when ignored; irritated when unheeded; combative when challenged; and obstinate when denied.

They Will Likely Ask for Your Opinion

People who tend to yield in their interpersonal interactions are often described as unassuming and non-confrontive. They may listen readily, and are generally interested in the opinions of others. They may appear to be low keyed and somewhat easy going. They may tend to withdraw when ignored; be resigned when unheeded; give in when challenged; and recoil when rebuffed.

THE SOCIABILITY SCALE

The tendency to be reserved in social situations or to be outgoing is another aspect of interpersonal style. At one extreme are the observable behaviors which indicate a minimum display of feelings and emotions in one's interactions, and at the other, a maximum show of feelings and emotions. This is the second dimension of the *Interpersonal Style Model*.

They Are Cool, Calm, and Collected

People who are perceived as socially reserved tend to be formal and business-like in their approach to social situations. They display an exacting, methodical manner, and are more than likely inclined to focus on the task at hand.

They Are Informal and Easy to Know

More socially responsive people tend to readily display emotions and show feelings. They are usually characterized as informal, agreeable, and open. They are approachable and tend to get involved with others on a personal basis.

THE INTERPERSONAL STYLE MATRIX

Actions that can be observed and agreed upon for describing a person's behavior in terms of *Dominance* and *Sociability* fit together into a convenient model called the *Interpersonal Style Matrix*. The *Matrix* depicts the 4 distinct behavior patterns.

Pattern I: Directive Style

Combines high dominance and low sociability. Their behavior is action-oriented, they get results through assertive and controlled behavior. Competitive and resourceful, they prefer to deal with immediately relevant issues and tend to excel at defining goals along with a plan for reaching them.

They are goal oriented and think in the immediate time frame. They want to achieve. They will make quick decisions especially in operational matters and like to be allowed to do so. Because of their zeal to get things done, they are often viewed by others as insensitive to feelings.

Pattern II: Counseling Style

Reflects a combination of yielding and outgoing behavior. They display feelings openly but are not typically aggressive. Their behavior is relationship-oriented. They tend to be supportive and they willingly show their own feelings. They are team players and as leaders of their own team they encourage team participation among their work group.

They have strong social drives and may base their decisions more on personal considerations than fact or necessity. People generally find them to be cooperative and supportive. Since this style is characteristically non-confrontive, they may have a tough time implementing unpopular decisions.

Pattern III: Collaborative Style

Exhibits dominant and outgoing behavior. People of this style have a tendency to dominate but they are given to a show of feelings and emotions. Intuition-oriented, they thrive on the interplay between themselves and others. They are persuasive and respond well to incentives and rewards.

They are usually extraverted and ambitious. They may take pride in their "gut feel" style of decision-making. Their enchantment with concepts and ideas may hamper their effectiveness in handling day-to-day activities.

Pattern IV: Deliberative Style

Shows the tendency to be reserved and controlled. This style is thinking-oriented. They are good planners and organizers. When performing tasks, they generally prefer to work alone or in small groups. Their decisions are based on critical thinking and the examination of the relevant data for each situation.

They are non-confrontive and tend to avoid conflict. When pressed, they will use facts and logic to reinforce their position. They will take a firm stand when sure of their ground, but they will usually exercise authority reluctantly. This style does not delegate authority easily. Their motto may be "inspect, don't expect."

The Interpersonal Style Matrix

Reserved	
Pattern IV Deliberative	Pattern I Directive
Yielding	Dominant
Pattern II Counseling	Pattern III Collaborative
Outgoing	

FALL BACK BEHAVIORS

All of us experience tension to varying degrees in our relationships. Most tension carries with it the positive effect of motivating us to perform better. The emotional interplay between players as they urge each other on to win a game carries with it positive stress. The praise of the coach, and the cheering of the crowds further raise the level of tension felt by the players. If the sporting event is important enough to us, we feel the tension, even though we may be 3,000 miles away watching the game on television. There are many examples of how tension provides motivation in almost any aspect of our lives.

We can also think of countless examples in our day-to-day relationships when tension has a negative effect. When negative tension develops, our actions may become defensive and we may slip into our *Fall Back Behavior.*

They Will Hold Their Ground

The two styles on the high side of the *Dominance Scale* tend to exhibit *Fall Back Behavior* in the form of *fight*. When *Directive* or *Collaborative* people experience tension build-up they usually exhibit aggressive behavior. The *Fall Back Behavior* of *Directive* and *Collaborative* styles, while in a fight mode, are different in character. *Pattern I* people tend to *fight* when pushed, but maintain emotional control. Their actions become *autocratic*. *Pattern III* people also fight when pushed, but show emotion combined with confrontation, usually directed personally at the other party. Their actions are in the form of a personal *attack*.

They May Fight the Battle Another Day

Counseling or *Deliberative* people express tension in the form of escape or avoidance behavior. The two styles on the low side of the *Dominance Scale* tend to exhibit *Fall Back Behavior* in the form of *flight*. The *Fall Back Behavior* of *Counseling* and *Deliberative* styles, while in the flight mode, are also different in character. Pattern II people will take flight when tense, but their behavior will be in the nature of *acquiescence* or giving in. Pattern IV people will also take *flight*, but the behavior will be in the nature of *avoidance* of emotional involvement.

Fall Back Behaviors

Pattern IV Deliberative Avoidance	Pattern I Directive Autocratic
Pattern II Counseling Acquiescent	Pattern III Collaborative Attacking

ACTION PLANNING STRATEGIES

As you develop skill in creating productive relationships, you will learn to establish action planning strategies. Here are concise action planning strategies which contain 3 basic elements.

1. The style needs that call for *support*
2. How you should manage your *time*
3. What you need to *provide* in the process of decision-making

Pattern One, Directive

Pattern I people need to be allowed to act. With their goals in mind they will move toward an objective with urgency and persistence. You should *support* their conclusions and actions, and use your *time* efficiently. When involved in the decision-making process *provide* them with options, along with your assessment of the probabilities, but let them decide. Focus on *what* the results will yield.

Pattern Two, Counseling

Support relationships and teamwork when working with the Pattern II style. Use your *time* to set up an agreeable framework for negotiating the task. In the decision-making process put forth an effort to assure them of your backing. *Provide* personal assurances concerning the outcome. Pattern II styles strive to develop trust and confidence in relationships. Show them *why* the decision is fail-safe.

Pattern Three, Collaborative

People of this style react favorably in situations where unique approaches to a problem can be explored. *Support* their ideas and concepts. Use your *time* to develop a stimulating dialogue, and avoid getting mired down in excessive detail. *Provide* a reason to decide in the form of an incentive and the rewards that a successful outcome will bring about. Don't be afraid to involve others in the process, show them *who* would be willing to participate.

Pattern Four, Deliberative

The need to be right, and the quality of the process are key to action planning with Pattern IV styles. *Support* their world of principles and thinking, and use your *time* to be accurate. Their decision-making process is careful and cautious. A quality decision is more important to them than an expeditious one. *Provide* evidence and avoid discussing personal issues. Be persistent, and emphasize how the plan will materialize.

20. *Styles of Business Leadership:*
The Gamesman and More

MICHAEL MACCOBY

WE EVENTUALLY CAME TO NAME four main psychological types in the corporate technostructure: the craftsman, the jungle fighter, the company man, and the gamesman. These are "ideal types" in the sense that few people fit the type exactly and most are a mixture of types. But in practically every case, we were able to agree on which type best described a person, and the individual and his colleagues almost always agreed with our typing. In fact, our discussion of these different character types sometimes crystallized feelings about differences among people, feelings they had never been able to put into words. Once seen, interpersonal conflicts and problems of communication were better understood. In labeling these character types, I kept in mind the ancient observation that naming is a legislative act, and without putting the question to a vote, I tried to select names that corporate managers could identify with. Within those companies where we have reported the results, these types are now used as tools to better understand human reality. Here are brief introductions to each type.

1. *The craftsman.* The craftsman holds the traditional values of the productive-hoarding character—the work ethic, respect for people, concern for quality and thrift. When he talks about his work, his interest is in the *process* of making something; he enjoys building. He sees others, co-workers as well as superiors, in terms of whether they help or hinder him in doing a craftsmanlike job. Most of the craftsmen whom we interviewed are quiet, sincere, modest, and practical, although there is a difference between those who are more receptive and democratic versus those who are more authoritarian and intolerant. Although his virtues are admired by everyone, his self-containment and perfectionism do not allow him to lead a complex and changing organization. Rather than engaging and trying to master the system with the cooperation of others who share his values, he tends to do his own thing and go along, sometimes reluctantly, toward goals he does not share, enjoying whatever opportunities he finds for interesting work.

Some corporate scientists we interviewed are essentially craftsmen but there is a type of scientist who shares some of the craftsman's interest in knowledge and creating, but who is more of a prima donna, and is found exclusively in research labs. Although these scientists might be more at home in universities than in corporations, among them are some of the most independent contributors who work in corporations. Since so few are successful managers, and do not reach the top levels of the technostructure, the "corporate scientist" type will be sketched only in passing.

Some of the most creative and gifted scientists whom we have seen in the corporate world are included in this type, together with the most unhappy misfits, resentful failures whose gifts do not measure up to their ambition. What most distinguishes the "scientists" from the craftsmen is their narcissism, their idolatry of their own knowledge, talents, and technology and their hunger for admiration. They are the corporate intellectuals and many are fascinated by esoteric issues (e.g., outer space or eternal life) only tangentially related to either corporate goals or social needs. In exaggerating their own importance, some of the scientists we interviewed belittled those who were more down to earth. Yet beneath their narcissism we found a receptive and dependent attachment to those in power, both corporate and state leaders, the "decision makers" who could support them and make their ideas into reality. A grandiose scientist does not trust the public to understand him, and it doesn't occur to him that the reason may be that he does not create things that benefit the public. He invents what is demanded by those who pay him—the corporation and the state. Both at home and at work, the grandiose scientist seeks a protected nest. He wants an admiring mother-wife to meet his needs in return for a chance to share in his glory, and he seeks patrons at work who will agree to similar symbiotic relationships.

2. *The jungle fighter.* The jungle fighter's goal is power. He experiences life and work as a jungle (not a game), where it is eat or be eaten, and the winners destroy the losers. A major part of his psychic resources is budgeted for his internal department of defense. Jungle fighters tend to see their peers in terms of accomplices or enemies and their subordinates as objects to be utilized. There are two subtypes of jungle fighters, lions and foxes. The lions are the conquerors who when successful may build an empire; the foxes make their nests in the corporate hierarchy and move ahead by stealth and politicking.

3. *The company man.* In the company man, we recognize the well-known organization man, or the functionary whose sense of identity is based on being part of the powerful, protective company. His strongest traits are his concern with the human side of the company, his interest in the feelings of the people around him and his commitment to maintain the organization's integrity. At his weakest, he is fearful and submissive, concerned with

security even more than with success. The most creative company men sustain an atmosphere in their groups of cooperation, stimulation, and mutuality. The least creative find a little niche and satisfy themselves by feeling that somehow they share in the glory of the corporation.

4. *The gamesman.* The gamesman is the new man, and, really, the leading character in this study. His main interest is in challenge, competitive activity where he can prove himself a winner. Impatient with others who are slower and more cautious, he likes to take risks and to motivate others to push themselves beyond their normal pace. He responds to work and life as a game. The contest hypes him up and he communicates his enthusiasm, thus energizing others. He enjoys new ideas, new techniques, fresh approaches and shortcuts. His talk and his thinking are terse, dynamic, sometimes playful and come in quick flashes. His main goal in life is to be a winner, and talking about himself invariably leads to discussion of his tactics and strategy in the corporate contest.

In the sixties, the gamesman went all out to win. In the seventies, both the country and the corporations are more skeptical about adventurism and glory-seeking. Some of the biggest companies have discovered that sym-biosis with the military weakens their ability to compete in other markets. Watergate shamed those who flew the banner "Winning is not everything; it's the only thing," which in the sixties decorated corporate walls and desks. In the seventies, America no longer considers itself the land of unlimited abundance. Rising energy costs and international competition still call for competitive, risk-taking corporate gamesmen as leaders, but they have become more sober and realistic, more concerned with reducing costs than overwhelming the opposition with innovation.

The new corporate top executive combines many gamesman traits with aspects of the company man. He is a team player whose center is the corporation. He feels himself responsible for the functioning of a system, and in his mind, his career goals have merged with those of the corporation. Thus he thinks in terms of what is good for the company, hardly separating that from what is good for himself. He tends to be a worrier, constantly on the lookout for something that might go wrong. He is self-protective and sees people in terms of their use for the larger organization. He even uses himself in this way, fine tuning his sensitivity. He has succeeded in submerg-ing his ego and gaining strength from this exercise in self-control.

To function, the corporations need craftsmen, scientists, and company men (many could do without jungle fighters), but their future depends most of all on the gamesmen's capacity for mature development.

21. Five Management Styles: Balancing Concern for People and for Production

ROBERT R. BLAKE
AND JANE SRYGLEY MOUTON

THE LEADERSHIP GRID

A VARIETY OF THEORIES regarding managerial behavior can be identified. These theories—or sets of assumptions—are based on the way in which three organization universals are connected to one another.

One of the three is *concern for production*; the amount of emphasis supervision places on achieving production. A second is *concern for people*; the productive unit of organization. The third is *hierarchy*; the *boss* aspect. Whenever a man acts as a manager, he is in some way making assumptions about how to solve problems of achieving organization purposes of production through people.

The *Leadership Grid* shows these two concerns and a range of possible interactions between them. The horizontal axis indicates concern for production while the vertical axis indicates concern for people. Each is expressed as a nine-point scale of concern. The number *1* in each instance represents minimum concern. The *9* stands for maximum concern.

At the lower left corner of the Grid is the Impoverished Management (1,1) style. This has a minimum of both concerns; that is, of concern for production and concern for people. At the top left corner of the Grid is found the (1,9) style, Country Club Management. Here there is a minimum of concern for production but maximum concern for people. In the lower right corner is (9,1), Authority-Compliance. This style has a maximum concern for production and a minimum for human aspects. In the upper right corner is the (9,9) style, Team Management, where concern for both people and production reaches maximum. Then, in the center is the (5,5) style, which is a "Middle-of-the-Road" Management, or an intermediate amount of both kinds of concerns.

It should be emphasized that the manner in which these two concerns are linked together by a manager defines how he uses hierarchy. In addition, the character of *concern for* at different grid positions differs, even though the *degree* may be the same. For example, when high concern for people is coupled with a low concern for production, the type of people concern expressed (*i.e.*, that people be "happy") is far different from the type of high concern for people shown when a high concern for production is also evident (*i.e.*, that people be involved in the work and strive to contribute to organization purpose).

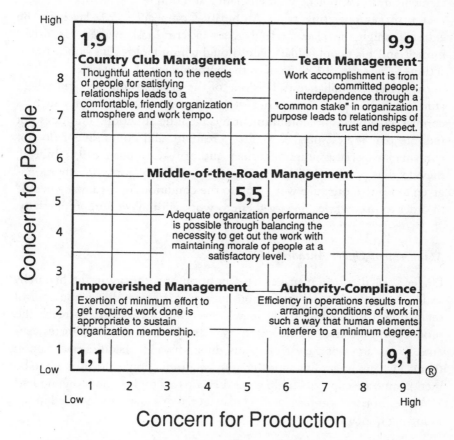

Concern for People

High

9 **1,9** **9,9**

Country Club Management ——— **Team Management**

8 Thoughtful attention to the needs of people for satisfying relationships leads to a comfortable, friendly organization atmosphere and work tempo. Work accomplishment is from committed people; interdependence through a "common stake" in organization purpose leads to relationships of trust and respect.

7

6

Middle-of-the-Road Management

5 **5,5**

Adequate organization performance is possible through balancing the necessity to get out the work with maintaining morale of people at a satisfactory level.

4

3

Impoverished Management **Authority-Compliance**

2 Exertion of minimum effort to get required work done is appropriate to sustain organization membership. Efficiency in operations results from arranging conditions of work in such a way that human elements interfere to a minimum degree.

1 **1,1** **9,1**

Low

1   2   3   4   5   6   7   8   9
Low   **High**

Concern for Production

The Leadership Grid® Figure

THE AUTHORITY-COMPLIANCE (9,1) MANAGERIAL STYLE

In the lower right hand corner of the Grid is 9,1. At this position a high concern for production, *9*, is coupled with a low concern for people, *1*. In the 9,1 managerial style, the assumption is made that, somehow, there is an inevitable contradiction between organizational needs of production and personal needs of people. If one is met, the other must be sacrificed. Yet, people must be used to attain the production for which the manager feels responsible. If he acts from an Authority-Compliance (9,1) orientation, he seeks to resolve the dilemma by arranging conditions of work which minimize feelings and attitudes. He does so in a way that prevents the "human elements from interfering with efficiency and output."

A manager operating at an Authority-Compliance (9,1) level, in the extreme, might be characterized as an exacting task master. He drives himself and his people alike. One thought monopolizes his concern and action—*production*. 9,1 personifies the entrepreneurial spirit.

Authority-Compliance (9,1) is one of the positions on the Grid where concern for people is low. Thus, it is not surprising that topics such as conflict, creativity, and commitment receive little attention. This does not indicate that topics such as conflict, creativity and commitment do not contain managerial assumptions under Authority-Compliance (9,1). Indeed, they do. The point is that they are weighted unevenly. Far more attention is given to how to organize work than to the conditions of organizing people in order to make it possible for them to work with maximum productivity.

Management Under Authority-Compliance

Under a 9,1 theory, a manager has a position of authority in the hierarchy and he knows it. He feels his responsibilities are to plan, direct, and control the actions of his subordinates in whatever way is necessary to reach the production objectives of the enterprise. The boss plans, subordinates execute. They carry out the various plans, directions and schedules placed upon them. The aim under this approach is to get production! Schedules are to be met! People are expected to do what they are told to do—no more, no less!

An Authority-Compliance (9,1) managerial orientation is typified in the following quotations:

> *Planning.* "I do planning by setting the production quotas and schedules to be followed by each subordinate. Then, I work out the procedures and operating ground rules and I make individual assignments. I also establish check points so I can ascertain that actions I have authorized are being taken as I intended them to be done."

> *Work Execution.* "I watch the work closely. I criticize as I see the necessity for it and authorize changes as needs for them arise."

> *Follow-up.* "I have plans laid for the next assignments and move people on to them as operations dictate. Recognition and corrective action are extended to individuals on a one-by-one basis."

THE COUNTRY CLUB (1,9) MANAGERIAL STYLE

In the upper left hand corner of the Grid is the 1,9 managerial orientation. Here a low functional concern for production, *1*, is coupled with high concern for people, *9*. As with 9,1, the 1,9 managerial orientation also is rooted in the assumption that production requirements are contrary to the needs of people. To a manager with a Country Club (1,9) style, however, the attitudes and feelings of people *are* important. They are valuable in their own right. They come first. Within this context, conditions are arranged so that personal, social and welfare needs can be met.

Management Under Country Club

When asked to describe his hierarchical responsibilities, a person operating under 1,9 assumptions is likely to use the same *words* as those the manager operating under 9,1 might use. He would say that his job is to plan, direct and control the activities of *his* subordinates. His aim as a manager, however, is to avoid pressuring for production at a rate higher than that which would win acceptance from organizational members. He leads by following. By deemphasizing production, the Country Club (1,9) approach avoids some of the conflict that arises from production decisions that disturb people. A deeper Country Club (1,9) attitude is seen in the feeling that, "You can't *push* people for production because if you do, they balk and resist," or "You can lead a horse to water, but you can't make him drink." "When people have turned against you, they are in trouble and you are, too." How he plans and directs subordinates and the way in which follow-up takes place are briefly outlined below.

> *Planning.* "I give broad assignments to my subordinates and convey my confidence by saying, 'I'm sure you know how to do this and that you will do it well.' "
>
> *Work Execution.* "I see my people frequently and encourage them to visit with me as their time permits. My door is always open. My goal is to see to it that they are able to get the things they want. That's the way to encourage people."
>
> *Follow-up.* "I hold a meeting with those who are on the job where I place emphasis on congratulating the group as well as individuals. We have fun and when we get down to business our wrap-up sessions usually revolve around why we did as well as we did do and how we can help things to go as smoothly or more so in the future. Criticism rarely helps. My motto is 'Don't say anything if you can't say something nice.' "

THE IMPOVERISHED (1,1) MANAGERIAL STYLE

Low concern for production, *1*, is coupled with low concern for people, *1*, in the lower left hand corner of the grid, where the 1,1 managerial pattern is located. Like Authority-Compliance (9,1) or Country Club (1,9) an incompatibility is assumed to exist between production requirements and needs of people. However, since concern for both is low, the manager with an Impoverished (1,1) orientation experiences little or no dilemma between production and people—he is more or less "out of it." But, the person managing 1,1 has learned to "be out of it," while remaining in the organization. Little is expected of him, and little is given by him in return. Impoverished Management (1,1) as an approach is rare in organization situations of non-repetitive action where each situation presents a different set of problems to be solved. It is far more common in routine operations, and in various staff functions.

The phrase "Impoverished Management of people" is an anomaly. A person who has adopted an Impoverished (1,1) orientation might better be described as "lost among," rather than managing people. Anomalous though it may seem, there are, today, many persons in managerial ranks whose supervision is best pictured as Impoverished (1,1).

The Impoverished (1,1) approach is unnatural. It comes to those who have accepted defeat. To permit oneself again to become involved and concerned over what happens in the work situation can only lead to deeper frustration and discouragement. It is an approach characterized, then, by low involvement with people and the contribution of minimum effort toward organization purpose.

Management Under Impoverished

The supervisory approach under Impoverished Management (1,1) is to put people on jobs and to leave them alone. He does this by letting people do their work as they see fit. He does not pester them. "Don't put your hand in a hornet's nest" is a motto characteristic of a manager who operates in the Impoverished (1,1) direction. His administrative responses are of minimum movement, enough to get the pressure off his back, but little more. The following show how an Impoverished (1,1) supervisor views his managerial responsibilities.

> *Planning.* "I give broad assignments though I don't think in terms of goals or schedules. I do little planning. A way that you might describe my job is I'm a message carrier. I carry the story from those one level

above to those one level below me. I put as little 'embroidery' or interpretation on what I pass as possible. I do what my job description requires."

Work Execution. "If I make the rounds, I take little on-the-spot action. People are free to solve their own problems. They like it that way. I do, too."

Follow-up. "If he inquires, I talk to my boss, who tells me what is to be done next and to find out how he wants it done and who he wants to do it."

THE MIDDLE-OF-THE-ROAD (5,5) MANAGERIAL STYLE

The middle of the Grid identifies 5,5. It is where intermediate concern for production, 5, is linked with moderate concern for people, 5. 5,5 also assumes conflict between organization purpose of production and needs of people. Rather than resolving the issue in the direction of production as in Authority-Compliance (9,1) or of people as in Country Club (1,9) or "leaving the field" as in Impoverished (1,1), satisfactory or workable solutions are found through equilibrium or compromise processes. Acceptable, even though not sound, production is possible from this approach without unduly disturbing people. The Middle-of-the-Road (5,5) orientation assumes that people are practical, that they realize *some* effort will have to be exerted on the job. Also, by yielding some push for production and considering attitudes and feelings, people accept the situation and are more or less "satisfied."

The Middle-of-the-Road (5,5) approach is based on a persuasive logic. It says, "What person or movement has ever had its exclusive way? Extreme positions are to be avoided. Doesn't experience show, again and again, that steady progress comes from compromise, trading out, and a willingness to yield some advantages in order to gain others? Democracy, as it has come to be interpreted by many today, operates quite well by yielding to the many and mollifying the few."

Realistically, then, the guiding assumption of Middle-of-the-Road (5,5) is *not to seek the best position for either production or people* ("that would be too 'ideal' "), but to find the position that is in between both, about half-way.

Management Under Middle-of-the-Road (5,5)

The key to 5,5 is found in placing some emphasis on production. Since recognition is given to the fact that, realistically, people cannot be ignored or disregarded, some deliberate consideration is given to the people side. Yet, this is different than Authority-Compliance (9,1), as can be seen in the managerial examples that will follow; the Middle-of-the-Road (5,5) approach holds to the responsibility to plan, direct and control, typical of Authority-Compliance (9,1). However, just as important, a major part of this responsibility is seen to be coupled with a need to communicate, to get understanding, and to elicit suggestions from subordinates. This aspect is different from Country Club. In other ways the Middle-of-the-Road (5,5) style is designed to open up the possibility of subordinates' thinking about their job in more than a Country Club social manner.

The way in which combining and splitting is done in a Middle-of-the-Road orientation can be seen in the following descriptions.

> *Planning.* "I plan work for each subordinate, more in a general way than down to details. After explaining aims and schedules, I make individual assignments. I insure that subordinates are agreeable with what is expected of them and that they feel free to come back if they need help in carrying my assignments out."

> *Work Execution.* "I keep up with each man's job and review his progress with him from time to time or when he asks for it. I give positive suggestions if a subordinate is having difficulty."

> *Follow-up.* "I meet with those involved in the job on a carrot-and-stick approach. I try to get discussion in order to point out good points as well as mistakes and to indicate how people can improve without *telling them.* Each individual gets the opportunity to discuss any reasonable suggestions he might have for improvement before I describe the next assignment."

THE TEAM MANAGEMENT (9,9) STYLE

In the upper right hand corner is located 9,9, where a high concern for production, *9*, is coupled with a *9* of high concern for people. Unlike the other basic approaches, it is assumed in the Team (9,9) managerial style that there is no necessary and inherent conflict between organization purpose of production requirements and the needs of people. Under Team Management (9,9), effective integration of people with production is possible by involving them and their ideas in determining the conditions and strategies of work. Needs of people to think, to apply mental effort in productive work and to establish sound and mature relationships on a hierarchical plane and with one another are utilized to accomplish organizational requirements. A basic aim of Team Management (9,9), then, is to promote the conditions that integrate creativity, high productivity, and high morale through concerted team action.

The Team (9,9) orientation views the integration of people into work from a different perspective than other approaches. In contrast with Authority-Compliance (9,1), the solution for a given problem is not necessarily defined by the boss's authority. Unlike Middle-of-the-Road (5,5), the Team (9,9) approach is oriented toward discovering the best and most effective solution in a given situation, not the one defined by tradition, etc. By utilizing both the mental *and* execution skills of people, this approach aims at the highest attainable level of production. This highest level is only possible through work situations that meet mature needs of people. Sociability for the sake of togetherness, status based on aspects unrelated to work, or power exercised for its own sake, or out of frustration, are not viewed as mature needs. Rather, *accomplishment* and *contribution* are seen as the critical aspect of organization performance and individual motivation. When one is met, the other is gratified automatically.

Management Under Team Management

Mutual understanding and agreement as to what the organizational goals are and of the means by which they are to be attained is at the core of work direction. In a real sense people and production *are* interconnected. The manager with a Team (9,9) orientation views his responsibility as seeing to it (but not necessarily doing it by himself) that planning, directing and controlling *are* accomplished soundly. Who are best qualified to do it? Those with the most stake in the outcome, regardless of level.

As in the examples following, a boss with a Team (9,9) orientation still retains the responsibility for such aspects of work direction as planning. There is no abdication of the Impoverished (1,1) variety, nor is there tolerance with "least common denominator" solutions of the kind that crop up under Country Club (1,9), nor of middle-road compromises of divergent interests as in Middle-of-the-Road (5,5). But in the Team (9,9) approach, others, where indicated, are drawn in on the actual planning of work activities. He might say that, "My job is not necessarily to *make* sound decisions, but it surely is my job to *see* to it that sound decisions are made." The Team (9,9) style is seen in the following:

> *Planning.* "I get the people who have relevant facts and/or stakes in the outcome to review the whole picture and to get their reaction and ideas. Then, I, with them, establish goals and flexible schedules as well as procedures and ground rules, and set up individual responsibilities."

Work Execution. "I keep familiar with major points of progress and exert influence on subordinates through identifying problems and revising goals and schedules *with* them as necessary. I lend assistance when needed by helping to remove road blocks."

Follow-up. "I conduct a 'wrap-up' with those responsible. We evaluate how a job went and probe what can be learned from it and how what we learned can be applied in future work. If appropriate, I give recognition on a team basis as well as recognizing outstanding individual contributions."

PART SEVEN

BODY TYPOLOGIES

EARLY GREEK PHILOSOPHERS BELIEVED that you are what you look like. Someone who resembled an animal was said to have that animal's personality. So, for example, if you looked like a fox, you were thought to be clever and cunning.

Over the centuries many philosophers and psychologists have assumed that personality patterns are related to physical characteristics, such as body build, facial features, and even the shape of the skull. Shakespeare reflects this common understanding in *Julius Caesar:*

> Let me have men about me that are fat;
> Sleek-headed men and such as sleep o'nights;
> Yon Cassius has a lean and hungry look;
> He thinks too much; such men are dangerous.

Our bodies are central elements in our lives, yet the body is often ignored in Western psychology. As we develop a more comprehensive view of human nature, we can begin to see how all human experience is embodied—feeling, thinking, relating, doing. Not only must we pay more attention to the body, we need to develop a more holistic view that emphasizes the functional unity of mind and body.

Our Western tradition has reinforced the dichotomy between body and mind. Even in our language we tend to separate "mind" and "body." In fact, it is extremely difficult to do anything else. In trying to avoid this

185

artificial separation, we end up with unwieldy terms like "body-mind." The separation of mind and body is related to a set of serious deficiencies in our culture, including the devaluation of the body, lack of awareness of how our bodies function, and guilt about our natural sexuality.

In this section, basic differences in physical and energetic structure form the bases of type differentiation. However, the theories in this section do not try to separate mind and body. On the contrary, each theory acknowledges the complex interactive unity of mind, body, and experience. Differences in body structure are related to differences at various other levels of functioning, including personality dynamics.

The American psychologist and physician William Sheldon pioneered the scientific examination of body build. Sheldon taught and conducted research at the University of Chicago, Harvard, Columbia, and the University of Oregon, and his main research interest was to establish a relationship between physique and temperament.

Sheldon and his research team analyzed photographs of four thousand individuals. He established three major axes of variation among those studied: *endomorphy, mesomorphy,* and *ectomorphy*. Endomorphs are soft, well-rounded, and tend to be fat. Mesomorphs are muscular, sturdy, and tough. Ectomorphs have fragile and delicate bodies, flat chests, and slender arms and legs.

To type each individual, Sheldon developed a 7-point scale for each dimension. A 7-1-1 is an extreme endomorph, a 1-7-1 is an archetypal mesomorph, and a 1-1-7 is a pure ectomorph. The vast majority of people have more balance among these three dimensions. Sheldon also found those who are 4-4-4, who are perfectly balanced in all three of his dimensions.

In this system, Sheldon provides one answer to the problem of overgeneralization in typing. Instead of trying to fit the entire world's population into a handful of categories, he empirically established both the extreme, or prototypical, cases and also the actual variation within a large sample population. He developed a statistical distribution in which each body type can be precisely defined. His three 7-point scales yield three hundred and forty-three different body types.

Sheldon then related body and personality type. The endomorph is sociable, relaxed, comfort-loving, generous, and calm. The mesomorph loves action and is independent, assertive, physically active, ambitious, and insensitive. The ectomorph is private, excitable, tense, sensitive, mentally active, and quick.

These three types have a great deal in common with the old humor-based temperament system of Hippocrates. The endomorph is very much like the phlegmatic, the mesomorph is similar to the choleric, and the ectomorph strongly resembles the melancholic.

Wilhelm Reich is the father of body-oriented psychology. A member of Freud's inner circle, Reich became interested in the role of the body in psychotherapy. He rejected the Cartesian mind-body split and viewed psychological defenses and physical armoring as a single, unified whole. Reich began by closely observing his patients' postures and movements and later started using pressure on chronically tight muscles to relieve directly physical tension.

Alexander Lowen, the cofounder of bioenergetic analysis, was a student of Reich's. Lowen sought to develop a balanced body-mind psychology, as Reich began to concentrate almost solely on body work. In Chapter 23 Lowen outlines the five major types of character structure in bioenergetic analysis theory. Each type defines the way individuals handle their need for love, intimacy, and pleasure. Each has its own habitual posture and pattern of handling energy flow in the body.

The *schizoid character* tends to avoid intimate closeness. The *oral character* can establish closeness only on an infantile basis, related to the need for warmth and support. *Psychopathic characters* can relate only to those who need them. The *masochistic character* can establish a close relationship, but only based on their submissive attitude. The *rigid character* forms fairly close relationships, but remains guarded, despite seeming intimacy and commitment.

Stuart Heller is a psychologist, dancer, mathematician, movement teacher, and a holder of two sixth-degree black belts in the martial arts. In his article written for this book, "An *I Ching* of the Body," he has combined the principles of the *I Ching*, the classic Chinese Book of Changes, with the martial arts philosophy of the *Book of Five Rings*, by Miyamoto Musashi, the great Japanese swordmaster, artist, and philosopher. Heller describes five fundamental styles of movement and relationship, each related to one of the five elements: earth, wind, water, fire, and space.

The earth style is solid and grounded and most suitable for those with large and powerful physiques. The wind style is light and quick and emphasizes the ability to turn or shift position almost instantly and effortlessly. The water style is soft, yielding, and receptive, and emphasizes blending with another's movement. The style of fire includes powerful focus and an emphasis on cutting through any obstacles or resistance. Space represents our ability to work with all of the first four elements. Mastery of space means the capability to access whatever element or combination of elements best fits a given situation.

Chapter 25 provides a discussion of Rudolf Steiner's approach to the analysis of temperament in children. The author, Roy Wilkinson, is a senior educator in the Waldorf School system in England and has worked with this system for many years.

Rudolf Steiner, noted philosopher and educator, pioneered in applying the four temperaments, originally discussed by Hippocrates, to working with children in the Waldorf School system, which he founded. Waldorf Schools, which aim to educate the whole child, are found throughout Europe and the English-speaking world. Their teachers are trained to use the four-temperament system to understand their students better and to help them with motivation, discipline, and interpersonal relations in the classroom.

The sanguine type was originally connected with "red humor" or the blood; the melancholic with "black choler" or bile; the phlegmatic with "white humor" or lymph and mucous fluids; and the choleric with "yellow choler" or adrenaline. The sanguine type is optimistic, outgoing, mobile, and volatile. The melancholic is pessimistic, inflexible, sober, and depressive. The phlegmatic is calm, even-tempered, kind, and detached. The choleric is decisive, energetic, impulsive, and erratic.

22. Three Body-Mind Types: Endomorph, Mesomorph, and Ectomorph

WILLIAM SHELDON

TRADITION HAS IT THAT FAT MEN ARE JOLLY AND GENEROUS, that lean men are dour, that short men are aggressive, and that strong men are silent and confident. But tradition is sometimes wise and sometimes stupid, for seldom does it distinguish between the accumulated wisdom of the ages and the superstitions of ignorance. Especially as regards physique and temperament have the conclusions of careful students been contaminated by the stereotypes of the street and by the dogmatism of the side-show phrenologist. But if we ignore these last and ask only about the opinions of the scholars, the writers, and the artists we find a persistent tradition that the shape of a man promises certain traits in his temperament.

Scholars have sometimes set off physiques and temperaments into *types*. Hippocrates may not have been the first to systematize his observations regarding the dependence of personality on morphology, but he long ago set forth a scheme that has reappeared under various forms in repeated generations. The writers and the artists establish their typologies more by implication than by argument and statistics. They cast their characters by rules mostly unexpressed, but seldom if ever do they put the temperament of a Falstaff into a lean and wiry body, or paint the face of a Scrooge as applecheeked and rolypoly.

THE ENDOMORPH

Given a measure of poetic license, we might describe the first dynamic component as a manifest desire to embrace the environment and to make its substance one with the substance of the individual's own person. At the most unsublimated level this is the drive to ingest and to assimilate food, which is

189

then transmuted into the flesh of the self. The predominantly viscerotonic personality generally remains close to the earth. Viscerotonia means earthiness. Such a person seems to express a dominant mood not far from the mood of the nourishing soil: he is unhurried, deliberate, and predictable. At high levels of culture he radiates warmth, stability, and (if cerebrotonia is low) indiscriminate amiability. At low levels he is gross, gluttonous, and possessive. In any event he knows what he wants, and his wants are tangible.

The viscerotonic's craving is for food, for comfort, and for the mental and somatic relaxation which accompanies the digestive process at its full best, when the main blood supply is withdrawn from the brain and from the peripheral somatic structures, and is vested in the digestive viscera. For cultured viscerotonics, the food-taking time is the high spot of the day, and the principal focus of feeling-awareness is in the assimilative business. The soul has its seat in the splendid gut. The viscerotonic is likely to devote a tremendous interest to *cuisine*, and he achieves ecstasy in the imagination and anticipation of fine food. Furthermore, he is prone to carry into adult life his natural early childhood interest in faeces and in the eliminative functions, for viscerotonia loves all digestive activity, including the peristalsis of defecation.

At lower cultural levels the viscerotonic becomes simply the glutton, growing heavier and more hoglike in his obesity if the food supply holds out, and less so when kept on a limited diet or on a rigid schedule of work and exercise. Peasant stock from all lands appears to carry a heavy viscerotonic component. The great majority of the overly fat, full-gutted personalities so conspicuous in American urban and political life, have presumably sprung from stock which for many generations had lived on limited diet under sterner conditions. Rioting now in the rich spoils of a newly exploited continent, some of these men and women of strong first component fail to maintain the balance, and they go to gut and fat.

Viscerotonic people tend to be hypoattentional and to remain over-relaxed. The viscerotonic gives the impression of being slow. Yet although his conscious response may seem sluggish to the faster reacting cerebrotonic, the basic conscious orientation of the viscerotonic is surer and in some respects more accurate. Viscerotonics can always be trusted to maintain a close grip upon immediate practical reality. They are certain to know where they are at all times, in relation to their jobs, to their marriage, to their social status, to their basic likes and dislikes. Attitudes toward these things do not change readily or suddenly in the viscerotonic personality, and for some reason, both viscerotonic and somatotonic people possess a better sense of spatial orientation than do cerebrotonics.

Viscerotonics are remarkably susceptible to habit formation. Food taking and sleeping in overdoses become habitual, and if drugs once are taken, especially sedative drugs, there is danger of the development of a drug habit. The habit of constant dependence upon tobacco is very common among viscerotonic people, who often tend to use this drug to hold down their weight, thus substituting a habit for internal (cerebrotonic) discipline.

Viscerotonic people like alcohol. They are frequently connoisseurs of alcoholic beverages. But they are rarely drunkards.

Sir Arthur Conan Doyle pictured his immortal Sherlock Holmes as an indefatigable smoker, capable of smoking half a pound of strong tobacco in a single night. Yet the Holmes of Doyle's fertile imagination was *also* a cerebrotonic ectomorph who in most respects conspicuously lacked the viscerotonic component. But Doyle himself had a flourishing viscerotonic component, and he loved his tobacco. The Holmes he created, like many legendary heroes, was a composite ideal, but not quite psychologically probable. Holmes was partly Doyle, and partly what Doyle dreamed of being. Viscerotonics and somatotonics dream of being *also* cerebrotonic. We all dream of being *also* what we are not.

Viscerotonia means realism. Viscerotonic ecstasy lies in the achievement of a "real" surrounding made up of nice things that taste good, smell good, look good, sound good, feel good. The viscerotonic wants to dig in, to establish himself in a good place on his earth, and to feel the warming and nourishing earth juices flowing in his veins.

In summary, viscerotonia refers to a motivational organization dominated by the gut and hence by the function of anabolism. The primary desire seems to be to assimilate the earth and to merge with it. Viscerotonia means warmth, earthiness, and in general, *indiscriminate* good will.

Predominance of this component generally means a slowness of reaction, but it means also a tenacious grip on reality, especially upon social reality, and a sure orientation in the spatial and personal sense. Viscerotonia means practicality.

THE MESOMORPH

The second component is the "motional" element in life. Somatotonia is the craving for vigorous action and (when fully admitted to consciousness) the resolution to subdue the environment to one's own will. Successful somatotonics are conquerors. They conquer mountains, oceans, forests, wild beasts, Chinese, and other less somatotonic or less strongly united peoples. Somatotonic ecstasy is that of vigorously overcoming obstacles, and somatotonic hell is inaction.

Somatotonics love a vigorous life and are at their best when meeting physical hardship. Under such conditions they reach their peak of energy output and when in the best of training are capable of enduring great exertion for long periods without food, eating enormously when the opportunity is presented.

Somatotonics feel good in the morning. They love to jump out of bed, take a shower, make a lot of noise, and greet the sun. Normally they become sleepy or tired rather suddenly at about their usual bedtime, and typically drop off to deep sleep at once upon retiring.

Somatotonic people tend to lack introspective insight. They are like loaded guns and they want to be pointed somewhere and set off. Their function is action.

Somatotonia is characterized by vigorous muscular expressiveness. In infants, the second component can probably be gauged by the relative vigor of kicking and squirming which takes place. Somatotonic infants squirm and cry with great vehemence and when picked up by the arms will frequently strike out powerfully and repeatedly with the hind quarters.

In older children somatotonia gives rise to rough and dynamic play, to self-assertiveness, and to pugnacity and dominational qualities. As the child grows on toward maturity these somatotonic manifestations either yield to sufficient sublimation and "socialization" to render the emerging personality socially acceptable and to lend it the quality of leadership, or they settle it at relatively unsublimated levels and the individual takes on the nature of incorrigibility.

Somatotonic people who are free from cerebrotonic interference are singularly open, guileless people. (The open face is the somatotonic passport, the amiable face is the viscerotonic passport, and the cerebrotonic face has no passport, but wears a lean danger sign which arouses universal suspicion.)

Somatotonia means susceptibility to habit. The even regulation of habitual overt behavior in somatotonics is striking, but is perhaps relatively unimportant in comparison with the same habitual ordering of mental activities. Somatotonic people who have more viscerotonia than cerebrotonia think in orderly, habitual patterns, and they rarely change their minds or their internal attitudes. They are prone to wear the same mental clothes through life, and whatever cerebrotonia may be present is readily bent to the role of rationalization or self-justification.

In summary, somatotonia means dynamic expression of the soma. This component is closely associated with physical drive and endurance, with a relatively low sleep requirement, with infrequent food requirement, with high blood pressure and the danger of apoplexy, and with a youthfully athletic body which tends to become solid and heavy as life advances. Somatotonia needs exercise and loves a vigorous life.

THE ECTOMORPH

The third component is the element of restraint, inhibition and attentionality. The forebrain holds in check both visceral and somatic functions, apparently to maintain a closer and more sensitive attentional focus. The cardinal symptom of cerebrotonia is tense hyperattentionality. The physical foundation for it seems to lie in relative predominance of exposed surface over mass.

The cerebrotonic is tense, incapable of peripheral relaxation, and chronically aware of his internal tension, although not necessarily disturbed by it. Cerebrotonics are often called nervous or neurotic when they are quite normal, just as viscerotonics are sometimes accused of gluttony and lethargy when they are behaving normally.

The cerebrotonic uses up a great amount of "nervous energy" and flirts with the danger of "nervous exhaustion." He needs more sleep than a person high in one of the other dynamic components. His basal metabolic rate is usually high, and he tends to become chronically fatigued in the normal routines of life. The history of fatigability, poor sleep habits, inability to get up in the morning, abnormal caloric requirement, and a chronic sense of internal tension are good clinical indicators of cerebrotonia. These people sleep lightly. The forebrain seems never to let go its dominance completely even in sleep. Dreaming is constant. The dreaming is relatively close to the threshold of clear consciousness, and the process of going to sleep is invariably a slow one. All relaxation is slow.

The essential characteristic of the cerebrotonic is his acuteness of attention. The other two major functions, the direct visceral and the direct somatic functions, are subjugated, held in check, and rendered secondary. The cerebrotonic eats and exercises to attend, the viscerotonic attends and exercises to eat, the somatotonic eats and attends in order to exercise.

The cerebrotonic component finds its primary ecstasy and its freedom not in eating or drinking, not in fellowship or for long in sexual companionship, not in physical adventure or in the power of social domination, but in a certain intensification of consciousness which appears to arise from *inhibition* of all of these (somatotonic and viscerotonic) "freedoms."

23. Body Structure and Bioenergetic Type

ALEXANDER LOWEN

KNOWING THAT THE BODY is the person (and that its form and movement reveal the personality and contain the history of the person) makes it possible for a bioenergetic therapist to make a tentative diagnosis of the character structure that defines an individual's habitual way of being.

According to bioenergetic analysis theory, there are five major types of character structure: schizoid, oral, narcissistic, masochistic, and rigid. These types are based on libidinal organization and ego development as manifested in the body. The following is an outline of these types:

1. The *schizoid* character structure is characterized by a tendency to split and dissociate. Thinking is split off from feeling. This is manifested on the body level by a lack of good connection between the head and trunk. In many of these individuals the neck is elongated; in others, the head is tilted away from the line of the body. With training this split can be easily recognized. This dissociation between head and body means that a person doesn't feel connected to his or her body. In a severe case, it may result in the phenomenon of depersonalization. In the schizoid personality one also sees a split between the upper and lower halves of the body, manifested by a severe contraction in the region of the waist or a lack of proportion and harmony between the two halves of the body. The schizoid personality is characterized by a fear of falling apart if one lets go, countered by the need to hold one's self together through tension in all the joint muscles.

2. The *oral* character structure stems from a deprivation of nurturing and support in early infancy and is associated with a fear of abandonment. Fear of abandonment is most manifest in thinness, lack of support in the legs and feet, and underdevelopment of the musculature. The oral character has a strong tendency to be dependent, which can be denied through pseudo-independence. The oral character holds on to self through strong tension in the shoulder girdle and in the legs to prevent falling, which would symbolize being left alone and abandoned.

3. The *narcissistic* character structure is complex. It stems from an early childhood relationship in which the child was seduced by the parent into an intimacy that made the child feel special but in which the child was also used by the parent. Because the seduction was sexual, although not acted out, the child denies feeling as a way to prevent the danger of incest. From being special the child develops a sense of superiority and grandiosity. To be superior the narcissistic person has to hold self above others. This is reflected in the body as an overdevelopment of the upper half and a relative weakness in the lower half. The narcissistic character structure holds self up through strong tensions in the legs and back.

4. The *masochistic* character structure develops in a child who was nurtured but forced to be submissive to the parent. The masochist holds in all feelings through tension in the muscles that control the outlets at the upper and lower ends of the body. Masochistic attitudes are often associated with early toilet training—the need to hold in and the fear of letting out. On the

body level, the masochist is heavy and muscularly overdeveloped, with the main tension in the flexor muscles, which results in a collapse of the body's erect posture.

5. The *rigid* character structure, phallic-narcissistic in the man and hysterical in the woman, is characterized by a straight erect body with considerable pride. However, the erect posture is maintained through a rigidity of the back muscles that denotes an attitude of holding back. This holding back by the rigid character stems from early experiences of being humiliated by the parent of the opposite sex at the time in the oedipal period when the child felt a sexual interest in that parent.

Character types are neither pure nor individualistic. Many persons show a mixture of tendencies and belong to two or more types. In addition, no individual can be understood fully in terms of character type alone because it is only the framework for the clinical picture. As in working with a jigsaw puzzle, one starts with a border and slowly fills in all the pieces. The pieces of the clinical picture emerge as the person gets in touch with the body and, through it, with the experiences of life. Slowly the pieces are filled into the right places, and when nearly all are in, the picture emerges with unexpected clarity for both the patient and the therapist. Each insight, no matter how obtained, is a piece of the puzzle.

Seeing this picture clearly makes the character structure an objective reality for the patient and allows him or her to dissociate from it. At this point there is a major change in the personality, but this major change is also the culmination of many minor changes that have occurred as a result of the insights developed in the course of therapy. These changes are also related to increases in the person's energy level, in aliveness, and in feelings of pleasure.

24. An I Ching of the Body

STUART HELLER

WHO AM I? This question spontaneously arises out of our personal song and dance of becoming. This question often appears in the form **what is my type**?

What do we mean when we say, "This is me. This is how I am. This is my type." *Type of what?* Type can be viewed as a shorthand way of saying that a particular process or person tends to act, react or evaluate life's events in a consistent way over time. However, when we "type" a person, are we implying that they act the same in all realms and in all circumstances? Can a person have more than one type?

When I refer to my type, am I referring to a way of being or to a way of becoming? If it is to **being** that I point, then I am saying that this represents an irreducible "fact" of reality. If it is to **becoming** that I point, then I am referring to a process that is flexible and changeable.

Certain questions arise at this point. First and foremost, **why do you want to know your type**? Do you want a label or do you want a direction to travel? Are you sure that the type that you believe you are is your "essential quality," or are you open to relating to it as representing your norm or habits of action?

These questions refer to your goals. In particular, **what are you going to do with this new information**? Knowledge of type can be used for appreciating human differences. It can be used as a mirror to reveal both your strengths and your weaknesses, or it can be used for either self-importance or self-flagellation.

The approach taken in this article is rooted in the traditions of Asia. It emphasizes the intersection between the Japanese warrior and the Chinese physician. From Japan we will draw upon the mandala of the Five Rings. From China we will draw upon the dynamics of the *I Ching*, the classic text on change and changing.

My commitment in writing this article is to make accessible a non-Western understanding of typology. Ordinarily, it is difficult to track down this material. The practitioners who know it refuse to **talk about it.** They will only **speak from it.** To paraphrase the first line in the *Tao Te Ching*, the Rings that I could describe exactly would not be the real Rings. If I could write about them with "objectivity," I would deprive you of their real power and magic. I have chosen to walk a middle way between the cultures. I encourage you to risk engaging with the movement that underlies the concepts.

The most familiar version of the Five Rings was written by Miyamoto Musashi in the 1500's in Japan. Musashi was a great swordsman and also a highly acclaimed, Zen-trained philosopher and artist. He recognized that human beings had biases, likes and dislikes. He realized that most warriors tend to act from their favorite styles, weapons, etc. This makes them both predictable and vulnerable to their opponents.

Musashi felt that by mastering the principles of strategy in the body, one would become unconquerable. He considered the five basic strategies of Fire, Ground, Water, Wind and Space to be consistent with the observable ways of Nature. The essence of his message was that you had to master each of these ways if you were to achieve your full power and potential.

The *I Ching* points to a way of looking at and participating in life. Its foundation is the everpresent movement of everything. For as Einstein said it, "Nothing happens until something moves."

There are two *I Chings*. One is the historical *Book of Change* that we can buy in bookstores and which contains the commentaries of Confucius. The other is not a book but a way of looking at life. It is the fundamental way of thinking that generated the written, codified *I Ching*. This primordial *I Ching* is written in flesh and bone and in the movements of heaven, earth and living beings. It deals with primordial tendencies of movement.

> *Chinese philosophy is built upon the premise that the cosmos and man . . . obey the same law. The very same laws rule for the one as for the other . . .*
> —*The Secret of the Golden Flower*, RICHARD WILHELM

The wisdom of the *I Ching* reminds us not to become fixated in the search for the singular unchanging atom of consciousness and life. It suggests that we relax into the endless movement of existence. If you imagine looking at a river streaming on by, you will notice that there are certain shapes that remain constant for long periods of time, even though every particle of the pattern is just passing through. In this context, **type** can be seen as a standing wave. I am continually moving and changing, yet I appear to have the same appearance over and over.

The world view in which the *I Ching* is embedded considers ongoing and endless change to be the "solid" platform upon which the world and our experience is built. The action of change is movement. Its substance is energy. There is only moving energy. Thinking and feeling are as much movement as moving through space.

Masters of different martial arts styles tend to agree about the fundamental principles and experiences that lie at the heart of each of their styles. Every style, when done well, employs the movement qualities of all of the Rings: **Fire, Water, Wind, and Ground.**

Each ring represents a living way of **moving**, of responding to an encounter. These are dynamic processes that I can only hint at here without freezing a living process into a codified and easily understandable, but dead form.

Fire involves the process of **moving forward**. Moving toward another, you can **move through** an obstacle or attack. One important aspect of Fire is to act instantly and freely, as if your intention immediately translates into movement. You have a clear intention of where you want to go and you just follow that intention.

If someone tries to stop you or hold you back, a natural Fire response is to keep on going, to move through whatever obstacle is placed in your way. You act if if there *were* no obstacle. Your mind is not "stopped" at the obstacle, in fact it may not even catch your attention. This is like the karate expert thinking "through" a brick before striking in order to break it without injuring himself or herself.

Ground involves **solidity, remaining still**, immovability. The style of movement of someone strong in ground is also "solid." Each moment you know exactly where you are. Everything occurs step by step. Your attention is on the immediate present. The goal is not so important; where you *are* is where your mind is.

Also, Ground may mean not reacting until you absolutely have to. This may be to stay unmoving until the very last moment, just before an attack is about to land. Another classic Ground response is to stand firm and ignore trivial pressure, to absorb an initial attack, to "take" a punch, and then respond powerfully and inexorably.

Water includes allowing oneself to **be moved** by another, **flowing** with the pressure. The quality of movement is fluid, like moving *through* water or some other resistant medium. It involves an awareness of the space through which you are moving. In one sense, it is honoring the posture and the resistance of the other. Water is more relationship oriented than Fire, which tends to ignore or to penetrate the other's resistance.

Water allows itself to be shaped by another. It means not being afraid of contact. One Water response is to mold oneself to the form of an encounter. Another is to flow backwards under pressure. If going forward is a fundamental Fire action, yielding and **going back** is a basic Water movement.

Wind is to **move freely and lightly**. It is extremely hard to touch or to "catch" someone moving in the style of Wind. Movement is light and easy, hard to pin down. Wind may act by *moving around* an obstacle. The basic wind movement is *turning*, or turning aside, letting an attack go right past you and refusing to be a target.

Wind can be soft and powerless, like those individuals who are sometimes called "space cadets" or "air heads." They are never grounded enough to have a significant impact on their environment. They often seem blown about by whatever occurs around them. These people are often good at imagination and speculation, but weak at action.

Wind can also be powerful or even overwhelming, like a hurricane. This strong Wind shares the focused forcefulness of fire. This decisive style of wind is in some ways the opposite of the imaginative "soft Wind."

Space transcends the four preceding styles. It involves **versatility** and **freedom of choice**. There are three levels of Space—ordinary, learned and discovered.

The first level of Space is shared by everyone. It refers to whatever particular proportion of the preceding four rings you use at a given time. It is a combination of personal history and constitution. You are always exhibiting a blend of the four rings or elements in whatever you are doing. What most people mean by typology is this kind of Space.

For instance, someone strong in Ground but relatively weak in Water is solid, difficult to move, and also relatively inflexible. To be strong in Wind and in Fire is to be like the great boxer Muhammad Ali, who said, "I float like a butterfly and sting like a bee."

The second level, learned Space, comes only after considerable training and discipline. It comes when you have learned to have access to all of the four rings, and can shift consciously to whatever balance of ring qualities best fits a given situation.

The third level, discovered Space, is reached when you cultivate an even more complete mastery. You discover the primordial Space out from which the four rings emerge. Fire, Water, Wind and Ground are just particular shadings of one fundamental quality or dynamic. In a sense, Space is more watery than Water, more fiery than Fire, more grounded than Ground, and more wind-like than Wind. Without ever leaving Space, the other movement tendencies show up instantly, without thought or planning. You don't *do* it; your response is spontaneous, like breathing.

A Japanese term for this is *mu shin*, literally "formless mind." Instead of responding from our limited intellect, we respond from our full Mind. This is also called "Heart-Mind," the whole mind which includes head, heart and belly. Our Western term, "mind," tends to refer to the head alone. It is also oriented to static form. Heart-Mind consciousness is dynamic and also embodied. It is about "movement thinking," rather than abstract and static conceptualization.

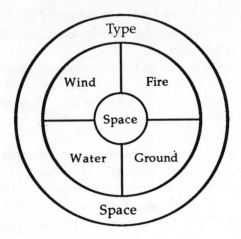

Every style, every type, every organization, every person is a Space in and of themselves. As we grow in our ability to flow from being passionately involved to objectively reflecting, our awareness of the flow and pulse of all of life also grows. Through this sense of connectedness, we are moved to express our uniqueness—our type—from our deepest heart. This is the **Space** at the center of the Rings.

In the martial arts community, students practice a wide range of Kung Fu styles. Among these are the animal systems and *I Ching* systems. Focusing our glance at these approaches may give us some insight into how type and shape are connected and what we can do to harmonize their relationship.

What we are calling "type" is intimately related to how we act and react. From the animal perspective, we are all animals. Our personal patterns of reacting are built upon the stress and encounter responses of the primordial human animal. Our type, therefore, can also be observed, appreciated and danced with, in the ordinary, everyday, taken for granted bodily experiences of being in the world.

Here are two more Five Ring maps. The wheel of Stress adds **faint, freeze and startle** to our usual vocabulary of **fight vs. flight**. These correspond very well to the Five Animals of Crane, Tiger, Dragon, Leopard and Snake.

The *leopard* leaping forward and the **fight** response to move into the encounter both partake of that quality we have been calling **Fire**.

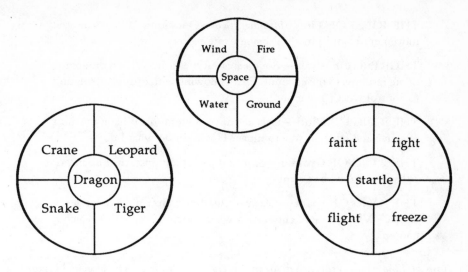

The *tiger* with its strength to resist and the **freeze** response holding its ground both partake of that quality we have been calling **Ground**.

The *snake* rippling away from your touch and the **flight** response of moving away both partake of that quality we have been calling **Water**.

The *crane* lifting up above the fray and the **faint** response of "leaving the body" both partake of that quality we have been calling **Wind**.

The *dragon* with its spontaneity and the **startle** response's reflex action both partake of that quality we have been calling **Space**.

While the animal systems explore the more earthy aspects of human experience, the *I Ching* systems turn to a more "heavenly" perspective. Instead of imitating the movements of animals, this orientation practices the movements of basic principles. It seems more abstract, yet to its devotees, nothing could be more concrete and practical.

THE RING OF **Fire**—*Intention leads*—Questions: Where does the movement begin? How is it being expressed?

THE RING OF **Water**—*Being moved*—Questions: What is the appropriate response to the encounter? Am I flowing with or am I attempting to control what's going on?

THE RING OF **Wind**—*Light and easy*—Questions: What is the most effective and efficient way to move? How do I do what I do?

THE RING OF **Ground**—*Step by step*—Questions: Am I balanced? What is the next best step?

THE RING OF **Space**—*Choice*—Questions: How did I arrive at my choice? When should I choose and when should I accept that which is chosen?

The *I Ching* styles often use diagrams as training devices. These visual images were used as kinesthetic mirrors. The body resonates muscularly with the shapes on the paper. From image to feeling to concept, there grows a deeper appreciation of the principles.

We can also use these images in a diagnostic-like fashion. When you look and contemplate the diagram below, notice: Which of the circular images is the most familiar? The least familiar? Which of the directional arrows attracts or repels you? What feelings or stories arose in you as you looked at the images?

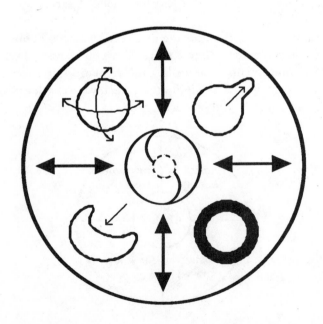

To embody fully the "best" qualities of your type requires that you seek it with all of you. But where is the all of you? As the poet Wendell Berry put it, "Unless you know where you are, you don't know who you are." You are here, now, in the flesh. And everything you do, no matter how large or how small, no matter in what realm of life, you do with your body. The body in this sense is much more than just the physical flesh. It is the dynamic, creative and responsive field or space within which human actions unfold.

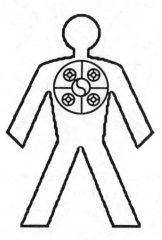

If we combine fundamental distinctions and geometry of the Five Rings with the *I Ching* view of the movement of life, we can build the following map. At the center, coordinating and connecting the four worlds within which we live and act, is our heart-mind's power of attention. To be alive is to think, to feel, to move and to stand.

From the dynamic perspective, thinking, feeling and moving can be understood as distinct configurations of muscle, nerve and energy. Life feels different in each realm or ring. Life moves differently. Life also evaluates differently.

From the heart-mind point of view, these worlds are always connected and always influencing each other. And within each ring are all of the rings. This unceasing relationship is occurring even when we cannot perceive it. Each individual or tradition emphasizes one of these worlds over the others.

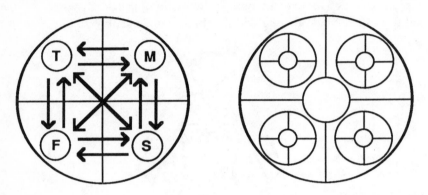

In this context, we may ask, "What combination of the rings makes up my style or type? How do I use the rings to express myself and respond to life?" With this new perspective, I can now observe and work with the building blocks of my style and experience. The question of whether a type is inherent or learned is now less important. Following the path of self-development, all that does not express my essence drops away. Being open to all styles, my uniqueness shines through and touches the world.

A major motivating force for the study of the martial arts or for traveling any other path of self-discovery is the felt sense that something is not quite right about the way life is unfolding. It all too often feels like you are going around and around in a circle, and that things are not really changing. And yet, there is a part of you that knows that life is supposed to be like a spiral path that circles ever closer to your goal.

Mu shin, or your dynamic heart-mind, is considered to be the essential human type. It is where we begin our journey and where we, hopefully, will end it. All other types are seen as particular aspects or faces of our Original Nature. In the Chinese martial arts, this is called **Dragon Style**. In the language of the Five Rings, it is the **Space**.

If asked, "which ring or style am I?" **the Dragon answers, "You are the one who is all of them."** *My type is a particular combination of the basic elements of action and response. It reveals itself in every action I make, whether I am acting in harmony with my essence or at odds with it.*

The process of polishing and refining myself as an instrument, a path which leads to the development of *mu shin*, begins with the observation and acceptance of my historical patterns and cycles. What is the world like for me when I am in a good mood? What is it like when I am in a "negative" mood? The practice is to let go of what I do not need, keep that which is important, and add on that which is missing.

Instead of just asking, "What is my type?" I begin to notice: How do I do

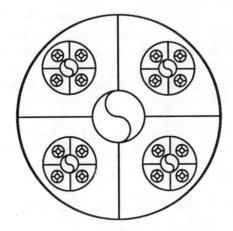

what I do when I do it best? How do I do what I do when I do it poorly? How do I get in my own way? And how can I get out of the way and allow my essential being, energy or type to manifest?

At the beginning of this article, the question was posed: Why do you want to know your type? The Five Rings system works well with the answer, *"I want to know so that I can enact and embody the best qualities of my type(s)."*

Therefore, I am interested in experiencing and knowing which postures, movements, feeling states, concepts and modes of attention will evoke or encourage the best of my type and myself. I also want to know which postures, etc., tend to encourage the worst of my type and myself.

> Aware of the danger (SPACE),
> I can move around it (WIND),
> I can move through it (FIRE),
> I can feel it (WATER) and
> I can resist it (GROUND).
>
> Aware of the danger
> I can change the game and
> move forward toward my goal.

Remember the words of the Dragon: "You are the one who is all of the Rings." The fifth ring is also the source or center from which the other four emerge. Space from the perspective of our historical selves appears dangerous and frightening. It seems like an abyss of nothingness, chaos and uncertainty, without any firm ground upon which to stand. Faced with this vision, no wonder we turn over control to the voices of familiarity.

However, this is not what Space is really like. Space is not empty, like a vacuum. Space is not a vast darkness that lies waiting to destroy you. Space is more like a pregnant pause, an enveloping fullness. It is filled with order, most of it beyond the brain's ordinary capacity to hold meaning. It is ever changing, like the phases of the seasons. It is from Space that we draw our power, awareness and compassion. Rooted in Space, we can become what we are meant to become.

25. Rudolf Steiner on Temperament in Children: Choleric, Melancholic, Sanguine, Phlegmatic

ROY WILKINSON

WHAT WE CALL TEMPERAMENTS today were known in Greek times as the four humours and medical science considered them of great importance. Knowledge of them seems to have fallen into the background until Dr. Steiner called attention to their importance in education.

Temperament has nothing to do with character or morals but is in itself a basic quality—a substance as it were, though not material. A person will do things or react in a certain way according to his temperament quite irrespective of his upbringing, education, standards, or knowledge.

There are four temperaments and these are related to the four elements, earth, water, air and fire. They are known as melancholic, phlegmatic, sanguine and choleric respectively.

The word Choler is the Greek for bile and the person described as choleric is one who is active, energetic and wants things done. He is also the one who rages, roars, and gets into tempers, as happens when the bile overflows. Like a volcano, he erupts and the fire manifests itself.

The sanguine has the rosy cheeks and fresh complexion denoting a healthy blood stream and he has the nature of an air bubble.

The phlegmatic is the one connected with the watery element, and is the methodical, placid type. However, like the ocean, he can become tremendously active if roused.

The melancholic is the one with black bile. This does not refer to the actual substance but a quality—meaning a person with black moods. This person has a peculiar type of earthiness.

Diagramatically the temperaments could be represented thus:

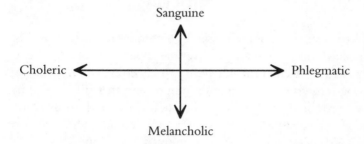

Sanguine

Choleric ← → Phlegmatic

Melancholic

Choleric and phlegmatic are opposites; so are sanguine and melancholic. Each temperament is likely to have traces of its neighbours but not of its opposite.

It must be emphasized that recognition of the temperament is not always easy and the teacher must not jump to conclusions on the basis of a few superficial observations. For instance, all children, being young, tend to be lively and as a general characteristic one could therefore say that all children are sanguine. But there are subtle differences which have to be discovered. In the present state of civilisation, it is also becoming more and more difficult to recognise what is basic. Children may be thought to be sanguine when they are really suffering from nerves. Domestic troubles may cause a child to be angry or vicious and the choleric temperament may be (wrongly) diagnosed. Apparent melancholia may be nothing more than too many late nights watching the television programmes. Apathy, caused by an overdose of sense impressions, might be interpreted as phlegma.

In dealing with the temperaments it is not only a matter of knowing the children in order that the teacher can handle them better, but of harmonising their natures. In a well-integrated, balanced, complete person, the four characteristics would be harmonised but since this is not the case it becomes one of the tasks of education.

. The following is a short guide to the study of the temperaments together with suggestions for dealing with them in the context of the school.

In general, when dealing with children individually, it is a case of treating like by like, i.e. following the homoeopathic principle. To the sanguine one must be lively; to the choleric, boisterous; to the melancholic, sad; and to the phlegmatic, indifferent.

It will be obvious that the descriptions are couched in general terms and not all the characteristics will fit all individuals. Modification can be brought about through a correct education. The adult can always improve himself through self-education.

CHOLERIC

This type is almost unmistakeable. In physique the choleric is short, stocky, bull-necked, upright and often gives the appearance of a stature bigger than it is in reality. He will probably have a ruddy complexion, firm jaw, and eyes radiating restlessness. He gives the impression that sitting is unnatural and that he must be up and doing. When he stands, he is firmly planted on the ground but ready to move at any time. In sitting he has his head forward, feet apart, hands on knees, ready to jump up at any minute.

When he walks, his heels dig into the ground as if he would pulverise the rock beneath him. One has the feeling that he has retained something of the rompings and the ravings of a baby and that the blood is pulsating too energetically through his veins. His gestures are short, energetic, purposeful and self-assured.

He speaks forcefully, emphatically, deliberately and to the point. The choleric feels that he has to be the leader in every enterprise. Only *he* understands what is required. Only *he* has the energy, the will and the insight. It is natural for him to want to rule. He must exert his ego in all circumstances. He is full of inner and outer activity, boisterous and impatient with fools, i.e. those whose opinions differ from his. As soon as he has thought of a plan he wants to put it into action without allowing time for second thoughts.

He feels that common things are not worthy of him and he sets himself difficult tasks which he then follows purposefully. His schemes are not always wise or successful and can result in bad temper; but any failure is always someone else's fault. Although a good organiser, he has no patience with detail. He will initiate things but then get others to do the work. He has the feeling that he can do ten things at once. Order is not his strong point.

He cannot stand criticism and will not admit being in the wrong. He may, however, recognise it silently and then correct the situation.

In his relationship with others, if he is the leader, then all is well. He must be considered indispensable and as long as this is understood, he will be friendly—in fact he will show surprising magnanimity and generosity.

He has the habits of his temperament—jollying other people along, doing things without thinking, fixed in purpose, going his own way noisily and with little respect for others. He sleeps well, is an early riser, has interest in practical activities such as building and engineering. He will dress to his own individual taste and enjoy spicy foods.

In painting or drawing, a choleric child's work will be characterised by dramatic situations. For instance, he might depict a volcano or precipice with himself climbing or standing on top.

The professions where cholerics are found are those giving opportunity to command, e.g. sergeants. Others are architects, surgeons, foremen, executives.

The choleric person will observe what is of interest to him and then forget it. He has no great power of memory. He will be good at games, probably making a good runner or something equally strenuous requiring physical stamina.

The negative aspects are a tendency to domineer, to be intolerant, despotic, obstinate, even blind to consequences, to get angry at other people for no reason. An extreme case would be a pathological persistance in following a certain course of action.

The treatment of the choleric child is to give him plenty of things to use up the characteristics of his temperament in a justified manner. He must be given activity, violent activity where necessary and possible. He must conquer the world. Opposition, competition, rivalry are food for his soul. Give him a challenge. The magic words are, "You can't do it."

Nothing will be achieved by admonition but much by humour. If the teacher can put on a choleric act the child will probably see the funny side of it and relate it to himself. If a child bursts out in rage, the teacher must remain quite unperturbed and talk over the outburst the following day. A teacher with an eye for these things will notice a certain restlessness developing. Before the breaking point comes, he must find a way of releasing the tension. He can ask the child to clean the blackboard or open a window.

The choleric child in particular needs a hero. He must think that the teacher knows everything and can do everything. The teacher must point out his own superiority. This child needs resistance to overcome, and to understand that there are difficulties in life. In some situations he could be consulted, particularly if he has been misbehaving. The teacher can put the situation to him objectively and ask, "What would you do?" Then the choleric would feel that an appeal is being made to his ego. He will become sensible and feel that the decision to make good is his.

Stories with great activity, whereby the teacher himself will get roused and excited, are food and drink to the choleric.

In school, he will have a special relationship to division sums and percussion will be his musical instrument. If he would wish to play another instrument, he will be inclined to want to play it solo.

Punishment, if necessary, should not be immediate. The choleric must get the red rag removed from before his eyes before he can be reasonable. Therefore his actions must be discussed after an interval of time and in a calm atmosphere.

SANGUINE

Sanguines are the talkers and chatterers.

The sanguine child is usually of an elegant, slender, harmonious and even build. He is well proportioned and mobile. He is good-looking with slender, well-formed hands, a bright, intelligent face with fair rosy skin and regular features. He is obviously happy in his body and for him the sun is always shining.

He does not walk so much as trip. He almost jumps and has a tendency to bounce on the toes as if buoyant, although he can walk firmly if he wishes. His breathing and rhythmic system are well developed. In fact the air is his element. He has quick-changing, dancing, expressive eyes which will suddenly light up with pleasure. He makes quick, varied gestures and has the peculiarity of sitting or lying in all sorts of awkward positions in which he apparently feels comfortable.

He speaks eloquently, sometimes uses flowery language, embroiders, but fails to come to the point. He is chatty and will give all sorts of information although his knowledge may be superficial and even incorrect.

His mind is like a butterfly. It flits from impression to impression. His interest is in all the events and features of the outer world. He finds great joy in something new but his interest soon wanes. He is friendly and forthcoming and hence makes a good companion. When hurt, he will yell hard and loud but is soon consoled. He cannot be angry for long. He likes change, will promise anything, and forget it immediately. He is imaginative and has lots of ideas which come and go. He is an incurable optimist living in a world of dreams and ideas for future plans touched off by his immediate experiences. He will notice everything and remember nothing.

It is difficult to speak of habits in a sanguine. His chief habit is that he has no habits. He changes, adapts himself, lives in the moment and in the immediate situation. He probably drops off to sleep quickly and wakes early. He will be birdlike in eating, with a preference for nicely prepared and served food, and he loves fruit. He will be interested in anything new—a new house, new friends, a new teacher. He will probably like poetry, acting, games. He will prefer colourful, fashionable clothes, even a uniform. A sanguine boy will be proud of his beautiful tie.

It is easy to recognise a sanguine child by his paintings or drawings. For instance, if he depicts a mountain scene, there will be lots of peaks and detail.

In a landscape there will be lots of birds and animals. The colours will be bright and beautifully arranged.

Eventual professions for sanguines would be those that have to do with people—actors, artists, caterers, social workers. But he is adaptable, and would slip into almost any sort of work and leave it again easily if not suited.

The negative aspects of the sanguine are that he lives in fleeting impressions which are not digested or re-lived. They do not, therefore, become experience. His changing humours overflow. He is impatient, he leaves things half-done, he forgets promises, overlooks responsibilities. He is unreliable and superficial and an extreme case would lead to insanity.

The treatment is to give lots of things to use up the temperament and then take them away again so that interest in one important thing can be reawakened. The temperament can be exhausted on things of little consequence but the educator should try to develop a lasting interest in what is essential by returning to it continuously. He must be serious and give strong, clear pictures. But the real key to treatment is to cultivate a personal connection. Although the sanguine will show only a fleeting interest in things, objects and events, he will develop a lasting interest in personalities. His interest for things will then be awakened through his connection with a person. He will not be bullied but will do things for love. He likes to give pleasure; he will do things as a personal favour. "Do it for me" is the magic phrase. If doubt is expressed as to his ability to carry out a task, he will be anxious to do it to show that he can.

In school he will have a special relationship to multiplication. Reeds and brass will be his musical instruments. As a sociable being, he will appreciate playing with the whole orchestra. Should admonishment be necessary, a friendly word will probably be sufficient. He will see the point and appreciate the consequences at once.

PHLEGMATIC

The phlegmatic is a comfortable sort of person, heavily built, rotund, perhaps a little flabby. He has his own unhurried, placid, loose-limbed way of walking which unkind people might call shambling. He does not gesticulate wildly but takes his own time in doing or explaining anything. This does not mean that he is lazy. If interested, he can be incredibly active. Phlegma is the watery element. The ocean can be placid but it is relentless. The tide may recede but it will return and if a phlegmatic is really roused, it is best for those in the immediate neighbourhood to take shelter until the hurricane is past.

There is no fire or dancing light in his expression. He looks out calmly on the world with a certain objectivity. He speaks in a good, measured tone, which can get monotonous but he expresses what he has to say clearly, concisely and in logical sequence. His information will be correct and reliable.

The phlegmatic lives very much within himself, not however like the melancholic. The latter is very much concerned with himself to the exclusion of the rest of the world. About the phlegmatic one would simply say that he is untroubled by what goes on around him. He is naturally calm and quiet with a general attitude to the world of "leave me alone." That does not mean that he is unfriendly. On the contrary, he is kind, thoughtful and helpful but a natural reserve holds him back.

He is good-humoured, easy-going, a good mixer if someone will break the ice for him; something of a dreamer but no fool. It is merely that he requires time to come to a decision, but then it will be sensible. He cannot reflect quickly and has difficulty in giving spontaneous answers. As a continual companion he can be a bore but he has many sterling qualities to counterbalance this and make him tolerable. He is honourable, faithful, reliable, truthful, honest, orderly, conscientious. One of his finest assets is a sheer inability to leave any job unfinished or badly finished. He likes routine, one job at a time, and order. He does not change ideas or jobs easily; therefore anyone requiring anything of him should give him due notice. He learns slowly but remembers everything. He is persevering to the point of obstinacy and could be considered old-fashioned in that he sticks to what he knows will suit his own comfort rather than trying anything fresh. He is not a born leader but excels in situations where careful detailed planning is required.

It is difficult to persuade him, but he will not refuse outright. He will just do nothing. Being considerate of other people he will not be quarrelsome but his annoyance will show itself in sulkiness. He is shy, living in his own world and is, therefore, grateful for anyone who takes an interest in him.

The phlegmatic is a creature of habit and keeps his habits. He likes regulated hours and a regulated life, good square meals at set times and he will eat anything. Actually he will probably never say no to a meal. He has no pronounced hobbies—perhaps a gentle walk with the dog; modelling, sculpture, reading and day-dreaming could be included. With his quiet unhurried way and his methodical mind the phlegmatic has the greatest possibility of acquiring wisdom.

A child of this type is the easiest to bring up. Eating, digesting and sleeping are the main occupations and provided there is regularity in these matters, he will be happy. In his paintings and drawings there will be a certain blandness. The picture will look somewhat unfinished and probably not very interesting although the colours will blend harmoniously. If it is supposed to be a mountainous landscape, we should see one big hill. In doing work of this sort, the phlegmatic will probably want to copy something or at least someone will have to give him the idea. He should be set a task because he would have very little consciousness of his own artistic ability and this might be quite considerable.

At work, the adult will probably have some subordinate position but one with responsibility. Detailed organisation and administration are his fields—teaching, research work, draughtsmanship, architecture.

The negative side of this temperament is a lack of interest and an extreme case would lead to idiocy.

The treatment, as with the other temperaments, is to exhaust what is there by nature. One should speak to the child phlegmatically of indifferent things but then awaken his interest through the interest of others. A child of this type should have lots of playmates so that his interests are awakened through theirs. He should be awakened at a reasonable hour and washed in cold water. Since he probably sleeps too much anyway, it would be a good thing to wake him up an hour early and give him something to do. He should not be overclothed or allowed to eat too much. Starch is not good for him.

He will develop a strong affection for a person which should be returned. He needs personal contact to awaken him to activity. He can be told directly what to do. The magic words are: "Get on with it" although in this case, and like everything else about him, there is precious little magic. He can be shocked into awareness by a sudden clapping of the hands or a banging on the desk. At such moments he is awake and some important message can be communicated to him. He can be pushed and ordered. He may grumble but he will obey.

His relationship to arithmetic is in the adding processes, his musical instrument is obviously the piano. To get him moving, he must be made conscious of the immediate present and, if punishment is necessary, it should be immediate. He will enjoy choral singing.

MELANCHOLIC

Although not necessarily big and bony, the impression that the melancholic gives is one of heaviness. There is a drooping sort of attitude and it seems difficult to move the limbs. The complexion is sallow and there is often a sad look in the eyes. The gestures are heavy, with a downward tendency of resignation. The melancholic takes a sliding, thoughtful step, giving the appearance of being a little distant from the world, as indeed he is. When he speaks, he stops and thinks, but then does not say what he thinks. His thoughts are only half expressed. He seems weighted by the substance of his body.

The melancholic is a quiet, withdrawn individual with an introspective mind. He is centered in himself and turns over and over in his mind what he has seen and heard, especially if he has received an injury to his amour propre. The egoism of the melancholic is such that he thinks his experiences are peculiar to himself and such things can and do only happen to him. It is therefore good for melancholics to read or hear stories to show that their experiences are by no means exceptional. In particular biographies of great personalities will be helpful. He never forgets injuries or insults even if these were not intended or are only the result of his own imaginings. He imagines catastrophes and has a morbid dread of dying of some horrible disease. He is sad, moody and lives in the past. He has the faculty of being so engrossed with himself that he does not hear what other people say and cannot see any other person's point of view. He is easily hurt by what people say of him and, in turn, hurts other people by speaking freely. He is amazed and annoyed if accused of selfishness, cannot realise that he can be in the wrong, cannot tolerate sarcasm or jokes at his expense. On the one hand he demands that the world serve him and he can be quite tyrannical; on the other hand, if his sympathies are aroused, he will be most helpful and self-sacrificing. He can identify himself with the suffering of other people.

When annoyed, he is spiteful. He is an object of self-pity and will be absorbed by every little ailment and bodily trifle.

He is slow to make friends and often has just one special friend who is more than likely to be a fellow-sufferer. He would like to join in the fun of others but too often feels he cannot and remains a spectator. He is fond of dark, shut-in places and is a voracious reader, seeming to enjoy reading particularly in a poor light. The child who sits in the branches of a tree to read is probably a melancholic.

In class the melancholic may easily get left behind. If asked to contribute something, he may well answer the last-but-one question.

A person of this temperament will enjoy sweet things and will have a great aversion to meat if the form of the animal is still there. He may suffer from constipation and will dread cold water. He will have a preference for drab clothes. His hobbies will be reading, painting, crosswords, jigsaws and solo card games. One could include thinking and brooding. He loves warmth and is happy to be looked after, enjoying attentions and kindnesses.

The melancholic is an intellectual, enriching everything with his own thought. He observes little but remembers what he observes and he has an extremely good memory for things that concern himself.

The melancholic child would reveal his nature in his paintings or drawings by getting lost in details which he could not complete in the media. He would paint with strong colours and try, for instance, to put in eyebrows and facial details even if using liquid water colours.

In professions, one finds the melancholics as doctors, parsons, gardeners, nurses and in the arts.

A negative aspect is an inability to appreciate the outer world and to show gratitude. In extreme cases what arises from within becomes overwhelming and acute depression or madness results, with suicidal tendencies.

The treatment consists of a mixture of sympathy with firmness. The sad traits must be played out. The child needs food for the soul and wants to participate in other people's sorrows. Stories with sad fates are the prescribed food.

The melancholic must not be "consoled." That is, it is no use trying to enliven or amuse him by optimistic "it will be better soon" remarks. He sees the sad and gloomy side of life and any attempt to jolly him will be resented and considered frivolous. It is the melancholic who is happy when he is miserable and one should allow him his happiness (or misery).

A melancholic will respond warmly if shown something or asked about something on which he can express an opinion. Attention must be drawn to the outer world and his interest in it awakened. The consequences of his actions must be brought home to him, particularly as they affect other people and cause them suffering. The educator must also be prepared to give a straight "yes" or "no" as the melancholic child will find a hundred reasons for some particular action or non-action. If difficulties are put in the child's way, he is led away from introspection in overcoming them.

The melancholic will be happy to do something for someone else if the request is put in such a way that he feels he is sacrificing himself. This also helps him to overcome his egoism. If the educator is a person who has suffered much in life and has been tested by fate, then the pupil will have a deeper relationship.

Some attention should be paid to the health. This type of child needs warmth, outer as well as inner, a good digestion and healthy bodily movements.

In arithmetic the melancholic has the closest relationship to subtraction and strings are the musical instruments of greatest appeal. He may have an inclination towards singing solo.

PART EIGHT

THE ENNEAGRAM TYPES

THE ENNEAGRAM HAS GROWN tremendously in popularity since the first enneagram books came out in the 1980s. The concept of the enneagram as a tool for self-understanding and inner growth was first introduced publicly at the turn of the century by the enigmatic esoteric teacher George Gurdjieff. Gurdjieff (1870–1949) claimed to have learned about the enneagram from a secret Sufi "wisdom school" in Afghanistan and compared it to the legendary "philosopher's stone" that could transform lead into gold. He claimed that it was considered of such great importance that it has been kept secret and cannot be found in any occult or Sufi literature. The term comes from the Greek *enneas* or "nine" and *grammos* or "points," and was almost certainly coined by Gurdjieff, who was an Armenian Greek.

The enneagram was later applied to personality by Oscar Ichazo, another enigmatic spiritual teacher who has been reticent about the origins of his theories. Ichazo grew up in Bolivia and Peru and, when he was nineteen, he began intensive training with an esoteric study group in Buenos Aires that was devoted, in part, to the study of Gurdjieff's work. He claims that he discovered the enneagram system of personality typology in a mystical revelation in which he experienced each of the enneagram points from the inside.

One of his early students was Claudio Naranjo, a Chilean psychiatrist who later came to the United States and became involved with Esalen Institute, the famous growth center, and with the human potential movement in general. Ichazo told Naranjo that he would accept a group of North American students for an intensive training program. In 1970 fifty-four North Americans, most of them connected with Esalen and invited by Naranjo, began a ten-month training with Ichazo in Arica, Chile. After the first six months, five of the original group, including Naranjo, were dropped from the training. The Chile training ended in April 1971 and the group returned to the United States.

Ichazo invited the group to help him open a school in New York and to continue work with him. The first New York training began in October 1971 with Ichazo and forty-four graduates of the Chile group. They founded the Arica Institute and began a national program of teaching, which, after several early years of rapid growth, is now relatively inactive.

Naranjo returned to his home in Berkeley, California, and began his own organization, called SAT, Seekers After Truth. One of his most potent tools was the enneagram personality system, which he had learned from Ichazo. Naranjo added his own knowledge of psychiatry to Ichazo's system and provided sophisticated psychological descriptions for each of the nine types. Many of Naranjo's students have gone on to teach and to write about the enneagram.

John Lilly and Joseph Hart were two of the original group of North Americans who worked with Ichazo. In Chapter 26 they present Ichazo's version of the enneagram of the personality. Ichazo defined each enneagram type in terms of ego fixation, which is highly similar to Gurdjieff's chief feature. Ichazo also specified for each type the "traps," or habitual ways of acting, the "ideas," or positive goals, the "passions," or emotional survival systems, and the "virtues," or essential feelings that counteract the passions.

Ichazo emphasized the importance of balancing head, heart, and belly, and stressed the necessity of beginning with work on the belly, which Gurdjieff called the moving center. It is here, Ichazo said, that we know and experience life directly, and we have to work hard to bring our consciousness out of our heads to do it.

Three of the enneagram types—8, 9, and 1—are oriented toward the belly center. They are related to Karen Horney's hostile, or moving against, types, and are concerned with power and justice and have relative little access to feelings of fear or anxiety. Types 2, 3, and 4 have strongly developed heart centers. They are comparable to Horney's moving toward types, and are primarily concerned with relationships, generally outwardly self-confident, happy, and harmonious. Types 5, 6, and 7 are the head types, related to

Horney's moving away character type, and tend to hide their feelings behind a façade of objectivity.

In Chapter 27 Naranjo relates this system to its Gurdjieffian roots and also to modern psychoanalytic theory. He also suggests different terminology for each type. His type names fit both the outstanding feature of each character structure and also its most typical cognitive operation.

Helen Palmer, the most popular enneagram author, is a counselor, a teacher of intuition, and a student of the Gurdjieff work. She has been teaching and working with the enneagram for over fifteen years and has a national program of enneagram training for therapists and other professionals. In Chapter 28, written for this book, she discusses the role of the placement of attention in each of the enneagram types. Because each type pays attention to different aspects of the world around them, each lives in virtually a different reality.

Like astrology, the enneagram is a map of consciousness, which provides clues to answer one timeless question, Who am I? It's always important to recall, when studying a map, that it is *not* the territory.

26. The Arica Enneagram of the Personality

JOHN C. LILLY AND JOSEPH E. HART

WHEN A CHILD IS BORN he is pure essence: a natural being in an ordered cosmos, one with all men and with God, instinctive, loving. This is the perfect state of innocence, but the child must grow. Under the influence of his surroundings, parents, society, he begins to develop a personality for survival, the ego, between four to six years of age. The awareness of the joy and harmony of his essence dims until he is conscious only of his ego, which is fighting for survival in a threatening world. This lack of awareness of the essence leads to the unhappiness which many feel as part of man's condition in this world. But if the ego with its constant fear can be eliminated, man can return to his original state of being in essence, with the addition of all the knowledge his life experience has given him. This knowledge and experience will now enrich the essence which can function more fully in harmony with the Cosmos and is now that of an "enlightened" man.

The ego affects the whole of man, his thinking, his emotions, his bodily movement and energy, which are represented by three centers: the intellectual center in the head; the emotional center in the heart region; and the movement, energy, instinct center about four finger-widths below the navel.

Consequently, one of the first steps toward enlightenment is to break the hold of the ego on the thinking center—since man in ego sees himself, others, and the world only in terms of his ego structure. The ego wants the mind to control the emotional center and the movement-instinct center, so it is necessary to learn to think with the whole body by the use of *mentations*.

To break the hold on the intellect, one must understand his personal ego structure. Each person in ego has a definite pattern of thinking—a fixation. There are nine basic fixations, usually shown in the form of an enneagram: the enneagram is a teaching device used by the Sufi school and developed by Ichazo. Far from being an arbitrary symbol, it has very carefully worked-out interior and exterior dynamic relationships between each point and the whole. It is the subject of constant meditation and study. The relationships are so complex and rich that it would be impossible to explain them in a limited article.

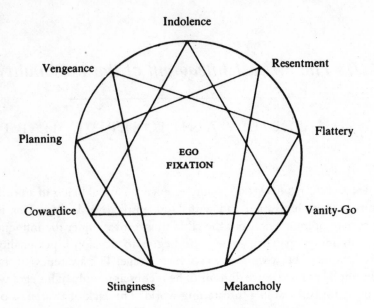

To overcome the feeling of unhappiness and emptiness, the individual in ego searches for something to fill the void according to his fixation:

Indolence: This person seeks love outside himself and makes no effort to find his essence and peace. Popularly called an Ego–In.

Resentment: Always angry with himself and others for not being perfect. Ego–Resent.

Flattery: Needs an approving audience. Many entertainers belong to this group. Ego–Flat.

Vanity: Strives for degrees, positions of importance, power over others. Ego–Go.

Melancholy: Never happy with the present, always looking toward a happy future. Ego–Melan.

Stinginess: Desires anonymity and to view life from the sidelines. Ego–Stinge.

Cowardice: Needs a strong leader to follow; one who can be protective. Ego–Cow.

Planning: Always planning what to do and what must happen; always disappointed at the outcome. Ego–Plan.

Vengeance: Destructive of self and others out of a sense of injustice. Ego-Venge.

The ego leads each person into his own fixation trap or false substitute for his experience of his own essence.

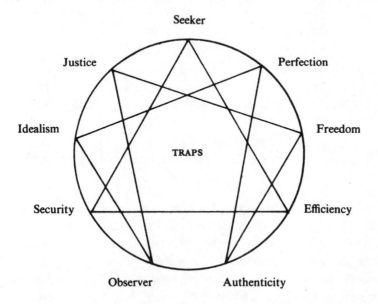

Each fixation has a "trap," a habitual way of acting that stems from the ego. A person who falls into the "trap" associated with his fixation will remain in that recurring action loop until such time as he realizes that it is getting him nowhere. At that point he is ready for the "idea" that will pull him through the door of the trap and into his essence.

Ego-In Seeker: He is always seeking outside himself for the solution of his problems, running from guru to guru.

Ego-Resent Perfection: While demanding perfection of himself he also expects perfection in others. Of course he always hates himself for not being perfect, and is always disappointed in others.

Ego-Flat Freedom: Although dependent upon others for constant approval of himself and his actions, he is fighting that dependency in order to be free from social disapproval and approval.

Ego-Go Efficiency: He has little patience with inefficiency in others, is looking for more effective and quicker methods of achieving his goals. Thus he may be rather inefficient himself.

Ego-Melan Authenticity: For this person, the really real mate will always be just around the corner of the next hour or day, or year. With such a mate, this person will then be fulfilled and, so, authentic.

Ego-Stinge Observer: For him life is fascinating to watch from a safe hidden place, but is much too terrifying to take part in.

Ego-Cow Security: Since such a person lives in fear—life is always threatening—he always seeks something or someone as protector against impending disaster. He will seek to build up a solid fortune or will become the devoted follower of a strong leader.

Ego-Plan Idealism: He is concerned with manipulating the present so that the future will be perfect and the fulfillment of his ideals. When the future becomes the present, he is disappointed and must begin working again toward his ideal.

Ego-Venge Justice: Being aware of living in a very unjust world, he is very sensitive to any unfair actions or thoughts directed at him. His immediate response is that of revenge.

When the "traps" are recognized as being a source of unhappiness, leading nowhere, the person is ready for and eager to accept the proper "idea" for him. These "ideas" are but particular facets of the eternal essence which can bring man to an experiential knowledge of his essential self and so to internal peace and happiness. Experiencing these ideas is dependent upon *Baraka,* divine energy, which must permeate the person. Drawing in Baraka is accomplished through meditation, breathing, chanting, and other exercises.

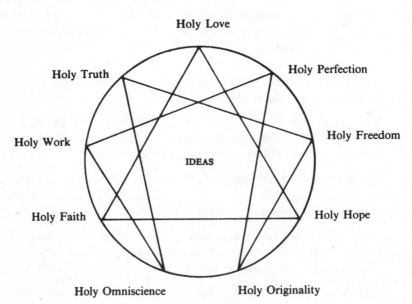

Ego-In Holy Love: The seeker is seeking for someone to truly love him, so that he can feel lovable. The experience of "Holy Love" reveals that his essence is pure love. Then he is both loving and lovable.

Ego-Resent Holy Perfection: The seeker for perfection from the outside experiences that his essence is perfect. He can relax.

Ego-Flat Holy Freedom: The experience of the essence forces man from a dependence upon the approval of others, and introduces him to the freedom of living the cosmic laws.

Ego-Go Holy Hope: The seeker for efficiency, resting in his essence, finds that all things are functioning and will continue to function most efficiently according to the cosmic laws. The continual functioning of the cosmos doesn't depend solely upon his efforts; there is hope for the future, whatever he does or doesn't do.

Ego-Melan Holy Originality: Once he realizes that his essence originates from perfect being, then he knows that he is "really real" now, and not sometime in the future.

Ego-Stinge Holy Omniscience: The observer, storing up knowledge of life by viewing it from the sidelines, steps into life when he experiences his essence. Then and only then can he truly have full knowledge of life.

Ego-Cow Holy Faith: For one seeking security, his essence will give him the assurance that nothing from outside him can hurt his essence, not even physical death, and he is truly his essence.

Ego-Plan Holy Work: For the idealistic planner of the future, the touch of the essence will bring him to live and work in the moment, fully and happily.

Ego-Venge Holy Truth: Once the seeker for justice realizes that his essence follows truly the cosmic laws which are imminently true and just, he will be satisfied and at peace.

Breaking the hold of the Ego on the emotions or heart center follows much the same pattern of becoming aware of one's predominant passion and counteracting it with the proper virtue.

The passions are the emotional survival systems of the ego. A person with a given fixation will generally react to life in a habitual way. He will feel all the passions at some time or another, but his predominant passion will set the emotional tone of his personality.

Ego-In Laziness: For the ego–indolent, the ego will persuade him to be very lazy in searching for his essence, though he may be hyperactive in finding ways to avoid working toward his essence.

Ego-Resent Anger: Again the ego will keep the person in resentful anger because he is not perfect, nor are the people around him.

Ego-Flat Pride: The Ego-Flattery is dependent upon the approval and applause of others, and he works hard to get them. The constant approval and flattery of others produce Ego Pride.

Ego-Go Deceit: One who wants to be known for his accomplishments, positions of influence, and efficiency finds it difficult to admit anything that might mar his public image, so he often is forced into deceit to protect his ego.

Ego-Melan Envy: The Ego-Melancholy person, hoping for the perfect mate or situation in order to feel really real and fulfilled, tends to think most others have achieved this and, of course, is envious of their seeming happiness and earthiness.

Ego-Stinge Avarice: Anonymity and security are important to the Ego-Stinge in order that he can safely watch the world from the peephole of his hiding place. Not only is he avid for the means to maintain his corner, he also is greedy for knowledge of what is going on in life, so that he can feel alive.

Ego-Cow Fear: There is a necessary instinctive fear of dangerous situations in order to safeguard our physical existence. We wouldn't last long without it. But for the Ego-Coward, all of life is threatening. Enemies surround him, so he must always be on the alert and find someone stronger to protect him. Though such constant fear is painful, yet it is familiar and safe. To live without it would leave one too vulnerable to unexpected attack.

Ego-Plan Gluttony: If a little of something is pleasant, then an unlimited amount should bring unheard-of pleasures, so the Ego Plan feels. This projection of present enjoyment into future ecstasy through more and more of the same is a recurring emotional reaction to the good, though each time it ends in uncomfortable satiation and physical distress.

Ego-Venge Excess: The person seeking justice and truth very often overdoes his vengeance in his great moral indignation at injustice. Just as he can punish too severely one who he thinks has wronged him, he can be even more punishing to himself when he feels he has failed in justice. Often he will do physical damage to himself.

To counteract these passions of the ego, which is trying to keep one from experiencing his essence, a person is led by special exercises to experience the opposite virtues or essential feelings.

The practical means used are meditation on the Virtues and the use of *mudras* or hand positions such as you see represented by figures of Buddha or

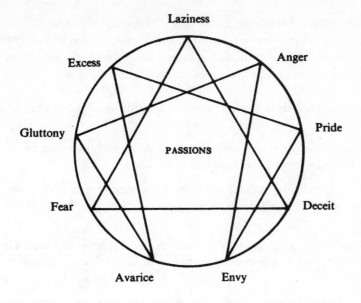

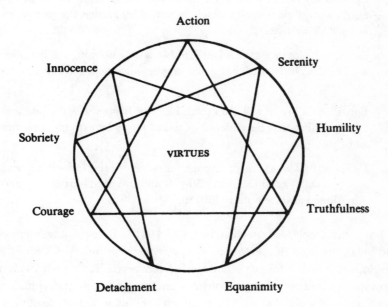

the Bodhisattvas. Much use is made of "ego-reduction exercises" which deliberately try to arouse the passions so that the person can become aware of his weak points. These reduction exercises are carefully prepared and given only when the person has been prepared to undergo them.

Ego-In: The virtue is action directed toward experiencing one's essence, overcoming laziness.

Ego-Resent: Serenity overcomes anger when one knows that his essence is perfect, as are the essences of all others.

Ego-Flat: Humility is the obvious means of overcoming pride. Basically, one can realize that he bears the same perfect essence as others; he is not unique.

Ego-Go: Truthfulness will help him to realize that he is what he is. He does not have to use deceit to maintain an outward image of importance.

Ego-Melan: Happiness in the present moment or equanimity will help overcome the envy of the happiness of others.

Ego-Stinge: Detachment from his secure hiding place and from the need to know everything will relieve him of his avarice, the struggle to protect his anonymity.

Ego-Cow: Courage can replace fear. No one or no thing can harm his essence; only he has the choice of strengthening his ego or experiencing his essence.

Ego-Plan: Sobriety will soon teach him that happiness is reached step by step and cannot be achieved once and for all by extreme measures and gluttony.

Ego-Venge: The excess of revenge on others and on himself can give way to a childlike innocence. "Why should I want to hurt anyone and why should anyone want to hurt me?"

For Ichazo, unless all men can be trained to live in their movement center, and break the hold of the ego, particularly on the mind, man's evolutionary development will come to a halt within ten years. But a man living in his movement center will know that he is one with all men; individualism will disappear, and with it the conflicts and self-seeking which are leading toward the destruction of our culture and our planet. All humanity must become an organic whole or planetary family living in harmony with the cosmos.

27. *The Roots of the Enneagram*

CLAUDIO NARANJO

THE BROADEST DISTINCTION in this body of psychology that I seek to outline is one between what Gurdjieff called "essence" and what he called "personality"—between the real being and the conditioned being with which we ordinarily identify. Where Gurdjieff spoke of personality, Ichazo spoke of ego—more in line with recent usage (ego trip, ego death, ego transcendence, and so on) than with the meaning given to "ego" in today's ego-psychology. The distinction is similar to that proposed today by Winnicott between the "real self" and the "false self," yet it may be misleading to speak of essence, soul, true self or atman as if their reference were something fixed and identifiable. Rather than speak of essence as a thing, then, we should think of it as a process, an ego-less, unobscured and free manner of *functioning* of the integrated human wholeness.

Though "ego" is the word I most often used while presenting these ideas in the early seventies, I expect to be using at least as often the word "character," which I consider an appropriate equivalent for the same notion without the disadvantage of a clash with the meaning of "ego" in modern psychoanalysis.

A derivative from the Greek *charaxo* meaning to engrave, "character" makes reference to what is constant in a person, because it has been engraved upon one, and thus to behavioral, emotional and cognitive conditionings. It has been one of the merits of contemporary psychology to elucidate the process of the deterioration of consciousness in early life as a consequence of early emotional frustration in the family context.

In reaction to pain and anxiety, the individual seeks to cope with a seeming emergency through a corresponding emergency response that, precisely in virtue of the perceived survival threat, becomes fixed, becoming a repetition compulsion, as Freud called it. This is a process that entails a loss of contact with all but the emergency foreground of experience (a dimming of consciousness) and at the same time an automatization, through which the person becomes to some extent a robot rather than a free agent in his life.

Together with the dimming of consciousness and automatization that set in in response to early pain, there is in the structure of the ego a polarity of over-desiring and hatred that, along with consciousness obscuration, have been emphasized in Buddhist doctrine as the three poisons underlying samsaric existence, i.e., three roots of egoic consciousness.

The theory of neurosis implicit in the Protoanalytic [enneagram] view is congruent with the Freudian and Reichian views of neurosis as a consequence of a curtailment of instinct, and also with the conception of health as unobstructed self-regulation generally shared by humanistic psychologists since Rogers and Perls. Though instinct theory has gone out of fashion in psychoanalytic circles since the rise of ethology, the present psychological theory acknowledges the pervasiveness of three goals in human behavior: survival pleasure and relationships.

Unlike traditional religions, which implicitly equate the instinctual with the sphere of the passions, the present view of the mind which conceives the healthy and optimal state as one of free or liberated instinct, could be adequately equated with the contemporary notion of self-regulation. It is a view in which the true enemy in the Holy War that the Fourth Way heritage prescribes against the false or lower self is not the animal within, but the realm of passionate drives that contaminate, repress and stand in place of instinct—and also, most decisively, the cognitive aspects of the ego, "fixations," which in turn sustain the passions.

Let me say something about the enneagram—a geometric structure that became known in the west through Gurdjieff and which the esoteric school behind him and Ichazo conceived as a pattern embodying universal laws, discernible in all manner of processes.

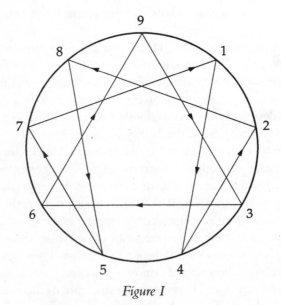

Figure I

More specifically, the triangle inscribed in its circle alludes to a universal threefoldness permeating all existence in the form of an "active," "passive," and a "neutralizing" force; while the points around it, with the exception of those in the 3 and 6 positions called "shock points," stand for a sevenfold pattern in natural cycles. The "Law of Three" is said to apply to the Divine Principle, the "Law of Seven" to Creation. The "invisible" shock points constitute a link between the realms of being and becoming, an influence from a higher level than that in which a given process unfolds.

Inspection of the enneagram of the passions in Figure II (page 232) shows that three of them occupy a position more central than the others. Because of the symbolism of the enneagram—according to which the different points along it correspond to degrees and intervals in the musical scale—psychospiritual laziness, at the top, stands as the most basic of all, being, as it were, the Do of the passions.

While the proposition of a psychological inertia, laziness, echoes the learning theory of neurosis as conditioning, the other two points in the inner triangle summarize the Freudian theory of neurosis—as an expression of childhood anxiety—and the existential one—that envisions inauthentic being and "bad faith" as the basis of pathology.

The fact that these three mental states are mapped at the corners of the triangle in the enneagram of passions conveys a statement to the effect that these are cornerstones of the whole emotional edifice, and that the ones mapped between them can be explained as interactions in different proportions of the same. Anger, for instance, is a hybrid of psychological inertia with pretending, as is also pride, though with a predominance of inertia or vanity respectively.

The interconnections shown between these three points, in the form of sides of the triangle, constitute psychodynamic connections, so that each may be said to underlie the next in a sequence mapped by arrows between them in a particular direction.

If we read this psychodynamic sequence starting at the top, we may say that a lack of the sense of being, implicit in the "robotization" of sloth, deprives the individual of a basis from which to act, and thus leads to fear. Since we must act in the world, however, much as we may fear it, we feel prompted to solve this contradiction by acting from a false self rather than courageously being who we are. We then build a mask between ourselves and the world, we identify with it, and vanity thus arises. To the extent that we identify with our mask, however, we forget who we truly are, we perpetuate the ontic obscuration that, in turn, supports fear, and so on, around the vicious circle.

Looking at the enneagram of the passions, the reader will not have failed

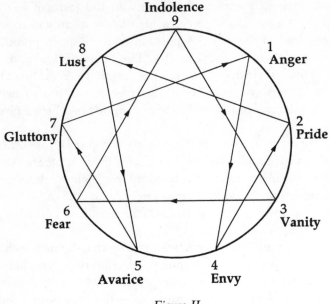

Figure II

to notice that seven of these are no different from the Gregorian capital sins (from *caput,* head). It may be observed that those not mentioned by the Christian tradition are precisely the cornerstones in the system, the shock-points, traditionally said to be invisible.

I think that the present conception of the lower emotional center or, in other words, the enneagram of passions, provides a more comprehensive account of neurosis than we find in theories that have proposed a specific one of these attitudinal atmospheres to be the ultimate background of all psychopathology—regardless of neurotic style.

Just as Freud elaborated a fear-centered interpretation of life and human relations and the existentialists have emphasized the need to be-for-others and inauthenticity, Karen Horney has claimed, like Christian writers, that pride is the crucial psychological defect; Melanie Klein has underscored envy, and Fairbairn and Guntrip have emphazised the schizoid phenomenon related with point 5.

Perhaps it is closer to the truth to say—as Protoanalysis implies—that a particular one of these interpretations will be more appropriate to the situation or character structure of a given individual, even though all points of view apply to each. Thus the diagnosis of the ruling passion can constitute a *central* interpretation, next in importance and transforming potential, according to this view, only to the pointing out of the cognitive ego or fixation, the main representative of "Satan" within the psyche, in the language of the vision transmitted by Ichazo.

Rather than characterizing the passions, I will only say now that we need to attune ourselves to an original meaning in the traditional words, seeing for instance, in "anger" a more inward and basic "standing against" reality than explosive irritation; "lust" as more than an inclination to sex or even pleasure: a passion for excess or an excessive passionateness, to which sexual satisfaction is only one possible source of gratification; likewise "gluttony" will be here understood, not in its narrow sense of a passion for food, but in the wider sense of a hedonistic bias and an insatiable desire for more. "Avarice," too, may or may not include money hoarding, and will designate a fearful and greedy holding on of a more generalized nature—a withdrawn alternative to the outreaching attachment of lust, gluttony, envy and other emotions.

28. Sacred Type:
The Nine Enneagram Personalities

HELEN PALMER

THE ENNEAGRAM is an ancient system of human development based on nine personality types and how they interact with one another. Each type is defined by a mental and emotional concern. The types correlate well with current personality theory, but describe normal and high-functioning people, rather than pathological trends. No type is better than another, and each is effective, but they differ radically in their point of view.

The outer study of the system highlights what the nine types think and feel, how they relate to one another, and what can help them flourish and grow. This level offers fundamental insight into ourselves and our relationships. But the Enneagram's deeper power lies in the ways that type is linked to aspects of the human essence. Our essence is the permanent element of being. An awareness of essence has also been called higher consciousness, or spiritual attainment.[1]

The inner study of the system concerns the linkage between the personality and higher consciousness. The task is to convert the energies spent in ordinary habits of heart and mind into capacities such as empathy, omniscience and love. The higher aspects of type are actually spiritual qualities. They properly belong to the realm of the divine and are not to be confused with talents, creative leanings, and high-functioning psychological traits. Spiritual qualities are not the same as the clarity of mind and emotional generosity displayed by people who are psychologically mature.

These gifts of the spirit appear when awareness is shifted beyond the boundaries of thought and feeling. They cannot be grasped by analysis or emotion because they are not of the same order of consciousness as psychological traits. There is, of course, a natural tendency to confuse aspects of essence with mature psychological functioning, because to describe essence at all, we have to name its many activities with words that describe ordinary events.

The *Abhidhamma,* the classic work on Buddhist psychology, is another ancient system that links type with spiritual life. The traits ascribed to the three Buddhist types correspond beautifully with the Enneagram's central triangle. The Greed type, like Enneagram Three, is motivated by gain: more money, more fame, more pleasure, etc. The Hate type, like Enneagram Six, sees life as a battle. The Delusional type, like Enneagram Nine, tries to function without paying attention. In the Buddhist system, the three deluded views are counteracted by cultivating their opposite tendencies, which are Non-Attachment, Compassion and Mindfulness.

THE PASSIONS OF SACRED TRADITION

Beginning in 1984, there have been several books about the system that describe the nine Enneagram personalities in ways that conform to Western psychological thinking. Each type is described in terms of mental and emotional habits and the ways in which those habits are acted out. An older approach sees type as a fixation of attention on one of the emotional passions that recur in sacred tradition. In this approach, a passion is the central axis of personality that organizes those thoughts, feelings and behaviors that are characteristic of type. Unlike emotions, which constantly change, the passion is the crux of a systematic perceptual distortion, the hub of a biased view of life.

There are seven historical passions, plus two "generic" tendencies that all types hold in common, for a total of nine. Each passion is the "fallen" or distorted version of an aspect of the human essence. The psychological task is to clarify and heal that distortion. The spiritual task is to transform the energy contained in the passion back to its original divine expression. The seven passions are widely known as Christianity's seven capital "sins." Gurd-jieff, the founder of the Enneagram in the West, believed that the "chief feature" of personality was based in the same vices.[2] As he said:

> Always the same motive moves Chief Feature. It tips the scales. It is like a bias in bowling, which prevents the ball going straight. Always Chief Feature makes us go off at a tangent. It arises from one or more of the seven deadly sins, but chiefly from self-love and vanity. One can dis-cover it by becoming more conscious; and its discovery brings an increase of consciousness.[3]

George Ivanovich Gurdjieff (1872–1949), a spiritual teacher of enormous personal magnetism, lived and taught during the period when Freudian ideas about unconscious life were barely in circulation. Stating that he learned the Enneagram from Sufi sources, he introduced the nine-pointed star diagram, including the internal flow pattern that unites the points in specific ways. The Enneagram diagram in use today became the signator of his work.[4]

Although the passions are named in the negative, as vices, or obscurations of mind, they are a primary source of energy for spiritual liberation. They are the raw material, the compost, the qualities of human nature that can be transformed to become aspects of divinity, or essence. It should be pointed out that the Enneagram names only those nine facets of higher being that can be experienced by transforming negative emotional energy. Joy, for example, does not appear, nor is there mention of inner states such as void or bliss. In this view of human development, the passion, as the axis of per-sonality, is the designated agent of change from ordinary to higher con-sciousness.

Richard Rohr, a Catholic priest and Enneagram author writes: "The juxtaposition of the passions with their positive alternatives has been promi-nent in the history of Christian spirituality. Geoffrey Chaucer (ca. 1340–1400), the greatest English poet before Shakespeare, offers an especially interesting list in the Parson's Tale from the *Canterbury Tales*. Chaucer writes from the assumption that there is at least one specific virtue as an antidote to each capital sin. His ideas are very close to the Enneagram teaching, in that the corresponding pairs of his 'sins' and 'virtues' are practically identical. Chaucer designates a remedy, or healing virtue for each 'sin.' Humility helps against pride, true love of God helps against Envy, the remedy for anger is patience, laziness (sloth) is overcome through fortitude, avarice through compassion, gluttony through sobriety and moderation, lechery (lust) through chastity."[5]

Continuing the concept of passions as potential agents of liberation, the poet Dante describes the seven areas of purgatory in practically the same language used in Enneagram studies today. Purgatory can be conceptualized as a "transit point" between earthly life and the heavenly realms. A "place" where sins are expiated in preparation for bliss, or permanent being.

Dante (1265–1321) *The Divine Comedy*— Purgatorio			Oscar Ichazo 1970 The Arica Training	
One	Anger	Meekness	Anger	Serenity
Two	Pride	Humility	Pride	Humility
Three			Deceit	Truthfulness
Four	Envy	Charity	Envy	Equanimity
Five	Avarice	Poverty	Avarice	Detachment
Six			Fear	Courage
Seven	Gluttony	Abstinence	Gluttony	Sobriety
Eight	Lust	Chastity	Excess	Innocence
Nine	Sloth	Zeal	Laziness	Action

Dante's attributions of the passions and their higher opposites from the Purgatorio section of *The Divine Comedy*[6] are placed next to the work of Oscar Ichazo, founder of the Arica School and noted Enneagram contributor, who successfully applied Christianity's capital sins to Gurdjieff's nine-pointed star. The "generic" types of Deceit and Fear are also described as states of consciousness in Dante's Purgatorio, and were placed by Ichazo on the Gurdjieff diagram to total nine.[7]

THE TRADITIONAL PASSIONS AS PLACED BY OSCAR ICHAZO ON THE GURDJIEFF DIAGRAM

Deceit and fear appear at what Gurdjieff called the "shock points," or anchors, of the Enneagram's inner triangle. These are the points of the diagram that model the influx of energies from the realms of essence or grace, to the material dimensions of life.[8] According to sacred tradition, we have all become deceived that our personality is our real self, and afraid when we lost our spiritual nature.

Deception is the result of identifying with the personality as our true self. Identification is a psychological mechanism that is necessary in the formation of personality. We all identify with the characteristics of our type and, through identification, we are *deceived,* or convinced, that our personality is our true nature.[9]

People who *identify* with role and image as the chief feature of their psychological life place themselves at the Three point in the diagram. Their

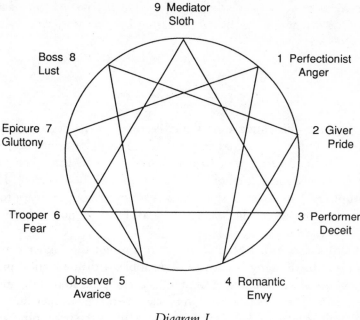

9 Mediator
Sloth

Boss 8
Lust

1 Perfectionist
Anger

Epicure 7
Gluttony

2 Giver
Pride

Trooper 6
Fear

3 Performer
Deceit

Observer 5
Avarice

4 Romantic
Envy

Diagram I

life stories highlight the self-deception of taking on a false persona to gain approval and love. Their observations remind us that we have all forgotten our Spiritual nature by identifying with the characteristics of our type.

Fear is the second "generic" quality that factors into the formation of type. Sacred tradition reminds us that children are born with the potential for physical trust and faith in the goodness of others, and that a child contracts when that security is invaded by distress and pain.

People who identify with fearfulness as the chief feature of their inner life place themselves at the Six point of the diagram. Their self-observations remind us all of the role of anxiety in the formation of any type. Sixes say that fear arises first in themselves, and is then projected outward. They say they assume that something external has caused them to be afraid, and they therefore scan the environment to find "the reason for" their sense of inner threat.

Projection is the major psychological defense mechanism for Six (Paranoid style), and also plays its part in all biased perception. We all share the generic tendency to look outside of ourselves to explain why we feel the way that we do. It is our fear that makes us project, or look outward to find "the source" of our distress.[10]

The generic factor of fear in the formation of type is highlighted in the universal fear of change. It is very difficult to change a behavior even when we see ourselves act it out. When it comes to change, we are afraid. We doubt. We deceive ourselves that the problem is trivial. Most of all, we forget. Our orientation to change is fearful, because we have to shift the defenses of our type.

THE CENTERS

Gurdjieff framed his concept of "Chief Feature" or the passion of type, in a model straight out of sacred tradition. His model describes humankind as a three-brained being. The "three brains" refer to three kinds of ordinary awareness: mental, emotional and instinctual (body-based). He saw spiritual progress in terms of shifting consciousness from ordinary to more subtle realms of perception, mediated by a higher mental and emotional center.

To Gurdjieff, spiritual life is conducted through the higher centers of perception. His thinking is entirely compatible with meditation practices that recommend the quieting of thought and emotions so that the inner, or "higher," intelligence of heart and mind can open. The deeper study of the Enneagram concerns quieting the mind, developing the inner observer, and shifting placement of attention so that the higher centers of perception activate.

Diagram II suggests one approach to activating the higher centers of perception. The energies usually expended in sex, instinctive well-being, and movement (orientation) are "accumulated" as a single force, in the abdominal center through specific meditation practices. When the three vital energies are consolidated in the abdominal center, they rise as one force, to activate the higher mental and emotional centers. In this way, the energies that are ordinarily expressed through the mental emotional and physical habits of type are transformed to "awaken" activities of the abdominal center and the higher mental and emotional centers. In spiritual parlance, the abdominal center has been variously called the Belly center, the center of the Body, the Hara, the Tantien and the Kath.

In my opinion, if it is so that the rising force of the consolidated abdominal center is fed by three separate "instinctual" energies, then those energies are mediated by the subcenters described in the physiology of sacred experience. These subcenters are located at definite physical sites in the body, and their activities are commonly described in the physiology of sacred experience. These subcenters are located at definite physical sites in the body, and their activities are commonly described by meditators when they energize during practice sessions. The primary subcenters can be felt at the perineum, the solar plexus and at the base of the spine.

Whether Gurdjieff's body-based "instinctual" centers are in fact related to the stages of psychological growth that depend upon maturing instinct is open to question by developmental theorists.

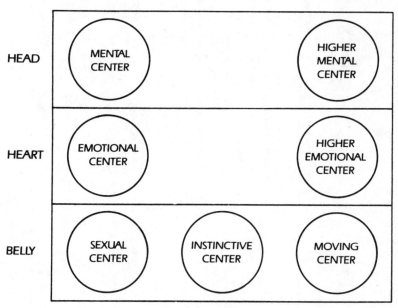

Diagram II: Sacred Type—The Center of Ordinary and Higher Awareness

Diagram III (page 240) shows how the nine sacred types can be overlaid on Gurdjieff's core model of three kinds of ordinary intelligence with their corresponding higher aspects. This overlay was developed by Oscar Ichazo, who correctly positioned Christianity's seven passions and the two more general traits of deception and fear, to a total of nine.

Ichazo fulfilled Gurdjieff's model of humanity's possible evolution by adding a cognitive component to the emotional passions. A mental preoccupation and its corresponding higher possibility are named for each type. He finalized his version of the Enneagram model of human development by assigning each of Gurdjieff's three vital energies or "instincts" to a specific sector of practical life, which he called the areas of Self-preservation, Sexual and Social relating.

Self-preservation concerns personal day-to-day survival, the sexual sector of life concerns survival through time (genetic), and the social sector concerns survival in the group (herd). Whether the key behaviors that Ichazo has assigned to each sector are actually mitigated by instinct is open to question. They may be simply type-related concerns about personal, sexual and social survival.

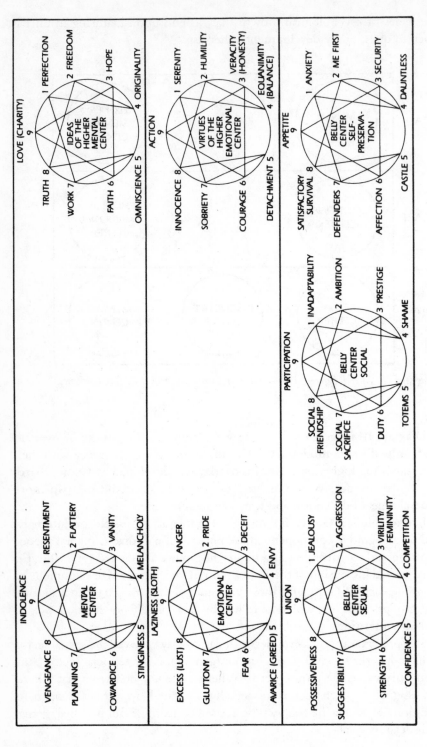

Diagram III

THE ORAL TRADITION

By synthesizing the Gurdjieff model with the traditional description of Christianity's capital "sins," and drawing on Western personality theory, Ichazo produced a description of the types that was transmitted at a training held in 1970, at Arica, Chile.[11]

The major preoccupations of type and their relationship to current psychological ideas were amplified by his student, psychiatrist Claudio Naranjo, who attended the Arica training. Naranjo aligned the types with current diagnostic criteria. He also demonstrated the effectiveness of an oral teaching approach by interviewing good self-observers who could describe their own inner condition.[12]

Oral teaching relies on the self-descriptions of people who can watch their inner world at work. Good observers can report on far more than their superficial behaviors. They can also report on the thoughts, feelings and motives that underlie their actions. In the oral tradition we rely on a method of inquiry to develop a conversation between the types. The conversation produces colorful firsthand examples of the ways in which differences in personality type affect decision making, professional life, and relationships of all kinds.

For close to twenty years I have taught the Enneagram by holding conversations between speakers who represent their own type, myself and those in the audience who want to propose questions. My role is to keep the conversation on track and to draw out specific facets of the personalities. Over time, the format of conversation has become far more than an impressive way to demonstrate the nine types. It has become an arena for people who approach life from different angles to develop compassion for each other. It is, for example, immensely impressive to hear the level of self-disclosure that develops between long-standing couples as they converse with each other. Often enough I have seen an audience of people who never really saw the importance of looking at themselves suddenly rise in their seats and applaud after an honest conversation.

I see the conversation format as the backbone of Enneagram teaching. The most obvious reason is that it's a fast and effective way to deliver immediately useful insight to large groups of people who may not be psychologically sophisticated. A second reason is that being able to personally question and interact with the types helps to eliminate many of the false ideas that develop from written descriptions about them. Many people who come to Enneagram classes know very little about their own type or those of the people who are close to them in life. The advantage of being able to see several people of the same type on a panel is obvious. We can compare our own lives to the speaker's stories. We either identify with them or we don't.

I also like talking with the types because it's fun. The conversation is never the same and it can turn in any number of interesting directions. Over the years I've talked with panels on topics ranging from sexuality to parenting styles to questions of spiritual development. We set up live interactions in class between the types and their parents, spouses, children, bosses, employees and friends. The wealth of information that a good conversation can produce leads directly to the real reason that I like to talk with the types. The real agenda is an inquiry about the role of type in spiritual life.

The panels make it abundantly clear that each type has its unique approach to professional and intimate living, but good self-observers continue to be a reliable source of information when asked about their experience in meditation and prayer. Panels say that the passion affecting their outer life also impedes their meditation and inner reflection. If we use the diagram's central triangle as an example: the Self-Deceiving type (Three) confuses the activity of *doing* a meditation with being affected and moved by the silence. The Fear type (Six) is afraid to let thoughts go, and the Sloth type (Nine) has difficulty in staying focused.

PLACEMENT OF ATTENTION

To me, each passion can be described by the habitual way that attention becomes organized when the passion takes hold. When attention is "caught" we automatically yearn with envy, or inflate with pride or contract with avarice. Energy automatically explodes when we are angered, and we fight or flee when we are afraid. Attention becomes fixated on the object of our passion, on what we envy, or who has made us angry, or what we desire. At those times, the object of attention becomes so energized that we respond reflexively, without realizing that our perceptions have become narrow and biased.

It is important to me that each type can literally name the automatic placements of attention that characterize their passion. The Envy type (Four), for example, remembers the missing object of love, and yearns emotionally, specifically naming an absent figure, and a special way of reacting to that figure. Another of the Enneagram's "feeling types," the Pride type (Two) focuses attention on the needs of others, and emotionally recognizes "which self to become" in delivering what people want. Since the passions are simply a more compulsive version of spontaneous and appropriate human reactions, we can all identify the placements of attention that underlie each emotional bias. Every one of us has yearned like Fours, and Twos are not alone in altering self-presentation to please. It seems that each of the passions reflects a way of attending that is entirely natural and familiar to us all.

My own addition to the Enneagram material concerns the placements of attention that underlie a range of perceptions, especially emotional, intuitive and spiritual perceptions. I think that the placements of attention that underlie personality type, and that unfortunately limit perception to a small sector of information, are actually self-serving versions of the attention placements that characterize specific meditation practices. The way that I explain that idea to students is by demonstrating ways in which the effects of each passion can be shifted by specific meditations. All inner life practice is at some level based on placements of attention, including those practices that specifically evoke each passion's opposite condition.

The Enneagram is based on the traditional concept that the passions can be converted to their opposite or "higher" condition. The higher aspects of type are conceptualized as being actual aspects of divinity, and in fact, there is a vast technology of sacred tradition that is organized to specifically cultivate qualities of essence such as Humility, Love and Faith, which in Enneagram terms are the opposites of Pride, Sloth and Fear. The goal of this work is to shift consciousness from the familiar habits of type so that the action of essence or grace is unimpeded by the passions.

The following short descriptions and lists of key preoccupations were developed from the statements of thousands of speakers who have appeared in Enneagram groups. They described themselves on panels to help an audience of newcomers discover their own type in the oral way. Like that of every teacher, my line of inquiry flows from my own ideas about the material. I am interested, of course, in demonstrating the preoccupations of type, and I continue to be fascinated by people's interactions with each other. But because I think that type is a strategic access point to higher consciousness, I am less interested in the behaviors and motives that preoccupy the panelists' attention, and more interested in the chronic placement of attention that organizes their world view. But to get to higher consciousness, we have to start with the ordinary consciousness that is familiar to us. We have to start somewhere, and to me the most advantageous starting place is focus of attention. We want to know *what* the types pay attention to, describe *how* they pay attention, and gradually shift that limited placement of attention to include the full range of objective information.

ONE—PERFECTIONIST

The passion of anger is focused on a violation of standards. The internal commitment to perfection is at stake. In extreme cases, we know this type as the Compulsive personality type.

One types earn love by becoming better people by doing what's right. They measure themselves against the highest standards in search of an ethical platform on which to build their lives. Thinking centers on "should," "must" and "ought to." "We should have a faultless relationship. We must have a spotless record at work." At its best, their commitment to goodness serves as a humane guide to improvement. As a defensive gesture, Ones can feel morally superior by finding fault with others.

FOCUS OF ATTENTION

- *A search for perfection. Avoiding error and evil.*
- *Conscientious. An emphasis on ethical and moral character. Think Right. Do Right. Be Right.*
- *Think Right. "Should, must and ought to."*
- *Do Right. Emphasize the practical virtues: work, thrift, honesty and effort.*
- *Be Right. Severe internal critic. An internal judging voice.*
- *Compulsive work loads can block out unacceptable feelings.*
- *Anger develops from unmet needs. Self-denial generates resentment. Not aware of their own anger. "I'm just energetic today."*
- *Excessively worried about decisions. Afraid to make a mistake.*
- *This focus of attention ensures an ethical and moral platform for life. It can also lead to:*
- *One Right Way thinking. Right or Wrong. Black or White. No greys.*
- *Superb powers of criticism and an intuitive sense of how perfect things could be.*

TWO—GIVER

The passion of pride is an inflated sense of self-worth that masks a dependency on gaining people's approval. If the compulsion becomes extreme, we know this type as the histrionic personality.

Love is ensured by being indispensable. Givers are helpful in other people's lives. They're supportive and pleasing with intimates and like to be the power behind the throne at work. Many different selves emerge to meet the needs of others. A self for the home, a self for the boss, many selves for private life.

At its best, this giving is altruistic and generous. As a defensive maneuver, giving is geared to get something you want in return.

FOCUS OF ATTENTION

- *Gaining approval. Adapting to please people. Avoiding own needs.*
- *Pride in being needed. Being central in people's lives. Being indispensable.*
- *A sense of having many different selves to meet the needs of others.*
- *Confusion can arise between the different selves. "Which one is really me?"*
- *Hard to recognize own needs. Gets own needs met by helping other people.*
- *Wants freedom. Feeling confined by having to give support to others.*
- *Self-presentation alters to meet the needs of others. This way of paying attention can lead to:*
- *Empathic emotional connections, or*
- *Adaptation to the wishes of others as a way of assuring their love.*

THREE—PERFORMER

The passion of deceit involves maintaining an image of success in the eyes of others. If the compulsion becomes extreme, we know this type as one of the Type A profiles.

Performers win love with achievements and image. They emphasize Doing. Doing things with the family and doing high-profile work. Threes are preoccupied with role and professional status. They want to count, to lead, to impress and be seen. Work is the area of interest; feelings are suspended while the job gets done. At its best, the performance orientation produces effective leadership. As a means of defense, image is tailored to promote personal success.

FOCUS OF ATTENTION

- *Achievement, product and performance. Goals, tasks and results.*
- *Competition and efficiency. Avoid failure.*
- *Poor access to emotional life. Your heart is in your work.*
- *Convergent thinking. A multitrack mind focused on a single product or goal.*
- *"I am what I do." Confusion between the real self and one's job or role.*
- *Learning to "do" feelings. Doing the look and learning the lines.*
- *Chameleon. Changing roles and changing image.*
- *This way of paying attention can maximize success. It also leads to:*
- *Self-deception. You begin to believe your own public image.*

FOUR—TRAGIC ROMANTIC

The passion of envy reminds us that others enjoy the happiness that seems to be missing from our lives. If the compulsion becomes extreme, this type becomes a Bi-polar or Depressed personality type.

A Romantic longs for love at a distance, becoming disappointed when love is near at hand. The feeling is: "We were connected—but now it doesn't feel right. What happened between us? Where did it go?" There's a lifelong search for heart connection, filled with attractions, hate and pain. Loss is cushioned by an elegant lifestyle, special treatment, and unique personal views. At its best, the passionate quest leads to authentic emotional depth. As a posture, shifting moods make Fours too precious for ordinary life.

FOCUS OF ATTENTION

- *Wants what's unavailable, far away and hard to get. Avoiding the ordinary.*
- *Mood, manners, luxury and good taste to hedge low self-esteem.*
- *Attracted to the mood of melancholy. The flavor of longing.*
- *A disdain of ordinary life. The "flatness of ordinary feelings."*
- *Amps up ordinary life through loss, fantasy, artistic connection and dramatic acts. Drama Kings and Queens.*
- *Push-pull relationships. Wants the best of what's missing. Pushing it away when it's available again. This alternating focus reinforces:*
- *Feelings of abandonment and loss, but also lends itself to:*
- *Emotional sensitivity and depth. An ability to support others during crisis and pain.*

FIVE—OBSERVER

The passion of avarice is a greed for the resources that support independent and private survival. Protecting knowledge, money, energy and time becomes psychologically important. If the compulsion is extreme, this type becomes either a schizoid or avoidant personality.

Fives detach from charged emotions and retire into privacy to find out what they feel. Drained by public encounters with people, they crave isolation to recharge themselves. Often positioned as thinkers and strategists, Fives like protected work environments with no interruptions. They prefer limited contact and agendas announced in advance. At its best, the stance of detachment produces clear-minded analysis. As a psychological strategy, detachment restricts emotional contact.

FOCUS OF ATTENTION

- *Preoccupied with privacy and noninvolvement.*
- *Stores knowledge and the essentials of survival. Avoiding emptiness.*
- *Tightens the belt to maintain independence. Do with less.*
- *Values emotional control. Prefers structured events. Known agenda and time frame.*
- *Compartments. Keeping the departments of life separate from each other. Predetermined time slots for emotionally charged events.*
- *The power of knowing. Values analytic systems and special information. Wants to find the keys to the way that the world works.*
- *Tries to figure out feelings.*
- *Often confused between spiritual nonattachment and the need to detach from emotional pain.*
- *Watching life from the point of view of an outside observer. This way of paying attention can lead to:*
- *Feeling isolated from the events of one's own life, or an ability to:*
- *Assume a detached point of view that is unaffected by fear or desire.*

SIX—TROOPER

The passion of fear involves a loss of faith in authority and situations more powerful than ourselves. If the compulsion is extreme, this type becomes the Paranoid personality.

Six types question the love of others. Why believe and then be betrayed? The mind is doubtful. Can I be certain? Do you like me? Should I stay? Loyal to the people they trust, Troopers turn to their intimates for reassurance. Mistrusting authority, they expect to be taken advantage of by people in power. Well used, a questioning mind produces clarity of purpose. As a life stance, inner doubt interferes with progress.

FOCUS OF ATTENTION

- *Procrastination. Thinking replaces doing. Avoiding action.*
- *High goals, often with a history of incompletes.*
- *Anxiety peaks with success. Success equals exposure to hostile forces.*
- *Amnesia about success and pleasure.*
- *Authority problems. Either submitting to authority (phobic), or rebelling against the power structure (counterphobic).*
- *Suspicious about other people's motives, especially authorities.*
- *Identified with underdog causes. Leader of the opposition party.*

- *Afraid to recognize own anger. Afraid of other people's anger.*
- *Skepticism and doubt. Similar to the Buddhist category of "doubting mind." A mental "Yes, but . . ." or "This may not work."*
- *Scanning the environment for clues to explain the inner sense of threat. This way of paying attention will confirm:*
- *That the world is a threatening place, but also leads to:*
- *A recognition of the motives and hidden agendas that influence relating.*

SEVEN—EPICURE

The passion of gluttony is a hunger for the many delights of worldly experience. If the mind becomes fascinated with outer life, then inner work deteriorates. Contrary to the usual concept of gluttony, this passion is only occasionally focused on food. If the compulsion becomes extreme, this type is known as the narcissistic personality.

Sevens feel entitled to love and attention. Disappointments barely surface when the mind is filled with plans. If option A doesn't work, we'll shift to B as a backup. If B's a bore, we'll fall back on C. Buoyed by a sense of personal worth, it's natural to follow your attractions. Why get mired in difficulty? When life's too hard, you're using the wrong approach. At its best, the dedication to adventure conveys its enthusiasm to others. As a self-serving tactic, the commitment to pleasure is a way to run from pain.

FOCUS OF ATTENTION

- *Stimulation. New and interesting things to do. Optimistic. Avoids pain.*
- *Maintains multiple options. Hedging commitment to a single course of action. Fears limitation.*
- *Replacing deep or painful feelings with a pleasant alternative. An escape into mental pleasure. Talking, planning and intellectualizing.*
- *Charm as a first line of defense. Fear types who move forward into friendly contact with people. Avoids conflict by going through the cracks. Talking your way out of trouble.*
- *A way of paying attention that relates and systematizes information, such that commitments can include many options. This style of attention can lead to:*
- *Rationalized escapism from a difficult or limiting commitment, or*
- *The ability to find connections, parallels and unusual fits. A talent for nonlinear synthesis of information.*

EIGHT—BOSS

The passion of lust is the single-minded urgency to satisfy needs. If the compulsion is extreme, this type becomes sociopathic.

Eights show their love through protection and power. They like the truth that comes out in a fight. They're at home with anger and will push to get contact. They stand up for "their people" and secure the bunker at work. Gravitating to positions of authority and control, Eights set the rules in love and business life. At its best, the take-charge stance develops leaders who use their power wisely. As a protective stance, the best defense is a good offense.

FOCUS OF ATTENTION

- *Control of possessions and personal space.*
- *Concerned about justice and power. Avoid weakness.*
- *Excessive self-presentation—too much, too loud, too many.*
- *Poor impulse control—hard to set limits.*
- *Difficulty in recognizing dependency needs and softer emotions.*
- *Boundary issues—learning the difference between self-defense and aggression.*
- *The denial of other points of view in favor of the "truth." Confusing objective truth with a subjective opinion that serves the Eight's agenda.*
- *An "all-or-nothing" style of attention which tends to see the extremes of a situation. People seem to be either fair or unfair, either warriors or wimps, with no middle ground. This style of attention can lead to:*
- *An unconscious denial of personal weakness or:*
- *Exercising appropriate force in the service of others.*

NINE—MEDIATOR

The passion of sloth is a way of forgetting oneself by investing energy in inessentials. Sloth is a desire to remain comfortable and undisturbed that is only occasionally acted out by literal laziness. If the compulsion is extreme, this type becomes an Obsessive or a Passive Aggressive personality.

Nines lose their boundaries by merging with loved ones. They take on many points of view. Saying "Yes" brings up a stubborn anger, but why say "No" and have to fight with you? Nines can relate to all sides of an argument, which derails their own agenda. "Yes" means "yes, I'm reflecting your opinion," "Maybe" could mean probably "No." At its best, the merging habit offers genuine support. As a protective measure, adopting many points of view avoids commitment to any one of them.

FOCUS OF ATTENTION

- *Replacing essential needs with inessential substitutes.*
- *Comforting self with secondary pleasures. Avoids conflict.*
- *On the fence with personal decisions. "Do I agree or disagree?" Seeing all sides of the question. Decisions are easy when not personally loaded, for example: emergency actions or political opinions.*
- *Postponing change by repeating familiar solutions. Acting through habit. Ritualism. Seems like there's plenty of time. It can wait until tomorrow.*
- *Hard to initiate change. Easier to know what you don't want than what you do.*
- *Can't say "no." Hard to separate. Hard to be the one to go.*
- *Damping physical energy and anger. Diverts energy to trivia. Delayed reaction time for anger. Passive aggression. Anger equals separation.*
- *Control by becoming stubborn. Do nothing. Wait it out.*
- *Control by using time. Wait some more.*
- *Paying attention to other people's agendas, which leads to:*
- *Difficulty in forming a personal position, but also develops:*
- *The ability to recognize and support what is essential to other people's lives.*

TYPE AND HIGHER STATES OF CONSCIOUSNESS

It would be comforting to think that an intact teaching can be transposed from the past without modification. Nothing could be further from the truth. In our time we look at ourselves through a psychological lens, but that perspective is less than a hundred years old. The Enneagram, with its psychological anchor in the ancient Spiritual passions, is a far more mature model of human development. From the vast perspective of consciousness that this system portrays, what we might think of as a "high-functioning" personality looks more like being mired in a pathological compulsion.

There is no traditional "Enneagram technology" available to us. How could there be? The lens changes with each generation. What was once sound advice is dated when better strategies emerge. The model that first appeared in the West through Gurdjieff was at one time exclusively grounded in the approach to higher consciousness that he taught. There was no psychology as we know it during Gurdjieff's time, so his understanding of type as an access point to higher consciousness was necessarily different from our own.

The contemporary authors and contributors to the system each have taken a personal perspective on the material. Each has a different way of working with the types. Some are focused on psychological interventions and treatment strategies, while others, like myself, are attracted to the ways in which type can act as a transformer from ordinary to higher consciousness.

What was once a closed teaching is now rapidly moving into the public arena. This is a fascinating phase for Enneagram studies, and the reason for its sudden popularity is quite simple. This is a mystical system that is anchored in psychological type but that goes well beyond conventional parameters. By linking the preoccupations of type with specific aspects of higher consciousness, the Enneagram joins the power of a Western psychological model with the agendas of sacred tradition.

NOTES

Chapter 1/Greene

1. C. G. Jung, *Psychological Types*. London: Routledge & Kegan Paul, 1971.
2. June Singer, *The Boundaries of the Soul*. New York: Anchor Books, 1973.

Chapter 12/Hillman

1. C. G. Jung, "Psychological types." In *Collected Works*, vol. 6, pp. 554–555.
2. *Ibid.*, pp. xiv–xv.
3. *Ibid.*, p. 555.
4. *Ibid.*, p. 494.

Chapter 16/Springer and Deutsch

1. Sri Aurobindo, quoted in J. E. Bogen, "The Other Side of the Brain. VII: Some Educational Aspects of Hemispheric Specialization," *UCLA Educator*, 17 (1975), pp. 24–32.
2. R. Ornstein, *The Psychology of Consciousness*. New York: Harcourt Brace Jovanovich, 1977.
3. R. Ornstein, "The Split and Whole Brain," *Human Nature*, 1 (1978), pp. 76–83.

Chapter 28/Palmer

1. Webster defines consciousness as an awareness that something was or is happening or existing. The Enneagram system implies that there are different orders of consciousness in which one can be aware of nonhistorical and nonpresent events. A classic work on defining states of consciousness is Charles Tart's *States*

of Consciousness (El Cerrito, CA.: Psychological Processes, 1983), originally published in 1975. Another treatment of levels of consciousness from the Gurdjieff point of view can be found in Tart's *Waking Up* (Boston: Shambhala, 1986).

2. Gurdjieff's concept of Chief Feature, or vice, continues the teaching that a negative feature of personality can be transformed into its higher opposite. Gurdjieff believed that our Chief Feature could be converted to our greatest asset.

3. C. S. Nott, *Journey Through This World: The Second Journal of a Pupil*. New York: Samuel Weiser, Inc., 1969, p. 87. It is useful to note Nott's choice of Vanity as a generic source of personality bias in conjunction with the seven capital sins. Vanity was placed by Oscar Ichazo at the Three point on the diagram. Ichazo also placed the generic characteristic of Fear at the Six point, for a total of nine capital vices.

4. Gurdjieff Foundation schools are active today and can be found in most major cities.

5. Richard Rohr and Andreas Ebert, *Discovering the Enneagram: An Ancient Tool for a New Spiritual Journey*. New York: Crossroad Publications, 1990, p. 25.

6. Paolo Milano, ed. *The Portable Dante*. New York: The Viking Press, 1947, Purgatorio section.

7. John Lilly and Joseph Hart, "The Arica Training," in *Transpersonal Psychologies*, Charles Tart, ed. New York: Harper & Row, 1975, reprinted by Psychological Processes, Inc., 1983.

8. The invisible shock points at Three and Six are involved with movements of energy within the diagram. They also point to links between the planes of ordinary awareness and the realms of essence, or pure being. The energy patterns of the diagram are not under discussion here. For a concise summary of these patterns, see Kathleen Riordan Speeth, *The Gurdjieff Work*. Los Angeles: Jeremy Tarcher, 1976, pp. 21–25.

9. In sacred tradition, personality is seen as a false self system that arises out of the need to cope with physical and emotional life. Sacred tradition points to the "real" as the full spectrum of awareness that lies beyond the private boundaries of thought, feeling and physical sensation. From this perspective, the real self is far more expanded than the attributes of a type.

10. David Shapiro, *Neurotic Styles*. New York, London: Harper Torch, 1965. See Section Three, Paranoid Style, pp. 54–107.

11. Lilly and Hart, "The Arica Training."

12. Claudio Naranjo, M.D., *Ennea-type Structures: Self-analysis for the Seeker*. Nevada City: Gateways/IDHHB, 1990. This is a summary of Naranjo's original work with the system.

BIBLIOGRAPHY
AND TYPOLOGY
RESOURCES

Astrology

WESTERN ASTROLOGY

Liz Greene, *Relating: An Astrological Guide to Living with Others on a Small Planet.*
York Beach, Maine: Weiser, 1977.
Dane Rudhyar, *The Astrology of Personality.* New York: Doubleday, 1970.
C. G. Jung, *Synchronicity: An Acausal Connecting Principle.* London: Routledge &
Kegan Paul, 1972.

NATIVE AMERICAN ASTROLOGY

Sun Bear and Wabun, *The Medicine Wheel: Earth Astrology.* New York: Prentice-Hall,
1980.
Sun Bear and Wabun, *The Path of Power.* Spokane, WA: Bear Tribe Pub., 1983.
For more information about Earth Astrology, write to Sun Bear and Wabun, c/o
The Bear Tribe, P.O. Box 9167, Spokane, WA 99209.
Theodora Lau, *The Handbook of Chinese Horoscopes.* New York: Harper & Row,
1979.

255

Eastern Traditions

YOGA

Ram Dass, *Journey of Awakening: A Meditator's Guidebook*. New York: Doubleday, 1978.
Ram Dass, *The Only Dance There Is*. New York: Doubleday, 1974.
Swami Radha, *Kundalini Yoga for the West*. Boston: Shambhala, 1985.

AYURVEDIC MEDICINE

Deepak Chopra, *Perfect Health: The Complete Mind/Body Guide*, New York: Harmony Books, 1990.
Vasant Lad, *Ayurveda: The Science of Self-Healing*. Wilmot, WI: Lotus Press, 1984.

CHINESE MEDICINE

Harriet Beinfield & Efrem Korngold, *Between Heaven and Earth*. New York: Ballantine, 1988.

Psychological Typologies

Sigmund Freud, *New Introductory Lectures on Psychoanalysis*. New York: Norton, 1949.
Erik Erikson, *Childhood and Society*. New York: Norton, 1963.
Karen Horney, *Our Inner Conflicts*. New York: Norton, 1945.

Jungian Types and Archetypes

TYPES

C. G. Jung, *Psychological Types*. New York: Harcourt, 1923.
C. G. Jung, M.-L. von Franz, Joseph Henderson, Jolande Jacobi, Aniela Jaffé, *Man and His Symbols*. Garden City, NY: Doubleday, 1964.
Lawrence Gordon, *People Types and Tiger Stripes: A Practical Guide to Learning Styles*. Gainesville, FL: Center for Applications of Psychological Type, 1984.
Isabel Briggs Myers, *Gifts Differing*. Palo Alto, CA: Consulting Psychologists Press, 1980.
Isabel Briggs Myers, *The Myers-Briggs Type Indicator*. Palo Alto, CA: Consulting Psychologists Press, 1962.

ARCHETYPES

Jennifer and Roger Woolger, *The Goddess Wheel*. New York: Ballantine, 1989.
Jean Shinoda Bolen, *The Goddesses in Every Woman*. San Francisco: Harper & Row, 1984.
Jean Shinoda Bolen, *The Gods in Every Man*. San Francisco: Harper & Row, 1989.
Robert Moore & Douglas Gillette, *King, Warrior, Magician, Lover*. San Francisco: Harper San Francisco, 1990. See also *The King Within* (1992), *The Warrior Within* (1992), *The Magician Within* (1993), and *The Lover Within* (forthcoming).

TAROT

Angeles Arrien, *The Tarot Handbook: Practical Applications of Ancient Visual Symbols.* Sonoma, CA: Arcus Publishing, 1987.

James Wanless & Angeles Arrien, *Wheel of Tarot: A New Revolution.* Carmel, CA: Merrill-West Publishing, 1992.

J. Kelley Younger, ed., *New Thoughts on Tarot: Transcripts from the First International Tarot Symposium.* Los Angeles: Newcastle Publishing, 1989.

Mental Typologies

LEFT AND RIGHT BRAIN

Sally Springer & Georg Deutsch, *Left Brain, Right Brain,* revised edition. New York: Freeman, 1985.

Robert Ornstein, *The Psychology of Consciousness.* San Francisco: Freeman, 1972.

Daniel Goleman & Richard Davidson, *Consciousness: Brain, States of Awareness, and Mysticism.* New York: Harper & Row, 1979.

LEARNING STYLES

Thomas Armstrong, *In Their Own Way.* Los Angeles: Jeremy Tarcher, 1987.

Howard Gardner, *Frames of Mind.* New York: Basic Books, 1983.

HUMAN DYNASTICS PRINCIPLES

For more information on Sandra Seagal and David Horne's approach to individual differences, you can contact them at Human Dynamics International, Inc., 20304 Croydon Lane, Topanga, CA 90290.

Relationship Typologies

RELATIONSHIP TYPES

For more information on the four relationship types of dominant, yielding, outgoing, and reserved, you can contact John Corbett at International Learning, Inc., P.O. Box 907, Roswell, GA 30077.

BUSINESS LEADERSHIP STYLES

Michael Maccoby, *The Gamesman.* New York: Simon & Schuster, 1976.

Michael Maccoby, *The Leader: A New Face for American Management.* New York: Ballantine, 1983.

MANAGEMENT STYLES

Robert R. Blake & Jane S. Mouton, *The Managerial Grid III.* Houston, TX: Gulf Publishing, 1985. For more information on the Leadership Grid® approach to management styles, you can contact Robert Blake at Scientific Methods, Inc., Box 195, Austin, TX 78767.

Body Typologies

BODY-MIND TYPES

William Sheldon, *Varieties of Temperament*. New York: Harper & Bros., 1942.

BIOENERGETIC TYPES

Alexander Lowen, *The Betrayal of the Body*. New York: Macmillan, 1969.
Alexander Lowen, *Bioenergetics*. New York: Penguin Books, 1975.

AN *I CHING* OF THE BODY

Stuart Heller, *The Dance of Becoming*. Berkeley, CA: North Atlantic Books, 1991.
For more information on Stuart Heller's approach to body movement and function-
    ing, you can contact him at The Institute for Movement Psychology, 513 Santa Fe
    Avenue, Albany, CA 94706.
Miyamoto Musashi, *The Book of Five Rings*. Victor Harris (transl.), Woodstock, New
    York: Overlook Press, 1974.
Richard Wilhelm, *The Secret of the Golden Flower*. London: Routledge & Kegan Paul,
    1962.

TEMPERAMENT IN CHILDREN

Roy Wilkinson, *The Temperaments in Education*. Fair Oaks, CA: St. George Publica-
    tions, 1977.
Rudolf Steiner, *The Four Temperaments*. New York: The Anthroposophic Press,
    1968.

The Enneagram Types

Charles Tart, ed., *Transpersonal Psychologies*. El Cerrito, CA: Psychological Processes,
    1983.
Kathleen Riordan Speeth, *The Gurdjieff Work*. Los Angeles: Jeremy Tarcher, 1989.
Claudio Naranjo, *Ennea-type Structures: Self-analysis for the Seeker*. Nevada City, CA:
    Gateways/IDHHB, 1990.
Helen Frings Keyes, *Emotions and the Enneagram*. Muir Beach, CA: Molysdatur
    Publications, 1992.
Helen Palmer, *The Enneagram*. New York: Harper & Row, 1988.

PERMISSIONS
AND COPYRIGHTS

CONTRIBUTORS

Thomas Armstrong is a psychologist, learning specialist, lecturer, and university teacher. He writes a regularly featured column for *Parenting* magazine, and is the author of *Creating Classroom Structure, The Radiant Child,* and *In Their Own Way: Discovering and Encouraging Your Child's Personal Learning Style.*

Angeles Arrien is a cultural anthropologist and author of *The Tarot Handbook: Signs of Life* and *The Four Fold Way.* She is a core faculty member at the Institute of Transpersonal Psychology.

Harriet Beinfield was one of the first Americans to be trained at the College of Traditional Acupuncture in England and to be licensed as an acupuncturist in California. She maintains a private practice in San Francisco and is the coauthor of *Between Heaven and Earth: A Guide to Chinese Medicine.*

Robert R. Blake is president of Scientific Methods, Inc., and was formerly a psychology professor. He is the author (with Jane Srygley Mouton) of over a dozen books, including *The Managerial Grid III, The Grid® for Sales Excellence,* and *The New Grid for Supervisory Effectiveness.*

Deepak Chopra has practiced endocrinology since 1971 and is the former chief of staff of New England Memorial Hospital in Stoneham, Massachusetts. He is a Fellow of the American College of Physicians and the president of the American Association for Ayurvedic Medicine. He is the author of *Creating Health, Return of the Rishi, Quantum Healing, Perfect Health, Unconditional Life,* and *Ageless Body, Timeless Mind.*

John Corbett worked for Xerox for ten years and then became vice president of sales for Microcard Editions, a division of the Indian Head Corporation. He is the founder of International Learning, Inc., which publishes behavioral tests and measurements and develops related business trainings, and the founder of International Learning Affiliates, a worldwide consulting network.

Georg Deutsch is a neuropsychologist who tests and evaluates neurologically damaged patients. He is the coauthor of *Left Brain, Right Brain*.

Erik Erikson, winner of both the Pulitzer Prize and the National Book Award, is one of the leading figures in the field of psychoanalysis and human development. His many books include *Childhood and Society, Dimensions of a New Identity, Gandhi's Truth, Identity and the Life Cycle, Identity: Youth and Crisis, Insight and Responsibility, The Life Cycle Completed, Life History and the Historical Moment,* and *Young Man Luther.*

Sigmund Freud is the founder of psychoanalysis. His writings include *The Interpretation of Dreams, Introductory Lectures on Psychoanalysis, The Psychopathology of Everyday Life, Civilization and Its Discontents, New Introductory Lectures on Psychoanalysis,* and the *Standard Edition of the Complete Psychological Works of Sigmund Freud* (24 vols.).

Douglas Gillette is a mythologist, a counselor in private practice, and a lecturer in the men's movement. He is the author (with Robert Moore) of *King, Warrior, Magician, Lover; The King Within; The Warrior Within;* and *The Magician Within.*

Liz Greene is a Jungian analyst, astrologer, and writer in London. Her books include *The Astrology of Fate, Relating: An Astrological Guide to Living with Others on a Small Planet, Saturn: A New Look at an Old Devil;* and *The Jupiter/Saturn Conference Lectures* (with Steven Arroyo).

Joseph E. Hart was formerly director of the Department of Humanities and Social Sciences of Parks College, St. Louis University. He was one of the fifty-four Americans who trained with Oscar Ichazo in Arica, Chile, and then served as a teacher and one of the directors of the Arica School in New York City.

Stuart Heller is a psychologist and consultant. He is also certified as a teacher of the Alexander Technique and as a hypnotherapist, trained as a mathematician and dancer, and has been awarded sixth-degree belts in two different martial arts. Heller is the founder of movement psychology and is the author of *The Dance of Becoming: Living Life as a Martial Art* and *Retooling on the Run: Executive Warrior* (Berkeley, CA: North Atlantic Books, forthcoming, with David Surrenda).

James Hillman is a Jungian analyst, lecturer, and prolific writer. He is the founder of Archetypal Psychology, which is based on the work of C. G. Jung. His books include *The Myth of Analysis, Suicide and the Soul, Insearch: Psychology and Religion, Re-Visioning Psychology, The Dream and the Underworld, Loose Ends, Anima: An Anatomy of a Personified Notion, Healing Fiction, Blue Fire,* and *Puer Papers* (ed.).

David Horne has worked for over twenty-five years as a therapist, administrator, writer, and producer of training films in the fields of psychology and educational therapy. He is a partner in Human Dynamics International and is coauthor of *An Introduction to Human Dynamics.*

Karen Horney was a practicing psychoanalyst and a pioneer in the exploration of feminine psychology and the social and cultural aspects of personality. She was the author of *The Neurotic Personality of Our Time, New Ways in Psychoanalysis, Self-Analysis, Our Inner Conflicts, Neurosis and Human Growth,* and *Feminine Psychology* (Harold Kelman, ed.).

Carl Gustav Jung is the founder of depth psychology. His many books include *The Collected Works* (20 volumes); *Modern Man in Search of a Soul, Man and His Symbols,* and *Memories, Dreams, Reflections.*

Efrem Korngold was one of the first Americans to be trained at the College of Traditional Acupuncture in England and to be licensed as an acupuncturist in California. He studied herbal medicine at the Kunming Research Institute in China and at the Shanghai College of Medicine. Korngold is a Diplomate and Examination Consultant of the National Commission for the certification of Acupuncturists and maintains a private practice in San Francisco. He is the coauthor of *Between Heaven and Earth: A Guide to Chinese Medicine.*

Theodora Lau was born in Shanghai and currently resides in Southern California. She is the author of *The Handbook of Chinese Horoscopes.*

John C. Lilly is a graduate of the California Institute of Technology, received his M.D. degree from the University of Pennsylvania, and was also trained as a psychoanalyst. He has done research in fields including biophysics, neurophysiology, electronics, neuroanatomy, and dolphin–human relations. He spent eight months in Chile studying with Oscar Ichazo. His books include *Man and Dolphin; The Mind of the Dolphin; Programming and Metaprogramming in the Human Biocomputer; The Center of the Cyclone; The Deep Self; The Scientist: A Novel Autobiography;* and *Simulations of God: The Science of Belief.*

Alexander Lowen is the cofounder of Bioenergetic Analysis and a practicing psychiatrist in New York and Connecticut. He gives lectures and workshops throughout the United States and Europe. His books include *The Betrayal of the Body; Love and Orgasm; Pleasure, Depression and the Body; Bioenergetics;* and *Narcissism: Denial of the True Self.*

Michael Maccoby is a psychoanalyst and a student of the late Erich Fromm. He is Director of the Project on Technology, Work, and Character, and Director of the Harvard Program on Technology, Public Policy, and Human Development. Maccoby practices psychoanalysis in Washington, D.C., and is on the faculty of the Washington School of Psychiatry. He is author of *Social Character in a Mexican Village* (with Erich Fromm), *The Gamesman,* and *The Leader: A New Fact for American Management.*

Robert Moore is a Jungian analyst and professor of psychology and religion at The Chicago Theological Seminary. He is the author (with Douglas Gillette) of *King, Warrior, Magician, Lover; The King Within; The Warrior Within;* and *The Magician Within.*

Jane Srygley Mouton is vice president of Scientific Methods, Inc. She is the author (with Robert R. Blake) of *The Managerial Grid III, The Grid® for Sales Excellence,* and *The New Grid for Supervisory Effectiveness.*

Claudio Naranjo is a psychiatrist, psychoanalyst, and gestalt therapist, and an accomplished student of esoteric psychology and spirituality, including Buddhism, Gurdjieff, and Arica. His books include *How to Be, Techniques of Gestalt Therapy, The One Quest, The Psychology of Meditation,* and *Ennea-type Structures.*

Helen Palmer is a leading teacher and practitioner of the Enneagram in America. She is on the psychology faculty of John F. Kennedy University, and has taught workshops and seminars around the country. She directs the Center for the Investigation and Training of Intuition in Berkeley, California, and is the author of *The Enneagram: Understanding Yourself and the Others in Your Life* and *The Enneagram in Love and Work* (forthcoming).

Ram Dass, formerly known as Richard Alpert Ph.D., has taught psychology at Harvard, Stanford, and the University of California. In the 1960s he was active in research on consciousness and psychedelic drugs with Timothy Leary and others. He studied yoga in India and, through his books, tapes, and lectures, has contributed to the integration of Eastern spiritual philosophy into Western thought. His books include *Be Here Now, The Only Dance There Is, Grist for the Mill* (with Stephen Levine), *Miracle of Love: Stories about Neem Karoli Baba, Journey of Awakening: A Meditator's Guidebook, Compassion in Action* (with Mirabai Bush), and *How Can I Help?* (with Paul Gorman).

Sandra Seagal has been a teacher, a school psychologist, and a psychotherapist. She is founder and president of Human Dynamics International, a management consulting firm, and has developed training programs for business, education, parenting, and crosscultural understanding. She is coauthor of *An Introduction to Human Dynamics.*

William Sheldon received both Ph.D. and M.D. degrees and was a professor and research scientist at the University of Chicago; Harvard University; Columbia University; the University of Oregon Medical School, Portland; and the University of California, Berkeley. He is the author of *The Varieties of Human Physique, The Varieties of Temperament: A Psychology of Constitutional Differences, The Varieties of Delinquent Youth,* and *Prometheus Revisited.*

Jim Shere is an astrologer and a psychotherapist in private practice. He was a student of Dane Rudhyar's and is a founder of Experiential Astrology.

Sally Springer is Associate Professor of Psychology at the State University of New York at Stony Brook. Her research includes work with brain-damaged and split-brain patients. She is the coauthor of *Left Brain, Right Brain.*

Sun Bear is a Chippewa medicine man who founded The Bear Tribe, which accepts Indians and non-Indians as members. He is the author of *At Home in the Wilderness, Buffalo Hearts, The Path of Power* (with Wabun and Barry Weinstock), and *The Medicine Wheel: Earth Astrology* (with Wabun).

Wabun is Sun Bear's medicine helper. She has written for magazines such as *Life, McCall's,* and *New York,* and is the author of *The People's Lawyers, The Path of Power* (with Sun Bear and Barry Weinstock), and *The Medicine Wheel: Earth Astrology* (with Sun Bear).

Roy Wilkinson has had over forty years of contact with the work of Rudolf Steiner and thirty years of practical experience in the classroom. He is the author of *Commonsense Schooling* and *The Temperaments in Education.*

Jennifer Barker Woolger is a psychotherapist and teacher who has worked with women, teenagers, and children for over twenty years. She is coauthor of *The Goddess Within: A Guide to the Eternal Myths That Shape Women's Lives.*

Roger J. Woolger is a Jungian analyst and a graduate of the C. G. Jung Institute in Zurich. He studied psychology and comparative religion at Oxford and London universities. He is the author of *Other Lives, Other Selves* and coauthor of *The Goddess Within: A Guide to the Eternal Myths That Shape Women's Lives*.

ABOUT THE EDITOR

Robert Frager, Ph.D., is the Founding President of the Institute of Transpersonal Psychology in Palo Alto, California, where he is currently Professor of Psychology and Chair of the Doctoral Program. He has taught psychology at Harvard University; the University of California, Berkeley; and the University of California, Santa Cruz. He is a past President of the Association for Transpersonal Psychology and is coauthor of *Personality and Personal Growth* and editor of *Love Is the Wine,* a book on Sufism. He lives with his wife and two of his four children in Northern California and is also a Sufi teacher and a sixth-degree black belt holder in Aikido.